Developing and Applying Study Skills

Donald Currie worked as a personnel officer for over 15 years before joining the Southampton Institute as a lecturer in personnel management. In 1990 he was appointed as a fellow in human resource management and, for over 10 years, led the CIPD Professional Education Scheme. Since retiring, in 1995, Donald has worked as a consultant to the Southampton Business School, and has been running the CIPD CPP Course.

The Chartered Institute of Personnel and Development is the
leading publisher of books and reports for personnel and training
professionals, students, and all those concerned with the effective
management and development of people at work. For details of all
our titles, please contact the publishing department:
Tel: 020–8612–6200
E-mail: publish@cipd.co.uk
The catalogue of all CIPD titles can be viewed on the CIPD website:
www.cipd.co.uk/bookstore

Developing and Applying Study Skills

Writing Assignments, Dissertations and Management Reports

Donald Currie

Chartered Institute of Personnel and Development

Published by the Chartered Institute of Personnel and Development, 151 The Broadway, London, SW19 1JQ

First published 2005

Design and typeset by Fakenham Photosetting, Fakenham, Norfolk
Printed in Great Britain by The Cromwell Press, Trowbridge, Wiltshire

British Library Cataloguing in Publication Data
A catalogue of this publication is available from the British Library
ISBN 1–84398–0649

The CIPD would like to thank the following members of the CIPD Publishing Editorial Board for their help and advice:
• Pauline Dibben, Middlesex University Business School
• Edwina Hollings, Staffordshire University Business School
• Caroline Hook, Huddersfield University Business School
• Vincenza Priola, Wolverhampton Business School
• John Sinclair, Napier University Business School

Chartered Institute of Personnel and Development, 151 The Broadway, London, SW19 1JQ
Tel: 020 8612 6200
E-mail: cipd@cipd.co.uk Website: www.cipd.co.uk
Incorporated by Royal Charter. Registered Charity No. 1079797

Contents

List of figures

List of tables

To my dear daughter
Annabel

Acknowledgements

I would like to acknowledge the work of the Study Assistance Department of Southampton Institute – University College, and to thank them for permission to use material that has influenced the content of this book.

For whom this book is intended

This book is intended for a broad range of students, including those undertaking courses at foundation, degree, professional and postgraduate levels. The following list gives an indication of the categories and levels of study for which this book is relevant.

- Students who are undertaking a business or human resources (HR) degree will benefit from this book. Such students are those who have chosen degree courses in business studies, marketing, or HR.
- Postgraduate level, in particular, Master's degrees such as the MBA.
- Those undertaking professional studies in similar subjects to those above, but with a view to gaining membership of, for example, the Chartered Institute of Personnel and Development (CIPD), or the Chartered Institute of Marketing (CIM).
- Students undertaking courses that qualify them for entry into higher education, such as pre-degree foundation students and those undertaking, for example a CIPD Certificate in *Personnel Practice (CPP)* or *Training Practice (CTP)*.
- Graduates undertaking *bridging* or *transition* courses such as the CIPD Certificate in Postgraduate Study Skills.
- Graduates or professionally qualified people who have decided on a career change and find themselves tackling subjects that are not related to their earlier studies.

Introduction – What this book is about

The idea for this book originally came from my students, albeit unwittingly on their part. In running seminars and tutorials with them at all academic levels in higher education it became clear to me that while they were well supplied with published texts on research methods, they had problems with understanding how to develop within themselves and apply the study skills they needed if they were to succeed.

This book sets out to offer practical guidance on developing and applying the skills that you need in order to succeed with your course work, which includes carrying out assignments and major projects; and writing essays and dissertations. It is intended for business and HR undergraduates and those undertaking postgraduate work such as a Masters in Business Administration (MBA). If you are undertaking another type of course or postgraduate work that contains elements of business or HR, you should find the book useful.

It may be that you are new to higher education and, perhaps, inexperienced in using research methods. If this is so, then I hope you will find that the research texts recommended in this book are relevant and useful. Researching specific subjects and carrying out extended written work, such as assignments, projects, essays and dissertations, are normal requirements of all courses in higher education.

APPLYING STUDY SKILLS

This is not a book about research *methods*, although it does include reference to research *skills*. For example, when you are presented with a workplace problem or issue that needs to be investigated, or when you have decided upon a topic for your dissertation, you have to devise an approach to tackling it. The research methods you choose have to be appropriate to the task.

In this book practical guidance is offered on developing and applying specific study skills needed to carry out the different types of work you have to do when you are working on your own. It is also designed to help you to get the best from working in the company of others, such as in tutorials, seminars, group work and informal study sessions.

To help you to clarify your understanding and practise the guidance that is offered here, you will find case studies and self-test questions at the ends of the chapters. Within the text there are exercises, examples, tables and diagrams designed to assist your understanding of theoretical concepts, task routines, structures and procedures. You are encouraged to put yourself through the exercises and case studies to extend your experience of tackling organisation-based problems objectively and addressing issues analytically. This increases your academic experience and helps you monitor your own progress. Experience shows that additional learning benefits accrue from carrying out such exercises in informal group sessions.

THE BENEFITS OF STUDY

There is only one kind of person who knows what it is like to complete a degree or a professional course, and that is someone who has done it. It is hard work, and much of it has to be completed by you in your own time; but you will enjoy the benefits you get from it for the rest of your life. Higher education is DIY education; it is a learning experience and nobody can learn for you. At times you may fear failure, feel stressed and alone, but once you are immersed in your chosen subject, you will begin to enjoy it and eventually experience the joy and satisfaction of having successfully completed a work of value. You will never forget the experience.

Chapter 1 – Getting started

This chapter introduces you to the concept of study skills by providing a brief overview. The main purpose of the chapter is to focus upon the skills needed in order to study purposefully and productively; and of course to learn from the experience. In this chapter you can follow a trail through the stages that lead to the completion of assignments, essays and dissertations and major projects. The chapter contains a list of the main study skills.

Chapter 2 – Getting the best from lectures and seminars

This chapter is about getting the best from lectures, seminars, tutorials and group work. It includes guidance on 'active listening skills', questioning and note-taking techniques, working with others on case studies (team work), in-class assignments and practical exercises carried out in small groups. Worked-through examples and mini-cases are used to illustrate this kind of work in a real situation. After studying this chapter, you should understand the purposes of lectures and seminars, and appreciate these events as important learning and information-gathering opportunities.

Chapter 3 – Working in groups

Regardless of the kind of course you are on, you will frequently find yourself working in groups. A wide variety of developmental and assessment techniques are used in universities today, with group work featuring strongly among them. Here we discuss the implications of studying as a group member, the differences between individual and group behaviour and the effect of that difference on the way you work. After studying this chapter you should be able to participate effectively as a group member, especially in terms of your contribution to tackling assignments and making oral presentations. By studying the worked-through examples, you will gain an insight into this kind of work.

Chapter 4 – Writing essays

This chapter discusses the purposes of essays, which include the tutor's purpose in setting the work and your own aims and objectives in producing them. An important feature of this chapter is analysing essay briefs in order to gain an understanding of exactly what is required of you. The chapter includes worked-through examples of carrying out these tasks, and finally there is a set of test questions and a case study, which includes examples of an essay brief and essay plan.

Chapter 5 – Carrying out assignments

Here we offer guidance on carrying out assignments. Unlike essays, in which the academic values predominate, assignments are usually concerned with the practical work that is involved in solving organisational problems. This chapter explains and discusses the study skills used when carrying out assignments, and there are examples and explanatory tables to aid your understanding. These include an example of an assignment brief and one of an assignment proposal and a table indicating the criteria against which your work may be assessed. There is guidance on analysing assignment briefs, identifying an organisational problem or issue that needs to be addressed and structuring an assignment report.

Chapter 6 – Searching for relevant literature

This provides guidance on carrying out a literature search, including the *literature search cycle,* which provides a structured approach to the task. There is guidance on using library and information services productively, developing a literature search strategy to access a variety of literary sources through the use of key words. We show how relevance trees may be used to generate these. We then define secondary data and explain how it might be used in your research. The chapter also contains a section on effective reading and concludes with an example of searching literature for a particular item of data.

Chapter 7 – Preparing the literature review

This chapter is concerned with analysing, comparing, contrasting and critically reviewing what other writers have said about a particular topic. Through the use of examples, the chapter shows how the review provides a context for the work and discusses how you may demonstrate where your work fits in to the general body of knowledge about the topic. After studying this chapter, you should be able to evaluate data in terms of its relevance to your topic and your research objectives. You should also be able to structure and organise data and decide where they may be integrated with your argument. The meaning of *scholarship* and demonstrating it in your work is explained.

Chapter 8 – Collecting primary data

In this chapter primary research, data and information are defined. There is a discussion about using primary methods, such as obtaining data from surveys, interviews and observational techniques. The skills explained include those of constructing statements for questionnaires and the questions for structured and semi-structured interviews. The chapter also contains guidance on preparing, setting up and applying observational methods of obtaining information. There are examples of questionnaire layouts and worked-through examples of how inferences may be drawn from the results of particular types of survey and from answers to interview questions. After studying this chapter, you should be able to draft a questionnaire, prepare for and carry out several types of interview and understand and apply observational methods. We also discuss a variety of techniques that may be applied in this kind of research and, in particular, you should gain an understanding of 'triangulation' and of how this may be used to support the reliability and validity of research results.

Chapter 9 – Dissertations and management reports

This chapter opens with a discussion on the nature of dissertations and management reports. We explain and discuss the role of your tutor and draw a distinction between work at this level and work you have carried out previously. We offer guidance on how to choose a topic, present a table that explains the criteria for making a good choice, and offer several techniques for identifying a topic. We then discuss the pros and cons of in-company delegation as a topic, after which we distinguish between the structures of dissertations and management reports and move into the area of drafting the copy. Several approaches to managing the task are suggested.

Chapter 10 – Writing it all up

The approach taken in this chapter is to offer guidance on all aspects of writing. This includes use of the language, handling citations, referencing, drafting a bibliography and the importance of the presentation of the document. The chapter includes sections on writing essays, assignments, reports, dissertations and major projects. A principal purpose is to advise readers what is expected of them in terms of the contents of such documents and their main purposes. Obviously, this is a major chapter and for this reason is the longest in the book.

Getting started

CHAPTER 1

CHAPTER OBJECTIVES

After studying this chapter you should:

- **understand the importance of managing your time throughout the course**
- **be able to identify the kinds of study skills you need to develop in order to complete your work successfully**
- **be able to select, from a range of study skills, those that are appropriate for particular tasks**
- **have acquired a sense of direction on the course in terms of how you are going to tackle your studies**

INTRODUCTION

It may be that this is your first experience of university and feel a little unsure about how academic work is carried out in higher education. The purposes of this chapter are to open the university doors to you and provide an initial introduction to the nature of study skills, focusing particularly on those that are commonly applied in business and HR studies. First-year undergraduates and those embarking on the initial stage of a professional course will derive most benefit from this chapter, although we do take a brief look at major projects, dissertations and master's theses. Browsing through it, therefore, may also be the beginning of a kind of refresher for the 'old hands' in their middle and final years and those undertaking postgraduate studies.

To increase the likelihood that your studies will be productive and lead to successful graduation, it is worth spending some of your time actually learning how to study. At this stage you need to learn how to study *purposefully* and *productively*, since it is your understanding of study skills and your ability to apply them (plus a little stamina, of course) that will ultimately determine the level of your success.

USING THIS BOOK

The fact that you are reading this book indicates that you are interested in developing and applying study skills. It may be that you need the book to assist you with a study skills course designed to aid your understanding of how to carry out an assignment or project, or write an essay. On the other hand, it may be that you are a mature graduate, have embarked on a career and decided to undertake a higher degree, such as an MBA and wish to refresh and update your understanding of study skills.

One approach to using this book is to scan it from start to finish – not to read in detail but just to see what it contains; to get to know the geography of the book so that the next time you are looking for something, perhaps when you need to know how to do a literature search or collect primary data, you can quickly find what you need.

'Where do I start?' is one of the main problems that concern students when they are first presented with the tasks of handling academic work, such as essays and assignments. From this chapter you should develop an initial understanding of *where* and *how* to start when it comes to carrying out this kind of work. The chapter is designed to give you a brief insight into the nature and application of the main study skills; the themes are developed further; the 'how to' type of guidance increases as we go into greater detail in the subsequent chapters.

Business and HR studies involve the use of the methods of the social sciences. These include, for example: data-gathering skills such as designing and carrying out surveys, conducting interviews and searching for literature that is relevant to the work in hand. Then, when you have the information, the literature has to be critically reviewed and analysed and the data have to be drafted and refined; finally, it all has to be written up.

GETTING TO KNOW THE UNIVERSITY

'I was sitting in the classroom trying to look intelligent, in case the teacher looked at me.' (Elton John)

Many first-year students are sitting in the classroom with pad and pen, waiting to be taught, which is unfortunate because there aren't any 'teachers' in universities; at least not in the sense that we think of those gallant folk in schools. University, however, does teach you one thing: it teaches you to think for yourself. Universities are set up to *facilitate* learning: there are libraries containing not only academic texts, but many different kinds of data source, and there are IT suites and other facilities, all waiting to be used by you. I said in the Introduction that higher education is a DIY process, but that is not to say that you are entirely on your own. The lecturers, the library staff and those in specialised departments are there to help you when you need them, but you do have to learn how to use what is there; and do not be afraid to ask for help.

SO, WHAT ARE STUDY SKILLS?

Having embarked upon a degree or a professional course, you need to develop and apply the skills that are required to gather data, such as searching for and reviewing literature and using a variety of methods and techniques to gather information, such as survey design and interviewing skills. You will need to know how to set up a research programme and how to analyse and draft the results. You also need to be a good written and spoken communicator in order to carry out your written work, interview effectively and make oral presentations. You also need to be able to structure, format and lay out the contents of reports and other written work in an appropriate sequence and to be able to make citations in your work and draft lists of references. The main study skills are listed in Table 1, although this should not be taken as exhaustive – it is just an indication of what we mean by the term study skills.

MANAGING YOUR TIME

A primary consideration at this stage is the importance of making sure that you know how to organise yourself so that you have sufficient time to do the work. Most first-year (and some second-year) students underestimate the importance of time management and fail to set aside enough time to finish their task. The whole purpose of 'being at university' is to *learn*, and to raise the level of your understanding of the subject/s you have chosen to study. Since most degrees and professional courses last only three years (some even less than that), you will find that one of your most precious commodities is time.

Obviously, time management is not a study skill *per se*, but if you learn how to manage your time effectively, you will give yourself the advantage of avoiding that last-minute struggle to meet a deadline,

Table 1   *List of the main study skills*

Skill to be developed	Application
Communication: written and oral	Writing reports, essays and dissertations; interviewing and making presentations
Searching for and critically reviewing literature	Providing a theoretical basis for your research and helping you review and refine the nature of your research
Collecting primary and secondary data; selecting and applying appropriate techniques	Conducting surveys and interviews to collect data; finding corroborative/contrasting evidence to support/ contrast with your argument
Learning with others in seminars and group exercises; debating and listening skills	Discussing issues, solving problems, handling case studies and exercises

which, incidentally, can lead to careless and at best mediocre work. Allowing sufficient time also reduces the risk of stress; in fact, managing your time is really an essential part of managing yourself.

Most courses today are made up of *subject units* (or *modules*). Every year you are tested in each unit by sitting examinations, carrying out assignments and writing essays, which have to be delivered in accordance with a timetable. The units run concurrently across any one year, so you find yourself juggling with your time.

Planning the work
Some people say, 'I work best when under pressure', but academic work should not be like that. It is best to start the work as early as possible, and it really is worth devoting some time to planning. You are given submission dates for the work, which are usually included in a timetable for the whole course, so in fact you can see the stretch of time ahead of you within which the work is to be completed.

You need to plan how you intend to use that time, not forgetting to allow slightly more time than you think you will need in case anything goes wrong or something takes slightly longer than you thought it would. For example, if, as part of your research, you are going to gather primary information by carrying out a survey, then you will need to issue the questionnaire early in the time span, since you will have to give respondents a reasonable amount of time in which to complete the questionnaire and return it to you, after which you have to analyse and collate the results. What you will find is that the tasks you have to carry out do not all fall into a neat and convenient sequence – you have to plan the sequence yourself.

Project management
One approach to doing this is to develop a schedule of the tasks in the form of a Gantt chart, which is a graphical representation of a project, broken down into tasks (see Figure 1). Gantt charts were originally developed for use in *project management* and are used extensively in civil engineering. Try to imagine, for example, all the tasks that have to be carried out when a house is built from scratch. Each task takes a particular amount of time and the tasks all have to be carried out in a certain order. For example, the trenches have to be excavated and the foundations built before anything else can be done. You would not, for

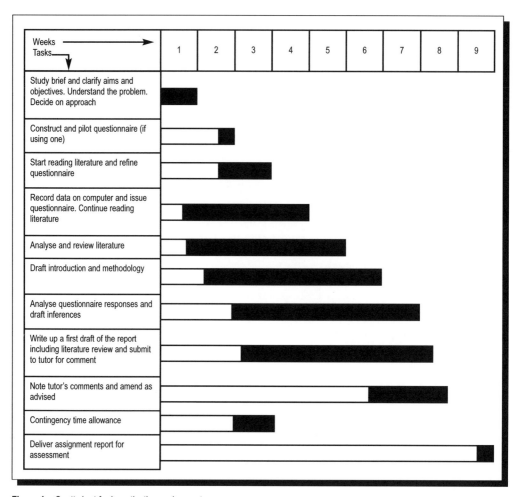

Weeks → Tasks ↓	1	2	3	4	5	6	7	8	9
Study brief and clarify aims and objectives. Understand the problem. Decide on approach									
Construct and pilot questionnaire (if using one)									
Start reading literature and refine questionnaire									
Record data on computer and issue questionnaire. Continue reading literature									
Analyse and review literature									
Draft introduction and methodology									
Analyse questionnaire responses and draft inferences									
Write up a first draft of the report including literature review and submit to tutor for comment									
Note tutor's comments and amend as advised									
Contingency time allowance									
Deliver assignment report for assessment									

Figure 1 *Gantt chart for investigative assignment*

example, bring in the plasterers until the plumbers and electricians have completed their work. The final tasks are usually the interior and exterior decoration and landscaping the garden.

If we examine the tasks that are involved in, say, completing an assignment or project, we find that each task will take a particular amount of time and that they have to be carried out in a certain order, just like building a house. You have to decide the order in which you will carry out the tasks and estimate how much time each will take. Now let us suppose you have been given an investigative assignment brief for which the deadline is in nine weeks. Figure 1 shows just a simple chart (there are more complex versions) and includes a contingency allowance for time. It is normal to allow more time than just a strict, end-to-end schedule; things can go wrong, people make mistakes and there are almost always delays for one reason or another. For major projects at all levels, and for dissertations, I always ask my students for a time schedule. They find that the Gantt chart works out well for them. Do not forget, either, to allow yourself sufficient time to relax, socialise with your friends and generally look after yourself.

First-year students are sometimes confused by the terms used to describe the different types of work they are required to carry out. Hopefully, the following sections will clarify the differences between assignments, essays, major projects, dissertations and theses and the kinds of course in which they feature.

As a general rule, students undertaking degrees are required to complete *essays* in all three years and a *dissertation* in the final year, while those undertaking professional studies are required to carry out *assignments* in each year of the course and a *major project* in the final year. On a degree course, it is the academic aspects of the subject matter that predominate, since you are expected to develop your knowledge and understanding, while on a professional course the practical aspects predominate, since in addition to developing knowledge and understanding of the principles underlying professional practice, you are also expected to develop competence in the application of the skills involved.

Assignments and major projects, therefore, are items of professional practice that you carry out in organisations where there are problems or issues to be investigated and resolved. On completion of the work, you present a *report,* which has its own special format. Drawing these distinctions at this stage is important, since the differences are reflected in the study skills you use for each type of work. This is not to say that you use one type of study skill for, say, assignments and another for essays; the difference is in the emphasis. Both include academic and practical values; it is a question of achieving the proper balance between the two.

ASSIGNMENTS

Typically, you will be given an *assignment brief,* which should include a clear description of what you are expected to do. It should also include the learning objectives, a reading list, a word or two of advice about studying and analysing the brief, and details of how the work will be assessed. The clarity and detail of the brief is usually regarded as sufficient to dispense with the need for an *assignment proposal*, although some universities do require this. Your aim will most likely be to resolve an organisational problem or issue. You may find a case study attached to the assignment brief, in which the task is to resolve the problems or issues that are apparent in the case. On the other hand, sometimes an assignment may be carried out as group work, in which you are divided into small groups of 3, 4 or 5 people. Whatever form the assignment takes, the final product is a report and sometimes a group presentation.

ESSAYS

Normally you will be issued with the essay topic or given a choice of topics. It is rare to be required to choose your own topic for an essay. When your tutor sets an essay, his or her purpose is to test your understanding of a particular topic. The *essay brief* may also require you to submit an *essay plan*, which should contain a description of the subject matter, the learning objectives, information about how the work will be assessed and an initial reading list. *Your* purpose in writing the essay is to answer a question to a particular standard. If the essay is set with a title, then you normally have to derive the question from this.

ESSAY PLANS

The *essay plan* should include your proposals for data gathering since you will need to know what other writers have said about your topic. Also, your proposals for data gathering should include citations of the literature you propose to read first. The essay plan, although important, is not usually a substantial piece of work; normally you will be asked for 1000 words or so. Finally, you need to include a list of all of the citations you have included in the text of the plan; in other words, a list of references showing the full bibliographical details of the sources you have cited (see Appendix 1).

DISSERTATIONS

Choosing a topic
Your first task here is to decide on a topic. This is not easy. It is, however, extremely important, since what you eventually decide to do will determine the entire direction of your research activities. Once you are clear

about your topic you will be able to choose the most appropriate research strategy and data collection and analysis techniques (Saunders *et al* 2003*)*.

On a Gantt chart, you would have to allow yourself a reasonable amount of time to choose a topic. Ideas (or at least *an* idea) may have occurred to you before you reach your dissertation year. It has been said that this is not something you can sit around and muse about, but in fact, what you eventually come up with will be based on an idea; so allow yourself time to muse. When you do, ideas will occur to you, and these will spawn further ideas and modified versions of them. Some of the ideas will be vague, while others will be clear. You may also like to discuss your ideas with your student colleagues and listen to what they are planning. It is essential for you to go for a topic in which you are truly interested. It should be something that excites your curiosity; something you will enjoy finding out about, since you are going to be immersed in it for a long time. When you feel that you have a topic, take it to your tutor and see if he or she thinks it is feasible; this is normally done by arrangement anyway.

Clarifying your aims and objectives
When you have finally settled on a dissertation topic you need to draft a title that embodies a succinct version of it. You may decide to draft a question for the dissertation that is based on the title. Doing this gives you a good focus on the tasks that lie ahead of you, which enables you to make a clear statement of your aims and objectives in carrying out the work; in other words, what you expect your investigation to achieve.

Deciding on an approach to the work
The work is best approached systematically. To achieve this you need to develop a programme of activities, a *methodology* that will lead you to the completion of the task. A method is a systematic and orderly approach taken towards the collection of data so that information can be obtained from those data (Jankowicz 1995). Central to your investigation is the literature search; you need to find sources of data that are relevant to your topic. Certain types of dissertation may be organisation-based, although in such a case, I would prefer to call them major projects. The point here is that working in an organisation, or in a number of organisations, not only opens the door to the collection of primary and secondary data, but may provide insight into the attitudes and idiosyncrasies of those organisations and their managers.

Searching for relevant literature
This is a task that you carry out several times. Firstly, you conduct a search when you are considering ideas for a topic in order to survey the research possibilities. Secondly, when you are planning your approach to the work, you conduct a more extended search, looking for relevant literature as prospective important information sources. Thirdly, when you have clarified your aims and objectives you will carry out another search. There is a systematic way of doing this, which is explained in Chapter 6.

DISSERTATION PROPOSALS

This is a very useful exercise. You write a proposal for your tutor so that he or she may gain an insight into, and assess the total viability of, what you propose to do. This should include a contents list, an initial summary and introduction; a statement of your aims and objectives; how you intend to approach the question, including the literature you propose to read and critically review; whether you intend to gather primary data and, if so, by what means; a brief statement of your anticipated possible findings; the conclusions you may draw from those findings; and finally, a list of references. When your proposal has been assessed, the tutor may suggest amendments, and you should expect to be tutored through to the final version. This is a very useful exercise because you should emerge from this process with a clear sense of direction and a sharp focus on what you are going to do.

THE MAJOR PROJECT

A major project is a significant item of practical professional work, which is carried out in an organisation. In a sense, it is a kind of large-scale, organisation-based investigative assignment, but the problem to be tackled or issue to be resolved has to be of greater significance than that of an assignment; in general, it is a larger piece of work. The problem or issue may be related to strategy, policy or operations, or it may be something that is carried out in one of the specialist departments, such as marketing, finance or HR. The breadth and depth of the work carried out should indicate that it could not have been done without the exercise of professional competence and good practice at the reputed standard for that particular profession.

THE MAJOR PROJECT PROPOSAL

For the same reasons as those stated in the dissertation proposal section (above), the major project proposal is also a very useful exercise. It clarifies your thinking and indeed your perception of the work. The proposal should include a summary of the contents of the report and a clear descriptive statement about the problem or issue you propose to address; a statement of your aims and objectives; your chosen methodology; including (i) the literature you propose to read, (ii) how it relates to the subject of your investigation, and (iii) how you intend to gather any primary data. Then add a brief statement of your anticipated possible findings; the conclusions you may draw from those findings and a set of recommendations for action designed to resolve the problem or issue, including a statement of the cost of implementation; and finally, a list of references, a bibliography and any appendices. Some professional institutions, such as the Chartered Institute of Personnel and Development, like to see a 'start-to-finish' timetable attached to the proposal.

INFORMATION-GATHERING

Most business and HR students and academics refer to information gathering as *research*. In a general sense that is what it is because, after all, your intention is to collect data in a systematic way. You conduct research in order to find things out – to *learn.* Your investigation may include carrying out a survey and/or conducting structured interviews to gather *primary data.* You may collect *secondary data* from a variety of sources. Secondary data already exists and can be found in company documents, such as policy statements and minutes of meetings, public records, statistics, and in research results, for example, from surveys conducted by others. Literature such as books and journals is often referred to as 'secondary sources', but some writers maintain that such sources really produce *tertiary data.* I call the process *information gathering.* We return to this in more detail in Chapter 6.

CRITICALLY REVIEWING LITERATURE

'It has become an annual ritual for graduate researchers embarking on their projects to ask about the literature review. They usually want to know what a review of the literature looks like and how they should do one' (Hart 1998). While the form of the critical review varies with different topics, the basic purposes remain constant. A literature review is an evaluative report of information found in the literature related to your selected topic (Ward 2003). The review should describe, summarise, evaluate and clarify this literature. It should provide a theoretical base for the research and help you to determine the nature of your research.

The literature review should also provide a context for, and justify, the research; show where your research fits in to the existing body of knowledge *by illustrating how the topic has been researched previously and enable the researcher to learn from previous theory on the subject* (Scown 2003). In fact, when you are drafting the literature review, you may find yourself refining and refocusing or even changing the topic. We return to this in greater detail in Chapter 7.

REPORT WRITING

There is no 'one shape, size or form fits all' blueprint for report writing. Reports may take many different forms. For example, your company may have its own format or 'house style' for reports; other examples include the so-called 'Civil Service' format, the Royal Navy format and the BSI, to name but a few.

When you have completed the work related to an assignment or major project, you have to write a report explaining the nature of the problem or issue that you investigated, how you carried out the investigation (your methodology), what you discovered, the conclusions you drew from those findings, and your recommendations for action designed to resolve the problem or issue.

There are well-known templates against which reports may be produced. Your university may recommend one of these, although to some extent, the subject matter of the report can influence the format and layout. The report has to be readable, well-written and presented, the sections arranged in a logical sequence and the pages laid out in a consistent and attractive, easy to read, format. It is a good idea to study a variety of report formats. Incidentally, if you select a format that is generally popular, such as that of the Civil Service or the BSI, you will find that your computer will recognise it and do the formatting for you. We explain the detail of all this, with examples of page layouts and a selection of the do's and don'ts, in Chapter 9.

DRAFTING ESSAYS

One of the purposes of an essay is to provide you with an opportunity to demonstrate your ability to research a subject. In a sense, therefore, you should have most of the essay written by the time you have completed your research programme, since you will have drafted and stored the results of your review of the relevant literature and any other data sources you may have used. Unlike a report, the essay is not divided into discrete sections; it is written straight through, although the sequence in which you present the information should be logical. As you progress in your research, you will notice that the topic has several internal themes, and it is a good idea to present these themes in a logical order. The essay should have a front cover bearing the title, which is often written as a question, and of course your name. Universities vary in terms of whether or not you should include a contents list and a formal introduction. In any case, your university will advise you about the essay format that it expects.

DISSERTATIONS, THESES AND MAJOR PROJECTS

This heading includes final-year dissertations, master's theses and major projects of the type required by professional institutions at the end of a study programme. According to the British Standards BS 4821: *Presentation of Theses and Dissertations,* the length of work at this level may range from 10,000 to 15,000 words. This is the level of work you will be expected to produce in your final year as an undergraduate or on completion of a master's degree. By the time you reach this stage in your academic or professional studies, you should have built up a breadth and depth of experience that will enable you to tackle work at this level. The rules, structures and procedures are similar, but the volume of work is greater and the standard is higher.

Reader friendliness is a critical factor in all forms of writing. The standard of your writing and the logic of your sequence, therefore, should go unnoticed; it will only be noticed if your standard is poor and/or your logic fails to appeal to your reader.

It is the writer's responsibility to be clear. It is not the reader's responsibility to understand (Eagleson 1990). This matter is dealt with in detail in Chapter 10.

SUMMARY

- The purpose of this chapter is to help you to get started with the work you have to do, by introducing you to the nature and applications of study skills.

- To help you towards successful graduation, the skills are explained in great detail in the chapters that follow.

- It is important to develop a sense of direction in your studies and to understand how a university is set up in terms of facilitating your learning.

- After reading this chapter you should be able to recognise the kinds of study skills that are appropriate to, and applicable in, carrying out particular tasks.

CHECK YOUR UNDERSTANDING
Questions

1 How would you structure your timescale for an essay?

2 What are the purposes of essays?

3 Having developed a selection of possible dissertation topics, how would you survey their research possibilities?

4 What is a methodology?

5 Why is writing a proposal useful to you and your tutor?

6 Name at least four different types of information source.

7 What is the difference between primary and secondary information?

8 What are the purposes of a literature review?

9 What are the main differences between a dissertation and a major project?

10 How does an essay format differ from that of a report?

Answers in Appendix 4

FURTHER READING

EAGLESON, R. D. (1990) *Writing in Plain English.* Canberra: Australian Government Publishing Service.

HART, C. (1998) *Doing a Literature Review.* London: Sage Publications.

JANKOWICZ, A. D. (1995) *Business Research Projects*, 2nd edn. London: Chapman and Hall.

SAUNDERS, M., LEWIS, P. and THORNHILL, A. (2003) *Research Methods for Business Studies.* Harlow: Pearson Education.

TORRINGTON, D. (1991) *Management Face to Face.* London: Prentice Hall.

WEBSITES

SCOWN, B. (2003) *What is a Literature Review?* Central Queensland University.

http//www.library.cqu.edu.au/litreviewpages/tips.htm

WARD, T. (2003) *Why do a Literature Review?* Central Queensland University.

http//www.library.cqu.edu.au/litreviewpages/tips.htm

Getting the best from lectures and seminars

> **CHAPTER OBJECTIVES**
>
> After studying this chapter you should:
>
> ■ **understand the purposes of lectures and seminars**
>
> ■ **understand what is expected of you in lectures and seminars**
>
> ■ **see these events as important learning and information-gathering opportunities**
>
> ■ **be able to take relevant and clear notes in a variety of sessions**

INTRODUCTION

The purposes of this chapter are firstly, to discuss lectures, seminars and other activities that contribute to your learning and secondly, to offer guidance on how to derive the greatest amount of learning from them. These events are exclusive, one-off opportunities to learn, gather useful and relevant information, discuss, practise and thereby develop and clarify your learning. We examine these learning opportunities separately because the purpose of each of them is unique.

THE PURPOSES OF LECTURES

Normally, there is a series of weekly lectures throughout each unit (or element) of your course. Each successive lecture deals with a different sub-discipline of the main subject area. For example, if you are on an HR course and the study unit is about recruitment and selection, then the lectures will cover such subjects as recruitment advertising, occupational testing, interviewing and so forth. In this way the lectures represent the planned route through the subject study unit. The content of the lectures themselves broadens the foundation on which the unit programme is based. Every lecture will introduce you to the underlying theory, analyse and explain complex issues and generally add to your knowledge of the central framework of the whole course. During his or her explanations, a good lecturer will offer guidance on reading in the areas that include further detail and alternative expert opinions.

THE FORMAT OF A LECTURE

In one sense, formal lectures are an anomaly because on the one hand they excite your interest and raise questions in your mind, but on the other hand, opportunities to ask direct questions of the lecturer are limited, so you have to be patient and ask your tutor at another time. The limitations are there for two main reasons: firstly, the amount of time allocated to the lecturer to deliver the main body of the talk is sometimes fairly tight. Secondly, the attendance at a lecture is usually greater than that of any other kind of session, and the lecturer simply does not have the time to respond with full and satisfactory answers.

What is said above refers to one particular type of formal lecture, but lectures may vary in their content and style of delivery. Sometimes, for example, in a one-hour lecture, the lecturer might leave 10 minutes or so at the end in order to take questions.

One of the purposes of a lecture is to present information, and different kinds of information lend themselves to particular media of delivery. So lectures may be given as PowerPoint presentations, or may include the use of overhead projectors and whiteboards. Additionally, the lecturer may have prepared handouts. Some lectures are interactive in that the lecturer may ask the audience to role play or participate in a brief exercise.

BEING AT A LECTURE

The fact that you have chosen to undertake a particular course implies that you have an interest in the main subject, so it is likely that you already know something about the topic of the lecture to begin with. A little reading in advance, however, will help you to assimilate into your existing knowledge more easily any new learning you gain from the lecture. This is because the literature you study will include the terminology of the subject, advance knowledge of which will allow you to concentrate on the essence of what is being said, rather than on the words being used. You will also come away with a clearer understanding of the lecture if you do a little advance reading around the subject.

ACTIVITY 1

Root through all of your stuff until you find your course programme. Open it and find the lecture programme and the course and unit reading lists. Make a time plan to go to the library before a lecture and read around the lecture topic. When you get into the lecture, you will be surprised by how much more comfortable and confident you are and how well you are able to concentrate on what is being said.

WHAT SHOULD I LOOK FOR?

We said above that the purpose of a lecture is to present information. Listen carefully to the *nature* of the information that the lecturer is presenting and classify each element of it as *facts* and *concepts*.

- *A fact* is something that is *known* to have happened and is universally accepted. The lecturer may present the facts about a topic through speech or with the use of visual aids.
- *A concept* is based on an idea or a series of linked ideas. A political idea, such as democracy, is a concept. The lecturer will link the elements of the subject together to formulate a conceptual integration of the material. Some writers believe that this is the most important part of the lecture, on the assumption that you will be able to collect the facts from literary and other sources.

Democracy, in the context in which it is given above, is *understood*; that is to say, we all know intuitively what people mean when they use the word. 'Intelligence' and 'freedom' are generally understood, but difficult to define or describe. In serious studies, such as yours, concepts are more or less complex, and if the lecturer feels that a particular concept will seem complex on a first hearing, he or she will usually provide contextual examples and alternative explanations so as to illustrate the point being made. Attaining a complex concept involves you in analysing and interpreting the material through which it is presented, which can sometimes be difficult.

ATTAINING THE CONCEPT

You can, of course, read in order to look up concepts as well as facts, but if you are struggling to attain a particular concept make sure that you note as much of it as you can in the lecture. Then, when you look it up later, you will be able to add to your notes the perceptions of it from the relatively different angles of various writers. If you still have difficulty, discuss it with your tutor.

BEING AT A SEMINAR

A seminar is a group discussion session, usually led by a lecturer with your full group in the classroom. Normally, the lecturer introduces the topic and will expect you and your colleagues to participate fully in the discussion. You will know the topic from your schedule of work, and it is a good idea to read it up in advance. Some lecturers believe that more learning takes place in seminars than in any other kind of session. Take a good supply of writing materials with you; this is another opportunity to exercise your note-taking skills, so that you can take away as much information as possible.

In a seminar, the atmosphere is more relaxed than that of a lecture. The role adopted by the lecturer is often that of a facilitator in which he or she will steer the conversation in helpful directions by asking the occasional question or making statements about particular aspects of the topic. The objective is to increase the depth of your understanding by analysing how the topic is currently presented by those who are recognised authorities on it. You also have the opportunity to compare and contrast your colleagues' perceptions of the topic with your own and those of the lecturer. When I say that you are expected to participate fully, you do have to observe the normal rules of conversation and allow others to express their views. The convention is to allow them to finish speaking before you present your own views and understanding. This, of course, involves you in listening, which is also a form of participation that is just as important as speaking, if not more so! (see later).

TYPES OF SEMINAR

Seminars may take a variety of forms. For a two-hour seminar, for example, I often divide the class into small groups of three or four, ask them to take a topic from the syllabus, learn as much as they can about it and prepare to lead a seminar in, say, three or four weeks. Typically, they will start with a 15 or 20 minute presentation and then open the seminar for discussion. Students tell me that they enjoy these sessions and that they are able to gather useful information from them.

Seminars represent an ideal opportunity to analyse what was said in a weekly lecture. I said above that opportunities to ask questions in formal lectures are limited, but in a seminar the reverse is the case. One approach taken by lecturers is for he or she to introduce the topic and then present the group with hypothetical situations in which there are questions to be answered. The class is formed into syndicates in which they develop answers to the questions and then present their answers to the reassembled class.

STRUCTURED SEMINARS

These are classroom activities in which you may be asked to participate in exercises. There is a wide variety of subjects and types of activity, some of which may include, for example, analysing exercises to find answers to relevant questions, commenting on particular organisational situations or responding with your comments on meaningful statements that have been made by authors, senior industrial managers, politicians and a variety of others.

A STRUCTURED SEMINAR BASED ON A QUESTION

The question is given a few weeks in advance of the seminar. Students are expected to prepare by gathering relevant information, which they bring with them into the session. The class is divided into pairs or triads. In their conversations, the pairs and triads exchange the information they have gathered, discuss it and try to draw a conclusion from what they have discovered. After about 15 minutes, the pairs and triads join to form small groups and the process is repeated. Half an hour is usually allowed for this, after which there is a plenary session led by the lecturer and conclusions are drawn. Normally, you will be asked to write up your perception of the conclusions. The obvious advantage of this kind of session is that it is an opportunity to analyse a question and gather useful and relevant information in the process.

An alternative to finishing with a plenary session is one in which the small groups are asked to carry out 10-minute oral presentations on their conclusions, but time often does not allow for this. It is, however, important to understand that planning a presentation reinforces and refines your learning (see Chapter 3).

I find this kind of session to be quite exciting. To hear the buzz of conversation in the classroom, knowing that my students are exchanging knowledge of a relevant subject makes me feel as if the ignition has been turned on and they are discussing something relevant and important. Experience shows that because of the continuous participation, a great deal of learning takes place in sessions such as these.

PARTICIPATION

It is safe to say that in most lectures, you play a passive role, while in seminars, you play a full and active role. Full participation is the secret for getting the best from seminars; the more you immerse yourself into it, the more you get out of it. The degree to which you are able to participate will be determined by several factors:

- Firstly, you have to research the topic or question as thoroughly as you can in the time allowed. Clearly, you are in a good position to participate if you are armed with plenty of relevant information that you have studied in advance.
- Secondly, you have to be motivated to participate. The degree to which you are motivated is determined by your interest in the topic or question along with your desire to learn from the experience. Also, of course, there is the anticipation of enjoying yourself because these sessions can be fun.
- Thirdly, your willingness to listen to the information that has been brought in by others. Remember that their information is important too. Obviously, there will be similarities within the accumulation of contributions made by you and your colleagues because the topic is common to all, but there are usually significant differences in how the information has been interpreted.

People vary in their ability and willingness to converse and generally relate to others, especially at the beginning of a course. If you were participating in a session such as the one described in the above example, you could find the first part of it hard going. On the other hand, of course, it could be stimulating; it depends on the type of person you happen to be sitting with.

In seminars, the advantage of having subject-centred discussions with individuals and in groups is that you learn from each other; in this way you can add to the knowledge you gained from your initial research of the topic or question. But you do have to learn to assess what others are saying and be selective in terms of the information you think is valuable and relevant. Clearly, all of this involves you in listening – and there is more to that than simply sitting with someone and hearing their words.

DEVELOPING ACTIVE LISTENING SKILLS

Face-to-face conversation is probably the most superior form of communication but most people do not take advantage of that. In a face-to-face conversation, people are sensitive to each other's reactions, and such sensitivity is an essential ingredient of satisfactory communication. It is the psychology of inter-personal perception that makes the conversational situation superior to other forms of communication. What is commonly referred to as 'body language' plays an important role in your perception of the meaning in what others are saying. Sadly and too often, however, the so-called 'listener', rather than listening actively, is thinking of what s/he is going to say next, and sometimes is either too rude or too impatient to allow the speaker to finish.

A seminar is a situation that is ideal for effective or *active* listening. Active listening takes place when one person hears and *understands* what another is saying, because he or she genuinely wishes to understand. It takes considerable practice – and often, patience – to develop and maintain active listening, but it is a high-quality learning technique that is certainly worth developing and applying. If you wish to understand the meaning of what is being said by colleagues and/or the lecturer, and to understand the implications for your learning, you may decide to develop active listening skills, in which case it is hoped that Table 2 will be helpful.

When you have developed these skills, they can be applied in a wide variety of situations. This includes a group situation such as a seminar – and do bear in mind that you will be expected to participate fully in other group sessions, such as case studies, exercises and group assignments (see Chapter 3). (There are additional advantages, which are not related to this chapter. For example, when you are interviewing someone to collect primary data from them (see Chapter 8), your interpretations of what they are saying are far more accurate if you have good listening skills. In such a situation, your main contribution is listening for 70–80 per cent of the time.)

Table 2   *Developing and applying active listening skills*

1	Keep your input to the conversation brief and simple without being discourteous
2	Do not interrupt the speaker: you may cause him or her to digress and fail in their true intention
3	Do not attack the speaker verbally. If something is unclear, rephrase the statement, ideally in the form of a question, and wait for an answer
4	Be sensitive to the emotional as well as the factual content of what the person is saying, but do not attempt to rationalise things on the speaker's behalf
5	If you wish to contradict what is being said, wait until the speaker has finished
6	Avoid confrontation at all costs – it puts people on the defensive
7	Study the person and observe what has not been said (avoidance, by the speaker, of some relevant fact or issue, may indicate his or her state of mind)
8	Ensure that there is mutual understanding of what is being said. Every now and then briefly summarise your understanding and wait for confirmation that you have got it right
9	Be honest. Do not search for reasons why the person could be wrong
10	Do not be judgemental about anything the person says, or says that he or she thinks
11	Be non-directive; that is, avoid giving advice or instructions; ask questions and just nod or smile to encourage the person to continue
12	Remain as unemotional as you can. Be supportive and encouraging, but beware of emotions; they are contagious and can cloud your understanding.

WELL, LOOK AT IT THIS WAY

Regardless of the format that is adopted for a seminar, the purpose is to learn from the conversations you have with the tutor and your colleagues. The most valuable by-product of this process is that actively listening to what others are saying may cause you to alter your perception of particular concepts. You have to be as sure as you can that the new information represents a reasonable and acceptable modification of your previous thoughts and, as noted above, you have to assess the information and be selective in what you choose to accept and incorporate into your personal knowledge bank. It is also wise to go to the library and check how the authorities on the subject interpret and present the information in question. If you are still unsure, you can always check further by discussing your refined perceptions with your tutor.

BE OPEN-MINDED

When you attend a seminar, the purpose is to learn; to gather information, discuss concepts and refine your own ideas. Try to open your mind to the perceptions and interpretations of others. One of your colleagues may have collected information that you missed, and the reverse could also be true. What you have to do, therefore, is to share what you have collected and actively listen to your colleagues and the tutor.

You should leave the session with copious notes. As soon as possible after the session, organise and collate them so that they make sense; then you will be able to complete any unfinished notes. This would be a good time to analyse what you have got and reflect upon what you learned from the session (see Chapter 7).

THE CRAFT OF NOTE-TAKING

This may seem to be a rather pretentious heading for what many may regard as a simple task. 'Surely,' they say, 'all you have to do is to sit there and jot things down as and when you think they are important'; but there is more to *effective* note-taking than that. You are at university to learn, and the opportunities to do so are available from many sources: lectures, seminars, tutorials, textbooks, papers, handouts, formal and informal discussions and, of course, the Internet. Collecting, collating and, in particular, *integrating* information from all of these sources is a major and important task. The ability to record and integrate this diverse range of material is probably one of the most important crafts you can possess in order to maximise the effectiveness of your studying.

Alternatively, you might occasionally find it helpful to take in a tape machine and record the whole lecture on it and then write it all up later. Obviously, you would have to arrive early to ensure that you could sit where the lecturer can be seen and heard clearly. You should always ask permission to record the lecture. Most lecturers will agree to allow this, but it is a normal courtesy to ask.

Truly, you should be selective in your note-taking, but remember that lectures are exclusive, one-off learning opportunities. This means that in each lecture you should grasp the opportunity to take away with you as much of the content and meaning of the lecture as you possibly can. It is no secret that the way to do this is to take notes. Hopefully, you will have developed the habit of taking notes from other sources of information, but it is particularly important to do so at lectures. You can revisit most other sources to check the material you collected, but lectures are transient – once they have gone there is no way back. Not only, therefore, are they 'one-off learning opportunities', they are one-off opportunities to collect notes that will certainly be useful to you at a later time in the course.

You can, of course, just sit there and write things down randomly and, perhaps, rely on handouts – if there are any! Realistically, it is fine to note down simple information such as facts and any references the lecturer may recommend, but it is worth bearing in mind that notes that you record *systematically* will help you at a later time, when you need to understand the context as well as the content of the lecture. If you really want to put together a comprehensive record of a lecture you may decide to *organise* your note-taking. You can do this by using a system that allows you to record material in a logical format. There are several valid approaches, but the two that are used most frequently are *linear* note-taking and *mind mapping,* the latter often being alternatively described as *diagrammatic* note-taking. Both types can be prepared in advance of whatever kind of session you are going to attend, be it a lecture, seminar or other kind of meeting.

LINEAR NOTE-TAKING

This may be compared to the note-taking of a shorthand writer from the era that preceded that of the computer. Typically, shorthand writers were female secretaries who sat opposite the boss while *he* (in those days it was almost always a *he!*) dictated letters and reports to *her*. She would use a pad and pencil as she dashed off his words in hieroglyphically styled shorthand, usually Pitman's. Since those days, of course, information technology has significantly changed office routines. You can make your linear notes in an organised fashion by laying out a standard page that will help you to identify the kind of information you are noting (see Figure 2).

If you laid out an A4 sheet similar to this, using a landscape page set-up, it could take quite a lot of material. You could photocopy it for future use, and, by the way, always take in to the lecture more pages than you think you might need. On occasions, you may have to use a different layout, depending on the subject matter of the lecture. From Figure 2 you can see how much easier it would be to put your notes in the appropriate places so that they were already categorised when you were reviewing them later. This is a simple system and you will become accustomed to using it fairly quickly. Here are a few tips on making good use of the page:

- *Shorthand.* For long words and phrases that crop up frequently, you can develop you own kind of shorthand through the use of well-known abbreviations such as HR (human resources) and OD

Lecture No ...	Speaker	Date
Topic:		
Facts	Concepts	
References	Arguments	

Figure 2 *Page layout for linear note-taking*

(organisational development) and a few of your own, all of which will enable you to write quickly. Make up your own shorthand by taking the vowels out of the word, eg 'mktg' instead of marketing; or you can shorten words by writing 'org' instead of organisations, and so forth.

- *Number the sheets.* If you use more than one page, number them so that you can file them in the order in which the lecture was delivered.

- *Writing while listening.* You only have one brain and, versatile as the brain is, you can only listen and write at the same time (like the shorthand writer) if the spoken and written words are the same; in other words, if you can write *verbatim*. Few students can do that. So, you have to find your own balance between writing and listening; the more you write, the less you can listen. You can overcome this by taking brief notes and filling in the gaps as soon after the lecture as possible.

- *Concentrate.* If you have laid out your pages according to your expectations of the lecture content, you will find that you are able to concentrate more easily because you are looking out for specific facts and concepts to be presented and points to be made about them.

- *Dealing with interruptions.* Nothing is more annoying than a colleague starting to chat to you when you are trying to concentrate on something at a lecture. It also irritates the lecturer, who will probably regard it as downright rude. Some students naively believe that the lecturer cannot hear them, but a lecture theatre has all of the physical qualities of the Whispering Gallery in St Paul's Cathedral (except perhaps for its beauty!) in that voices travel far, regardless of the pitch; indeed, that is the whole point of having a custom-built lecture theatre. Deal kindly with your colleague. Put them off by telling them you will have a chat later. If the interruption persists, then you may have to harden your tone a little.

ACTIVITY 3

You are going to attend a lecture entitled 'Eliciting Employee Commitment'. Carry out a brief literature search, beginning with your course handbook, and layout a page in readiness for linear note-taking at the lecture.

MIND MAPPING

Buzan (1974) proposed the use of a *diagrammatic* model for note-taking and for a variety of other purposes (see *relevance trees* in Chapter 6). This is a kind of road mapping technique in which the topic, or central theme of a lecture, is the starting point. It is placed at the centre of the page.

As you can see from Figure 3, the idea is that the routes to the related effects and disciplines branch out in a radial pattern from the main theme placed at the centre. If you have done your pre-lecture reading, you can prepare the centre and the main arteries of the diagram before you go into the lecture. As the lecture progresses, you may need to add a few side roads, since the lecturer may introduce facts and concepts that are branches of the sub-disciplines. Finally, to refine the concept even further, you can also link the arterial roads to each other and, where appropriate, the side roads too, in order to remind yourself of the interrelated concepts.

ACTIVITY 4

You are going to a study skills lecture on time management. Prepare a skeletal mind map that you might use for this session.

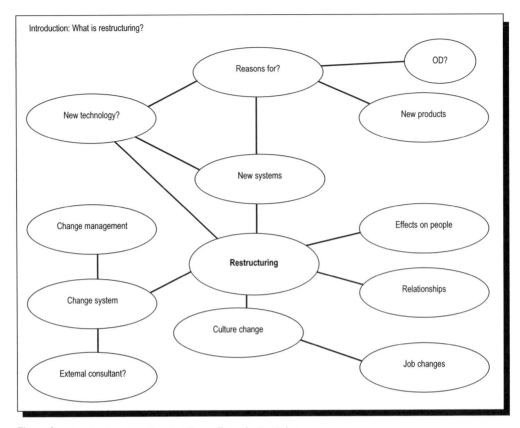

Introduction: What is restructuring?

Figure 3   *Example of mind map for note-taking – effects of restructuring*

USING A MIND MAP

Whatever form of note-taking you prefer to use, you have to be able to read and interpret your notes after the event, bearing in mind that you may need to refer to them in several months' time, or even longer than that. (For example, your notes may prove to be invaluable when you are wrestling with the problem of identifying a topic for your dissertation.)

Let us imagine that you are sitting in a lecture with the skeleton of a mind map that you prepared earlier. There is not much on it at that stage; in fact, you are probably looking at something you could call a *spidergram,* with the body in the middle, the legs radiating outwards towards the edges of the page and very little else. You are faced with the task of completing the picture. As you listen to the lecturer you can jot down the aspects of the talk that you regard as important. During your pre-lecture reading, you may conclude that the talk could consist of several main elements. In case this turns out to be so, take more than one mind map in with you as appropriate.

Looking at Figure 3, we can see that the words and phrases such as *Culture change, Effects on people* and *Relationships,* can be grouped into classifications. For example, the above phrases, taken from the figure, can be seen as possible consequences of restructuring; in other words, they are the *implications* of what is planned. But some of the pods are questions, such as *Reasons for* and *OD.* Why is the change being made? Is it because of the introduction of new technology; is it part of an organisational development programme? These are features that will occur to you as the lecture proceeds. You may decide to develop a code that you can use as soon after the event as possible so as to extend your notes in a way that will enable you to read and interpret them at a later date.

For example, you might decide to group the words and phrases into classifications such as:

- Facts
- Interpretations
- References
- Concepts
- Implications

Williams (1989) extends this idea by saying that additional emphases can be given to individual elements (of a lecture) by (i) enclosing items in boxes, (ii) using colour to highlight words and areas of interest, or (iii) using stars or some other graphic indicator. Additionally, you might underline or double underline words to indicate their levels of importance; or you can use asterisks.

The sum of these ideas may be turned into a kind of system for using a mind map, which may be summarised as follows:

- Go into the lecture with a prepared mind map/s
- Actively listen for facts, references, concepts, interpretations and implications and classify them accordingly
- Emphasise important points by using graphic indicators such as: underlining or double underlining words and phrases, stars, asterisks, using colour and boxes, etc.
- Try to note enough information to enable you to complete your notes at a later time by filling in any gaps you had to leave.

NOTE-MAKING

Write up your notes while the substance of the event is still fresh in your mind, or as soon as possible afterwards, filling in the gaps and expanding on the ideas presented. Do not forget to finish by filling the parts you did not have time to record during the lecture. This is *note-making* as opposed to *note-taking.* Do not be afraid to add your own comments; your ideas are important, and remember too that knowledge is about understanding concepts and ideas as well as learning facts.

On reading all that is said above about note-taking, it may seem to be an unnecessarily complex process. When you first see a linear page set-up or a mind map, it certainly appears to be complex, and when you start to use these note-taking aids, you may be anxious about how well it will all work. Rest assured that you will very quickly become accustomed to using them.

DEVELOP YOUR OWN FILING SYSTEM

Clearly, you have to take notes, since it is impossible for you to carry all of the incoming information in your head. Besides, you need to have the mental security of knowing that the information that you have gathered is useful and relevant to your studies, now and in the future, that it retains as much of its integrity as possible and is speedily accessible, Furthermore, it is clear that your notes will mount up as the weeks and months go by. For all of these reasons, having an effective and reliable filing system is an important tool in your study skills box. Some people can work effectively in a muddle, but experience shows that it is the organised rather than the disorganised students who are more likely to succeed.

GETTING IT SORTED!

Study the structure of the course, which you will find in your course handbook. Note how it is divided into separate disciplines and sub-disciplines. Create a hard copy file for each of the main disciplines and label it with a brief indication of the subject; give it a number; an envelope file that takes A4 paper will serve the purpose. Whenever you emerge from a session at which you have taken notes, write them up and place them in the appropriate file. In time, you will find that the volume of paper in each of the files needs to be cut down. When this happens, you can create files for the sub-disciplines.

Every now and then the contents of the files will need to be recollated so that access to specific information is fast.

At the front of each file, have a list of the contents; if you have numbered the files as suggested above, the speed of access to specific items will be increased.

I am recommending the use of cardboard files because there will be times when you need to take some of your notes to a classroom session, in which case you will manage more easily with tangible notes in your hand. You could, of course, copy it all over on to your computer, and you may prefer to do this for back-up purposes.

CHECK YOUR UNDERSTANDING

Questions

1 What are the main *purposes* of a lecture?

2 What specific types of information should you look out for during a lecture?

3 In what ways is your role at a lecture different from that at a seminar?

4 What are the main purposes of seminars?

5 What steps would you take to prepare yourself for a forthcoming lecture or seminar?

6 What is *active listening*?

7 Write down four different types of situation in which active listening would be an advantage

8 What are the main the differences between *linear* and *diagrammatic* or *mind mapping* techniques of taking notes?

9 What is the difference between *note-taking* and *note-making*?

10 What are the main advantages of creating your own filing system for your notes?

Answers in Appendix 4

FURTHER READING

BUZAN, T. (1974) *Use Your Head*. London: BBC Publications.

HINDERER, D. E. (1992) *Building Arguments*. Belmont, CA: Wadsworth.

SHARP, J. and HOWARD, K. (1996) *The Management of a Student Research Project*, 2nd edn. Aldershot: Gower.

WILLIAMS, K. (1989) *Study Skills*. Basingstoke: Macmillan Press.

Working in groups

INTRODUCTION

Regardless of the kind of course you are on, you will frequently find yourself working in groups. A wide variety of developmental and assessment techniques are used in universities today, and group work features strongly among them. In the previous chapter we touched upon working as a member of a small group, and what we discussed there will be relevant here.

WHAT IS A GROUP?

Modern researchers have invested considerable time and effort into acquiring an understanding of groups, the purposes of their existence, how the members interact and how groups interact with each other. This has developed into a very wide-ranging subject that we refer to as *group dynamics.* Over the years researchers have built up a typology that includes many different kinds of group, which makes it very difficult to put together an all-embracing definition.

In any case, it is not appropriate for us to delve deeply into current theories of group dynamics in this book, but if the subject attracts you or if you feel you would prefer to have a comprehensive understanding of it, there is an excellent analysis in Huczynski and Buchanan (2001).

When writers define groups they are most frequently concerned with small groups, each of which is of a size that does not hinder interaction between and among its members. When we refer to large groups, we usually mean the people in a whole organisation. For our purposes, we will say that a group is:

> A number of people who are together because they have a shared interest or an objective to achieve. They interact with and are aware of each other, and regard themselves as members of the group. This description represents the kind of group in which you will be working.

ACTIVITY 5

If you are accustomed to working in groups, think of two that you were in recently: one that worked well that you enjoyed, and one that you regard as unsatisfactory. Perhaps the first one was well-organised and made a good job of the task; and maybe the members of the second one lacked motivation or cohesion. Analyse both experiences and try to identify why you found one to be satisfactory and the other to be unsatisfactory.

The purpose of this chapter is to introduce you to several examples of group work and to offer guidance on your role within them, how to learn from them and how to work as a team member when the objective is to solve a problem or carry out a learning exercise. When eventually you leave the course and start to work in an organisation, you will find that your experience of working in groups – especially groups working as teams – has many benefits, because most people in organisations today are members of work teams.

TYPICAL STUDENT GROUPS

You will work in several types of group, but in the broadest of terms, they may be placed into three main categories: (i) *informal discussion groups*; (ii) *structured learning groups* and (iii) *assessment groups*. These are my descriptions, although you may find similar explanations of them elsewhere.

INFORMAL DISCUSSION GROUPS

Informal discussion groups usually form as a result of classroom friendships and the motivation to learn. These are small groups of three, four or five people with whom you have become friends. You have decided to have these meetings because you enjoy each other's company and are prepared to offer your perceptions of concepts, ideas and topics and to listen to those of your colleagues. The bonus at the end of the meeting comes in the form of useful learning outcomes and the modification and refinement of your previous thoughts and perceptions. Obviously, such meetings are opportunities to practise your note-taking skills (see Chapter 2).

Informal meetings are also an ideal forum in which to analyse a recent lecture or seminar, or to go through a concept that you find difficult to understand. I knew of one group that introduced a bit of fun into the meeting by finishing with a brief question and answer session. Naturally, the answers to the questions stimulated further discussion and often healthy but friendly argument.

A few of the criticisms that have been levelled at this kind of group are that (i) after several meetings, the members become accustomed to each other to the extent that they can at times predict what they are going to say, perhaps in response to a question or as their normal contribution to the session; (ii) because the members get to know each other well and have become good friends (and wish it to stay that way), they may decide to avoid argument in case it becomes too heated and is in danger of leading to a confrontation; and (iii) for these two reasons, the group members may become bored or dissatisfied with the meetings, and such groups have been known to dissolve by attrition.

Alternatively, if these problems are dealt with as soon as they are noticed, the group may be strengthened by purposefully increasing the level and frequency of argument. If they do this, the members have to learn to separate the heat of argument from the relative warmth of friendship; and the purposes of meeting on these occasions from the purposes of meeting on other perhaps purely social occasions. The ability to sustain this separation is important and need not lead to the breaking up of friendships. A good example of where is happens is in the House of Commons, where members of different parties have the most heated arguments and yet outside the House are the closest of friends.

You attend such meetings to make your contributions, which might take the form of your perception of a particular concept, the results of some relevant research you have carried out, or what you have gathered from what a particular writer has said about the topic or concept under discussion. You also attend to listen, consider and comment upon what the other group members are saying about the chosen topic. It is particularly important for you to find the right balance between the length of your contributions and the amount of listening you do. If you fail to find this balance, you risk criticism from your colleagues for either occupying 'the floor' for too long (being overbearing); or for being a passenger (giving nothing but taking everything away with you).

It is also worth bearing in mind that group members in these situations become interdependent and, in particular, they rely on each other to attend. If you know in advance that you are not going to be able to attend, try to find a way of letting the others know; in other words, don't let the side down by depriving them of your contributions. If you are frequently absent, they will doubt your commitment to the whole idea of meeting.

ACTIVITY 6

You are doing an assignment and need to research the relationship between organisational change and culture. The question is concerned with the several ways in which restructuring can affect employee commitment and motivation. Arrange an informal discussion with a few of your friends and carry out a brief trawl of the literature on the subject to see what you can contribute to the meeting.

STRUCTURED LEARNING GROUPS

In one sense, all groups are learning groups, but what we are discussing here are those formal sessions in which you are given cases and exercises to carry out in the classroom. The class is divided into small groups of three or four to carry out an exercise. Alternatively, the lecturer may set up a mock interview or a negotiating exercise. It may be a case study or a role play that takes you through an organisational situation. Yet again, the lecturer may have given you a case study with several questions at the end, say a couple of weeks in advance of the session. Here your task would be to analyse the case and answer the questions.

Structure of the session

As you can see from what is said above, there are many different approaches to a structured learning session. It is normal for the lecturer to give a brief introduction, divide the class into small groups and set an amount of time in which to reach your conclusions. Frequently in this type of session your group will be required to carry out a brief oral presentation at the end as a means of communicating everyone's conclusions to the whole class. Finally, the lecturer will make his or her concluding comments, which may include an indication of how well the groups have performed.

Reaping the benefits

These sessions are invaluable learning opportunities in the sense that you learn from the experience of carrying out exercises and analysing cases, and you learn from each other in the discussions that lead to your conclusions. At this point it is worth reiterating the importance of researching the subject of the case study in advance of the classroom session – otherwise you will not have a contribution to make. For the same reasons it is also important to study the situation and the context in which the case is set. Finally, when the tutor handed out the case study, he or she may also have included a short reading list.

ASSESSMENT GROUPS

An assessment group may involve the group members in demonstrating particular skills, dealing with a case study or carrying out an assignment. These are vitally important events since not only are they valuable learning experiences, but are also part of the formal assessment strategy and the results you achieve. Therefore, they count towards your overall marks for the study unit and the academic year.

The tutor may ask the students to form themselves in to small groups of four or five members. Naturally, when this happens, people choose those with whom they would prefer to work. Alternatively, the tutor may nominate the group members, in which case you may find yourself in the company of colleagues with whom you have not previously worked. There is a general belief among lecturers that there are advantages to varying the personnel of groups for different events. One advantage is that eventually the class becomes more of a cohesive whole; another is that the individual students experience a broader range of perceptions, views and ideas from their colleagues and, thereby, learn more.

TYPES OF ASSESSMENT GROUP

Today's universities have developed a wide variety of techniques for assessing the work of students in groups, and a variety of formats for structuring group activities. You may be required to work with others in several of the following types of groups and their activities:

> The assessment of specific skills. These are required most frequently by the professional institutions that have approved the learning centre as a provider of their courses. One of the grounds upon which this approval is given is the assessment strategy. For example, the Chartered Institute of Personnel and Development (CIPD) requires its student members to demonstrate competence in the application of particular skills, examples of which might be those required for (i) training and (ii) recruiting and selecting new employees.

The students are formed into small groups and given an *assignment brief*, which outlines what they are required to do (see Chapter 5). The exercise culminates in the delivery of an oral presentation by each group in which *all* group members must participate. Each individual student then has to produce a written report giving an account of the objectives of the whole group, how the conclusions were reached, and the nature of the contribution that was made by the writer of the report. The presentation and the report delivered by each individual are assessed together, so that each student emerges with his or her own marks. In carrying out this assessment, we always involve several lecturers (usually the whole course team), and an external adviser.

Assessed assignment groups. These are probably the most frequently used means of assessment through the use of group formulae. You carry out a group exercise in your own time; that is to say, the main bulk of the work is done outside of your classroom hours. If your fellow group members have been nominated by the lecturer, then you need to go through the important process of getting to know each other. Carrying out a group assignment is a social process, and for it to succeed, you need to work closely together. Normally, you only appear in the classroom as a group to deliver a presentation to your colleagues and at least one tutor.

All of the members of your group will have been given an assignment brief, which is a document that outlines what you are required to do. While the main parts of a *group assignment brief* are similar to those of an individual assignment brief, which is described in detail in Chapter 5, there are aspects of a group assignment brief that we can explain here. The group brief that you are given may contain any or all of the following:

- The title of the course and any study unit to which the assignment relates
- A description of the problem you are required to investigate, which may take the form of a case study
- An initial reading list (perhaps partly drawn from the reading list provided by the relevant professional institution)
- Details of the assessment strategy
- Where and when the work is due to be handed in
- The required length of the report
- The required duration of the oral presentation.

EXAMPLE 2: CARRYING OUT A GROUP ASSIGNMENT

Andrew, Margaret, Petra and Chetan are in the second year of the Chartered Institute of Marketing course and have been issued with a group assignment brief. This is based on a case study that describes a problem within the marketing department.

As a group, they are required to investigate the problem, draw conclusions as to its cause and make recommendations designed to resolve it. They also have to deliver an oral presentation of their findings and recommendations to the class and the lecturer. Each individual member of the group is required to produce his or her own written report of 1500 words in its main sections, describing their role in the group and the nature of their contribution to the investigation. The report is to be submitted for assessment two weeks after the classroom presentation. There was a short reading list attached to the case.

Their first step was to organise a meeting to develop a strategy that would lead to the completion of the work. This was a very important meeting; it set the tone within the group and started to establish a good working relationship between them.

To develop their strategy they first analysed the requirements of the assignment brief and then the case study itself. During their discussions they realised the importance of reaching a consensus on the strategic approach. From the results of their analyses of the brief and the case, they developed a list of the tasks that needed to be carried out in order to complete the investigation.

Their second step was to allocate the tasks equally and agree upon deadlines for their completion. The meeting ended and they agreed to meet again one week later.

The second meeting began with a review of the progress that had been made. As agreed at the first meeting, Chetan and Petra had been working together to refine the approach to tackling the problem. Andrew had started a literature search, and he reported on the data he had collected. Margaret had drafted the questions for a questionnaire to be distributed at her workplace, and she wanted to show it to the others, mainly to hear their thoughts about the questions she had drafted. They re-examined the appropriateness of the methodology. The rest of the time was taken up with reviewing what they had achieved and discussing their next steps, which included collating, writing up and studying the information they had gathered. They arranged another meeting in order to review their progress again and to start their preparations for the presentation.

The next meeting was their final get-together. They concluded that they had enough information to make the presentation and they worked together to develop it, using PowerPoint as the medium.

They all had to participate in the presentation, and it was logical for each of them to present an account of their individual contributions. Andrew gave a brief introduction, each of the others gave their accounts and Margaret did the summary, so that the overall effect for the audience was the presentation of a cohesive piece of work.

The presentation was a success and the group members then set about drafting their individual reports.

This example is just one type of group assignment. It does not need to deal with a specific marketing case study because the main points that the example makes are related to the ways in which the group members cooperated to produce a worthwhile result. For example:

- Everyone turned up to every meeting, thereby demonstrating their commitment to the task
- They all did what they had agreed to do and delivered their findings to their colleagues on time
- They helped each other out when necessary
- They worked together as a team to reach the objective.

DEVELOPING PRESENTATION SKILLS

When they first come to university most students are not very experienced at making oral presentations, and having to deliver material at a seminar means having to develop and apply new skills. The need to do so, however, should not be seen as a chore, a hurdle to overcome, or as some believe, a terrifying experience! In fact, it is an opportunity to develop skills that will prove to be of considerable value to you, not only while you are on your course, but later too, when you start out on your career. In today's business and public sector organisations, the ability to present a report orally has increased markedly in importance to the extent that every year, hundreds of employees are sent on courses to acquire the necessary skills. The importance of acquiring presentation skills is emphasised by Anderson:

You will find many opportunities to talk about your research on an informal basis, but the occasions on which you present your research more formally are likely to be talks to different groups of staff within the organisation, or a presentation made to a conference (Anderson 2004: 263).

COPING WITH NERVES

There are people who become gripped with terror at the very thought of having to stand up and make a personal presentation, even in a simulation exercise in the classroom. But if one is serious about entering one of the business or HR professions, then one should be prepared to 'stand and deliver'. In business, people are often asked to carry out project work; today, it is not at all unusual to be asked to make a personal presentation of the main features of the resultant report, perhaps to a group of senior managers or even the board of directors. Initially, there are steps that one can take to avoid disaster, after which it becomes a matter of experience. Delivering a presentation is a craft that can be learned. Where possible, however, those who are new to it are advised to take the opportunities to practise in the classroom during the course, when presenting to tutors and fellow students.

Many of the greatest presenters have suffered from 'nerves' when faced with the prospect of standing up in front of others. Actors, newsreaders, professors, demonstrators, company directors, trade union chiefs – whatever trade or profession they belong to and no matter how famous they are, it happens. Such fear is regarded by some as a healthy thing. 'It heightens your sensitivity and sharpens your performance,' some say. There are several keys to overcoming this affliction:

- *First and foremost*, ensure that you know your material thoroughly. Having a familiar route laid out in front of you stimulates your confidence.

- *Second*, learn to relax before you make the presentation. There are relaxation techniques that have to be learned, and there are plenty of books and classes on the subject.

- *Third*, be genuinely interested in your subject. Your enthusiasm for it will be communicated to your audience, you will become involved in what you are doing and will forget that you were ever nervous.

- *Fourth*, be aware of and control your speech. Talking too quickly (which for some students is an escape strategy) will make you feel even more nervous. Look at your audience and talk naturally, even a little more slowly than usual, without, of course, boring them. This can calm things down and give the audience the time to take in what you are saying. Then you can take charge of the session and run it to the best of your ability. The more often you do it, the less nervous you will be.

PREPARATION

Thorough preparation is the key to making a successful presentation. Good presentations do not just happen, you have to plan and rehearse them. Remember, you are to make a presentation that is important, because your colleagues may learn from it and, of course, it is going to be assessed. The approach to preparation should be methodical, just like the work you carried out to get this far with your assignment.

Writing your presentation notes

Initially, you should do this by following the logical sequence of the notes you made during the research process. This will ensure that your part of the presentation has been well researched, logically structured and supported by appropriate evidence and references. Once you have completed your notes, you can now restructure them for the presentation.

Drafting the presentation

To making an effective presentation, you need to consider the following factors:

- Who will be in your audience?
- How much are they likely to know already about the subject?
- How long is the presentation to last?
- What material will the other members of my assignment group present?
- Where am I to make the presentation: seminar room, lecture theatre?
- What facilities are there for presenting supporting materials: OHP, video presenter, slide projector, whiteboard, flipchart, PowerPoint projector?

The answers to these questions will affect both the content and the structure of your presentation. For example:

1   An audience that knows nothing about a subject will require more background material, whereas an audience with some knowledge of the subject will be more critical, requiring you to provide more detail and supporting evidence.

2   It would be a disaster if you turned up for your presentation with a box of beautifully prepared slides to discover there is no projector!

3   The size of room will determine where you place yourself in regard to your audience as well as your choice of visual media. A flipchart will appear quite large in a seminar room, whereas it may appear insignificant and difficult to read in a lecture theatre. Conversely, a small seminar room may not be

big enough to set up and properly focus a slide projector, while in a lecture theatre the size of the image obtainable can give your presentation considerable impact.

Important! If you have prepared a PowerPoint presentation on your home computer, *always* give it a dry run on the university's facilities well in advance of the date of your presentation. I have witnessed the horror experienced by students who stride confidently up to the front of the class, floppy disk in hand, only to discover that they cannot open up their presentation on the computer in the room. If, when you do test it, it does not work, take it to the IT department and ask them to 'fix it'.

Know your subject!

When your plan for the presentation is complete, learn it and practise going through it as if delivering it in the real situation.

Handling your notes

Work out what you are going to say and how you are going to say it. Ensure that you have written your notes in order of delivery. Some presenters have their notes on sheets of A4 paper and keep them in a file that they can flip through as each item is delivered and completed. Others use small cards, about the size of a postcard, with a hole in the top left corner for a treasury tag to keep them together. You need to get to know your notes so well that you never have to refer to them during the presentation; just take them in as your security blanket!

Important! You will lose marks if your delivery is a straightforward 'read-out' from your notes.

Reading directly from your notes will prevent you from making eye contact with members of your audience; it will also lose some credibility and make your presentation rather dull. Just in case you need to look at your notes, have them at your side already open. If you have included subheadings in bold capital letters, you will very quickly find what you need.

Communicating the message

To get a message across clearly, I always use the *sandwich approach*:

A Tell 'em what you're gonna tell 'em

B Tell 'em

C Tell 'em what you've told 'em!

(A). *Tell 'em what you're gonna tell 'em,* is the bottom layer of bread – it is the introduction, which is important. It should be designed to gain the immediate attention of your audience. However, on the basis that not everyone was listening or understood your opening, repeat it – not word for word but summarised to ensure that your audience has taken it in. This applies to all major points throughout your presentation. This is a technique that is understood and used by all good public speakers.

(B). *Tell 'em,* is the meat in the sandwich. This is when you deliver the main points of your presentation. Always use simple, everyday language. Avoid jargon and specialised terms except when it is necessary to be explicit. Speak slowly and clearly; you must allow your audience sufficient time to take note of what you are saying. Round off one idea – pause – then introduce the next.

There is a limit, however, to the amount of information you can impart to your audience orally. Do not confuse them with lots of facts and figures – use simple charts and graphs instead. Good visual support material is essential, particularly when you are putting across statistical information.

Focus your attention on concepts rather than detail. You can always provide detail in a handout at the end of your presentation. If you have included references on your OHP foils or PowerPoint frames, leave them up there long enough the audience to jot them down, or include them on your handout.

(C). *Tell 'em what you've told 'em!* is the top layer of bread. The audience had a summary at the beginning; they have had the main sections, so this is where you provide the summary again. You came in with a bang; this is your chance to go out with a bang. Your final summary may be slightly different from the first one. This is because you may not have stuck strictly to your script; things occur to you while you are speaking. They may be items you had overlooked when you were drafting your notes, or they may be fresh thoughts that occurred to you because of what you were actually saying at the time. You will see from several other chapters in the book that the same kind of phenomenon occurs when you are writing.

Still, you have to draw your little spell in the limelight to a conclusion and, despite what is said above about the summary, you have to work to the clock. The whole thing should finish on time. After your summary, invite questions (keeping your eye on the time) and then, when you are sure that your audience knows you have finished, distribute any handouts you may have prepared.

Important! There is only one way to get the timing of your presentation right and that is to practise. You will need to rehearse your final version at least twice – preferably with an audience of friends or relatives.

USING VISUAL AIDS

- Make sure you know how to use a white board, flip chart, overhead projector (OHP) and PowerPoint equipment. You also need to know how to prepare your OHP foils. Handwritten or hand-drawn foils are now almost unheard of, and producing foils on a computer makes for a far more attractive presentation. In this way, the print is clear; colour may be introduced to brighten up the proceedings and will also help to hold the attention of your audience. Never transpose an ordinary sheet of typewritten information on to an OHP foil, or any other presentation media for that matter. The type will be too small to read, it will carry too much information and it looks like lazy or last-minute preparation. If, however, you can only prepare your foils by hand the following tips may help:
- Use only block capital letters written with a colour-fast OHP pen
- To achieve straight lines, use ruled paper under the foil when writing
- Do not overload any one foil with too much information. This applies to all foils, whether handwritten or otherwise produced; four or five lines of writing on each foil are sufficient.

Using the OHP
Always remember to turn off the OHP and only remove the foil when you have delivered its contents *and* dealt with any questions that may give rise to showing it again. If you move on to the next section of your delivery while the OHP is still illuminated, with or without the foil, it will distract your audience.

Prepare notes to cover the contents of the OHP, but do not distribute them until the end of the session. If you do, your audience will be reading them while you are speaking. Tell the audience that you will be handing out notes; otherwise they may try to make notes when they should be listening to you.

PowerPoint
This has become the most popular illustrative medium through which to deliver a talk. Ideally, you will know how to use it. With PowerPoint, you can guide the audience through the whole presentation from the same

spot. It is usual to run off copies of the PowerPoint frames to hand out to the audience as *aide-memoires*. With this medium, you can vary colours and use animated techniques. Modern computers have a capacity that will accommodate the PowerPoint package, which includes instructions for use. However, if you have difficulty with the preparation of any visual materials, most universities have a *media resources department* to which you may go for advice and assistance.

USING STORYBOARD CARDS

You may have several visual images to present, and you will need to control the sequence and the timing of their introduction into your presentation. The most effective means of achieving this is to use a simple storyboard (see below). Storyboards are merely a development of your notes with prompts at the appropriate points in your presentation. Separate cards are used to represent (by what you say, show or do) each key point in the development of your theme. By shuffling these cards about, you will be able to develop a coherent and logically structured presentation. When you have finally settled on their order, number them sequentially to prevent errors later.

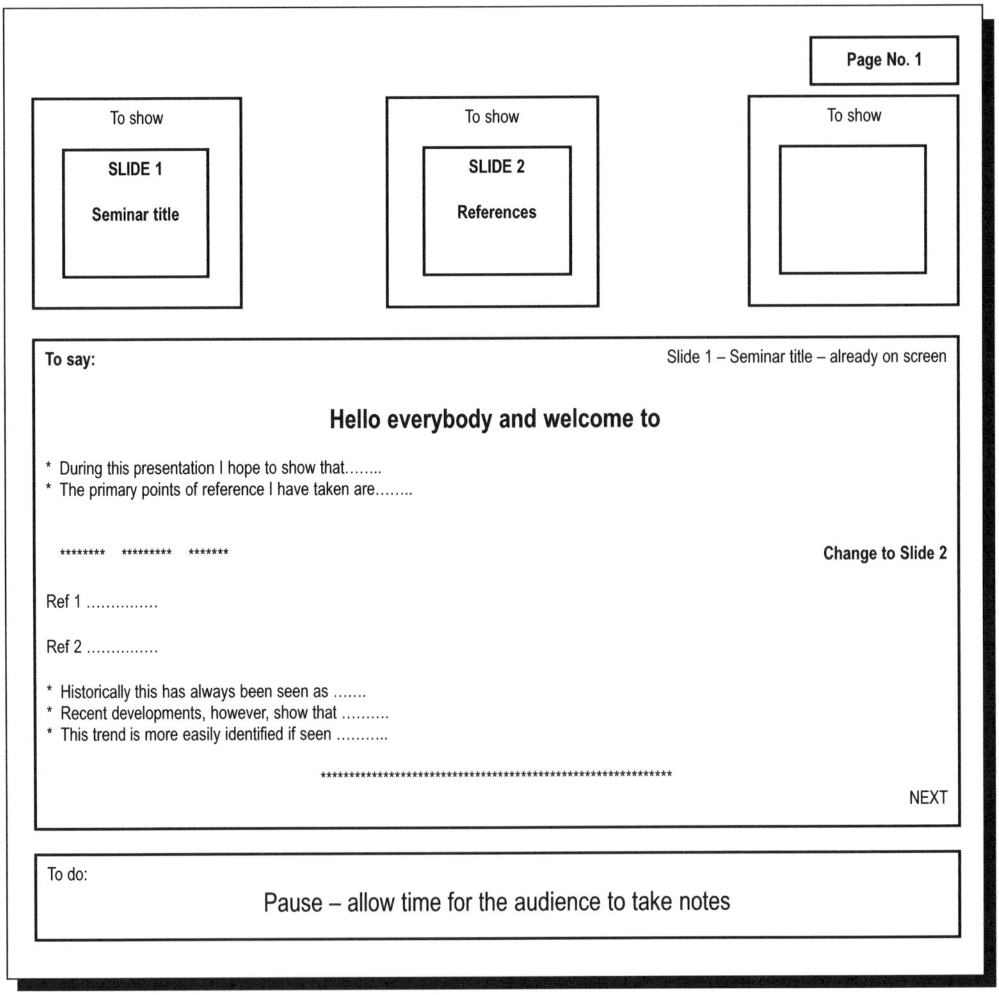

Figure 4   *Examples of storyboard cards*

Figure 4 shows how the storyboard is used to control the sequencing of your presentation. You may not need to use all of the elements on each card. If you do not need an item, cross it through, but do not obliterate it, so that you will know that you have not forgotten something.

HANDLING QUESTIONS

It is wise to lay the ground rules for questions from the very beginning of your talk. There are several ways of handling this. Firstly, are you willing to take questions at any point in your presentation? Secondly, would you prefer to take them at the end when you know how much time you have left? Thirdly, you may decide to ask for questions at sectional points when, for example, you have just finished explaining a concept, or perhaps, why you chose a particular methodology. There are advantages and disadvantages to all of these options.

Advantages

1 *Interruptions.* You may decide to turn these to your advantage. They may allow you to focus your argument on particular points of interest and engage your audience by allowing them to participate, which could make you forget any nervousness you may have had, and to change the pace and direction of your presentation; all of this might make the event more interesting for everyone.

2 *Taking questions at the end.* If you decide to do this, you can be sure of a free run through your presentation, which would allow you to focus exclusively on what you are doing, while avoiding any digressive discussions. At the end, you should know how much time you have left; if your time is short, you will be allowed to limit your answers to any 'difficult' questions.

3 *Inviting intermittent questions.* Again, this is an opportunity to engage the audience and give them a sense of participation. Also, it provides you with on-the-spot feedback on how your talk is being received. By using this method, you can regain control of the floor whenever you wish, especially if you feel it slipping away from you.

Disadvantages

1 *Interruptions.* If you take questions 'on-the-hoof', you may risk exceeding your allotted time or, worse still, it may cause you to have to cut short your delivery. Such interruptions can interfere with the smooth flow of your talk, giving your audience a 'stop-start' impression, but more importantly, interruptions can cause you to lose track of where you are in the sequence.

2 *Taking questions at the end.* If you decide to do this, you could leave your audience stranded and feeling isolated, especially if you have not planned sufficient time for this part of your talk. Furthermore, you could feel a little stranded yourself, because insufficient interaction with your audience will leave you wondering how well they thought you did.

3 *Inviting intermittent questions.* Students have been known to use this method if they feel that the content of their presentation is a bit thin, but if you use it for that reason, be very careful, especially if your programme really is lacking in substance, because if that is so, then you probably do not have the answers.

Most of what is said above applies equally to group and individual presentations. However, when you are carrying out a presentation with your group colleagues, you need to pay particular attention to several factors. Firstly, you must stick rigidly to the portion of the time that has been allocated for your contribution. Every minute you overrun is a minute off their time. Secondly, do not put your footprints on your colleagues' ground; in other words, only deliver the aspects of the presentation that were planned for you beforehand. Thirdly, do not try to answer questions that relate to your colleagues' subject matter.

This leads us to consider the advantages of making the decision for the whole group to take questions at the end of the presentation, rather than at the end of each individual's allocated time. Obviously, someone seeking clarification of a small point that can be dealt with very quickly should be answered, but if the main questions are taken at the end they can be deflected to the appropriate group member.

CHECK YOUR UNDERSTANDING

Questions

1 Name three of the types of group in which you work

2 How would you prepare yourself to participate fully in a *structured learning group*?

3 How might your group plan to carry out an assessed assignment – what steps would you take?

4 How might the experience of working as a team be valuable to you after you have finished the course?

5 How would you try to overcome the fear of making an oral presentation?

6 Who will be the beneficiaries of your presentation, and why?

7 What do you need to know about your audience before you make a presentation?

8 What is the *sandwich approach* to making a presentation?

9 What options do you have when deciding how and when you are going to take questions?

10 What are the main differences between an individual and a group presentation?

FURTHER READING

ANDERSON, V. (2004) *Research Methods in Human Resource Management.* London: Chartered Institute of Personnel and Development.

CAMERON, S. (2001) *The MBA Handbook*, 4th edn. Harlow: Pearson Education.

HUCZYNSKI, A. and BUCHANAN, D. (2001) *Organisational Behaviour – an introductory text*, 4th edn. Harlow: Pearson Education.

Writing essays

CHAPTER OBJECTIVES

After studying this chapter you should:

- **understand the purposes of essays as learning instruments**
- **be able to analyse an essay brief with a view to achieving a clear understanding of what you are expected to do**
- **be able to develop an essay question and title**
- **understand how essays are assessed**
- **be able to develop an essay plan**

INTRODUCTION

An essay is an answer to a question. Its purpose, from the tutor's point of view, is to test your knowledge of a subject and your ability to handle ideas and information; and to develop an argument that supports the case you make in your answer, all of which lead to a planned and logical response to the question. Your purpose is to take advantage of the opportunity to learn from discovering fresh information about the essay topic, to state your point of view and to demonstrate your ability to search for, find and review evidence that supports your view. This means searching for and reviewing relevant literature and other potential sources of information, such as academic and professional journals or CD-ROMs, all of which will be in your library. An essay, therefore, is an opportunity for you to develop your knowledge further as you search for information that enables you to answer the question; and a means by which the tutor assesses your knowledge and skills.

At the beginning of the course you will have been given several documents such as, among others, the course handbook for the year and the timetable. In our document pack we include the briefing papers for the work that needs to be carried out, which, of course, includes the *essay briefs* (see below). Tutors regard the documents in the pack as critically important, yet many students put them to one side, with 'I'll get around to reading those later' comments. For time management purposes it is essential for you to study the contents of the document pack since it contains details of the tasks you are required to carry out and what you need to know about those tasks in terms of delivery dates and so forth. I am often asked questions by students, and far too frequently I have to tell them to read the handbook.

On most courses, essays have to be submitted during the second half of the year. If you read the requirements and start early, you will be able to manage your time more easily. So, take a careful look at the deadline dates for your work, because in the 1990s many universities reprogrammed their courses across semesters, rather than terms, although there is now a drift back to terms. If your university uses a semester system, then your work will be due in at the end of each semester, rather than at the end of the year.

WHERE TO START

You start by studying the *essay brief*, which is a document that outlines precisely what you are expected to do. There is an example of an essay brief at the end of the chapter. The essay subject may be written as a *question, an instruction* or perhaps an *abstract* from the work of an eminent writer; in whatever form the topic is presented to you, the brief will define the essay subject. There is no universal format for an essay brief; universities have their own styles and they vary quite widely. The document, therefore, may contain any or all of the following:

- The topic in the form of a question, instruction or abstract
- Details about how you are expected to handle the topic
- The assessment criteria and information about what the examiner will be looking for
- The required length of the essay
- The date it is to be handed in
- Some guidance about the format and style of the essay
- An initial reading list.

ANALYSING THE ESSAY BRIEF

This is a critically important task since clarifying your understanding of the requirements of the brief will determine all of the activities you engage in before you actually sit down to write it all up. 'Formulating and clarifying the research topic is the starting point' (Ghauri and Gronhaug 2002). To achieve this it is essential to read the brief thoroughly – a cursory glance is not enough, nor indeed is just a single reading. Every time you go through it, you see something you did not previously notice.

ANALOGY: THE GIFT SHOP WINDOW

When you are strolling along the promenade at the seaside you may find yourself gazing into a gift shop window. The next time you walk past and glance into the window, you will see something you missed on the day before. Essay briefs are like that and so, by the way, are books. The second time you read them, read *into* them *purposefully*, and you will find meanings that you previously missed. Read the brief thoroughly several times and make notes.

So what are you looking for?

You are looking for information that will enable you to answer the question and plan the task of producing the essay. Below is an example from an essay brief that was issued to second-year degree students studying organisational development. In this brief the topic is based on an instruction.

EXAMPLE 3

Choose two different **types of organisation** and **compare and contrast** the **effects of the changes** that have been brought about by the introduction of new technology.

You will notice that I have highlighted several words; these were not highlighted in the original brief. Firstly, let us consider the phrase, *types of organisation*. How many students do you think wrote about two different organisations, such as Brown & Co and Smith & Co? The answer is too many – they failed to read it thoroughly. What in fact we asked for were *types* of organisation such as, for example, one in engineering and one in food processing, or perhaps one in retail and one in banking. The word 'types' did not seem to register.

Secondly, let us examine the words *compare and contrast*. I am drawing attention to these because they are key words and they need particular consideration. They are called *process words*, and you should ensure that you understand their real meanings because your tutor will have used them to tell you how he or she expects you to handle the topic. Notice too that process words are verbs, things for you *to do*. Other process words (verbs) that you might find in an essay brief are: *criticise, explain, justify, discuss, evaluate, assess, illustrate, construct,* etc. Look out for these words in the brief; they are there to guide you.

Thirdly, the *effects of the changes*. This means that the examiner is not expecting you to simply describe the changes. You may have to do that, yes, but the examiner will expect most of the emphasis to be upon what the changes mean for the organisation in terms of its success, what they mean to the shareholders, the board of directors, the managers and the employees. How might the changes affect them?

FORMULATING AN ESSAY QUESTION

When, as in Example 3, the topic is based on an instruction, you will be expected to develop a question from it. First, you have to think about what statement *you* wish to make about the topic. When you study the instruction ideas about how the subject might be approached will occur to you. This may lead you into a few blind alleys, but when you have decided on an approach the question will begin to emerge. The question you eventually decide upon should be strongly influenced by the point of view you wish to express about the topic. A question such as 'How might technology change organisations?' is what one might call a non-adventurous question, since it could open the door to nothing more than writing up a list of the kinds of change that each type of organisation may have to make. To follow such a line may not lead to a high mark from the examiner; it is a flat question. What about: *Does new technology always bring a welcome change?* The word welcome has introduced a hint of the approach you might have taken.

COINING THE ESSAY TITLE

This is derived from the question, and there are two main considerations here. The first is, 'does my title indicate the essay subject clearly?' The second consideration is the attractiveness of the title. Will it make the reader want to read on? One of the factors in generating a dynamic title is the number of words it contains. To be drawn to it, the reader has to be able to take it in at a glance. Advertising people are the experts in this field, and they will tell you that the average person can read and derive meaning from no more than five words when taken in at a glance. Captions in newspaper advertisements are designed to compel attention; so are those that are used in television advertising, as, of course, are book and film titles. But that is another field and, for our purposes, I would recommend no more than seven words for an essay title. Using only five words, you could, for example, entitle it: *New technology – a welcome change.* If this appeared on the title page, the reader would then turn the page and read the question, which heads up the first page of the essay, and he or she would find what they were expecting to find. The question and the title should be totally interdependent.

EXPLORING THE RANGE OF THE TOPIC

When you study the brief you start thinking about how you are going to approach the task. In this respect the *range of the topic* refers to the variety of avenues of possible enquiry you discover and may consider exploring further when you start to tap the information sources. It also refers to the breadth and depth of your study. How far you are able go in these terms is partly determined by the knowledge you have gained on the course and from your reading, the level of which will depend on the year you are in. An important factor, of course, is how far you are prepared to go yourself in order to achieve a mark that you would regard as satisfactory. Some students are not prepared to push themselves enough to achieve a high mark. Mind you, when they fall short of what they thought they would have achieved, they find themselves in some difficulty, especially with the tutor who has invested considerable time and effort into preparing the ground upon which they may study. The advice is always to aim high because, if you do not, you are not only being ungracious to your tutor, 'you are also being unfair to yourself because you are not giving yourself the maximum opportunity to have your ideas and plans scrutinised and subjected to rigorous questioning' (Saunders *et al* 2003: 29).

EXPLORING PROSPECTIVE AVENUES

Going back to *New technology – a welcome change*, below are a few examples of the directions in which your thoughts may turn when you are discovering and considering the range of the topic.

- The technology may be welcomed by all since, in both operational and administrative terms, it brings with it a cleaner, faster and more efficient way of doing things; and it speeds up the rate of business activity.

- It might be welcomed by those involved in corporate strategy because it may enable the organisation to do things it could not do before such as producing a new range of goods and services facilitating entry into new markets. 'For corporate management this (technological innovation) is a problem of costs and controls ... for employees, however, it is a problem of the dehumanisation of work' (Braverman 1974).

- The employees, therefore, may not be so welcoming; they may worry about their future in the belief that new technology reduces the demand for human resources. 'Computers and robots will replace people in manufacturing; the unstaffed factory is a reality ... where people are still required, work will be simple, routine, dehumanised' (Huczynski and Buchanan 2001).

- Employees may also worry about their skills being eroded and being expected to cope with technology they may not understand, even with training.

Preparing yourself in this way seems like a lot of work and can be a little time-consuming, but you have to be prepared to do this. Without spending time on this stage you are far less likely to achieve a successful project (Raimond 1993).

READING

Literature is the most important source of the information you need when writing an essay. There are other sources, which are detailed in Chapter 6, but when you start to gather information for your essay, you need to carry out an *initial literature search*. There should be an initial reading list in the essay brief; if there is not, go and see your tutor and ask for guidance on reading and other information sources. It is essential for you to know where to look for information.

You should not regard the reading list in the essay brief as a definitive list; rather it is a starting point. The texts on the list will lead you to further readings and broaden the scope of the information you gather. When you start to read you should try to do so *purposefully*; that is to say, you are looking for something that is relevant to the topic and the aims and objectives of the essay. First, however, you have to identify key words that will lead you to the data you seek (see Chapter 6). In a sense, purposeful reading is a little like looking something up in a dictionary because you know the topic and, armed with your key words, you know what you are looking for. Your purpose is to identify what other writers have said about your subject. Some of the books you find will be exclusively about the subject, while others will be related to it or may contain a chapter on it. When I issue a reading list I always divide it into three broad categories:

1   *Essential reading.* These are the books that I would include in an essay brief, since they are exclusively about the subject, they are up to date and by authors whose names the examiner would expect to see cited in your text and on your reference list. By studying these and noting the references they use, you can broaden the scope of your information since they will lead you to further readings.

2   *Recommended readings* are texts that are related to your subject but not exclusively about it. This also includes some older, but well-known texts that contain information that is still valuable and relevant to the subject.

3   *Supplementary reading,* which includes professional and specialist journals, especially those published by professional institutions.

THE ESSAY PLAN

In many universities, before starting on an essay, you have to submit an *essay plan,* which usually asks for:

- An essay title and question
- Your intended overall approach to the task
- Your approach to searching for and reviewing literature
- A reading list and details of other information sources you intend to use.

The essay plan is usually assessed, representing about 10–15 per cent of the total marks for the essay. The more care you take over your preparation, the more successful your essay plan and, ultimately, the essay itself will be. Even if you are not asked for an essay plan, you would be well advised to produce one anyway, for your own benefit. When you have produced an essay plan you have given yourself a set of guidelines to which you can refer as you progress through the planning and preparatory stages for the essay itself. There is an example of an essay plan at the end of this chapter.

ASSESSMENT AND STANDARDS

It is important for you to gain an understanding of the assessment criteria and the academic standards that are expected. Assessment criteria are the formal criteria against which your work will be marked, and they should be included in the essay brief. If they are not in the brief, then you need to get hold of them as soon as possible. As you will see from Table 3, they are not subject centred and they usually appear in the same format for all essays in each university.

Table 3 provides an indication of an examiner's comments *after* reading a student's essay. What it should convey to you is an indication of what the examiner regards as important, taking into account the year or level of the student concerned. This is particularly useful if you are a first-year student. Look, for example, at the phrase 'meets the requirements in all respects'; this relates to the requirements that are set out in the essay brief. However, the statements about the degree to which you have met the requirements is moderated as we move vertically down the scale from 70 per cent +. Similar treatment is given to other criteria, such as relevance and appropriateness, research, the writing standard and the citation and referencing system. As a student, however, this tells you little about what *you* actually have to do to get 70 per cent or more. One approach is to examine the elements that go towards creating a successful essay.

ELEMENTS OF A SUCCESSFUL ESSAY

The following is written as a checklist for use *after* you have completed your essay and are checking it over before submitting it. It is included here, however, since it would also be useful to have at your side even

Table 3 *Assessment criteria – whole essay: Business/HR-related*
Note: Does not take account of marks awarded for essay plan

Mark	Comment
70% and above	Meets the requirement in all respects. Academically appropriate and relevant to area of business/HR. Case is argued well and is supported by evidence from thorough research. Well-written. Recognised citation and referencing system
60–69%	Meets the requirement in almost all respects and appropriate to academic aspects of business/HR. Makes some good points in argument. Well-written. Recognised citation and referencing system
50–59%	Meets the requirements in some respects. Arguments appear feasible but lack sufficient evidential support. Would have benefited from more rigorous research. Fairly well-written. Recognised citation and referencing system
40–49%	Addresses the issues but the requirements met are few. Arguments are tenuous in places. Insufficient research to fully justify what is said. Fair standard of writing. Citation and referencing system mostly applied correctly
Fail: 39% and below	Fails to meet the requirements. Digresses from the central issues. Amount of opinion outweighs research results. Poorly written. Some citations and referencing correct

from the early stages of preparation – because if these are the important elements, then they are what you should be aiming to achieve as you do the work:

- Have I answered the question that was set?
- Have I covered all the main points and done so in sufficient depth?
- Is the content relevant, accurate and written plainly?
- Have I sequenced the material logically?
- Have I presented a convincing case, which I could justify in a discussion?
- Does the essay move smoothly from one section to another?
- Is each main point supported by research results, examples and argument?
- Have I acknowledged all sources and references?
- Have I distinguished clearly between my own ideas and those of others?
- Is the essay the right length?
- Are the grammar, punctuation and spelling acceptable?
- Have I read it aloud to myself to sort out clumsy or muddled phrasing?

Another approach to assessment, which is usually used in addition to the one described in Table 4, is to show how marks may be allocated in terms of the degree to which the student has responded to each of the main elements of the essay. This approach uses the main elements of the essay as criteria against which your work will be assessed. Table 4 should tell you something about the importance, *and the*

Table 4 *Assessment criteria – allocated percentages: Business/HR-related essay*

Criteria	70%+	60–69%	50–59%	40–49%	39% and below
Literature review: breadth and depth; validity of critique; comparing and contrasting	Wide range of texts and other sources; relates well to question; good and valid critique	Acceptable range of texts and other sources; mostly relates to question; could have been more critical	Good range of texts but few other sources; mostly relates to question; compares and contrasts what other writers have said, but lacks critique	Good range of texts, but other sources not used; mostly relevant to question; lists and comments on what other writers have said	Range of texts too narrow; other sources not used; simply lists what other writers have said; lacks analysis of literature
Argument: strength; feasible; logical; based on data; ideas; relevant to question; convincing	Well-formed; ideas handled well; based on data; logical and convincing	Well-expressed; ideas handled well; largely based on data; logical and fairly convincing; open to some debate	Well-expressed; some good ideas; mostly logically argued, but tenuous in parts	Related to question but not strong. Would be hard to defend in discussion	Tenuously related to the question; reiteration rather than argument
Supporting evidence: relevance to argument; sufficiency; authoritative	Based on good authority; relevant to argument; clearly presented	Mostly relevant to argument; authoritative; well-presented in most parts	What is presented is fine, but sometimes lacks relevance to argument; well-expressed	Basic and obvious, but mostly relevant to the argument; mostly drawn from standard texts	Some evidence is there but is not used to support argument; drawn from standard texts
Information handling: data collection, structure, manipulation; presentation	Demonstrates very good skills; clearly presented and well-structured	Demonstrates good skills; well-presented; some good manipulative skills	Demonstrates moderate skills; well-presented; fair manipulative skills	Demonstrates good skills; attractively presented	Demonstrates fair skills; style of presenting data could be improved
Presentation: writing standard; layout and format; sequence of themes; citations and referencing	Good writing standard; attractive layout and format; flows well; logically sequenced themes; citations and references match and are clearly shown	Acceptable writing standard; good layout and format; flows well; good logical sequence; most citations and references match and are clearly shown	Fair writing standard; good layout and format; sequences of themes open to question; citations and references poorly handled	Moderate writing standard; fair layout and format; sequence of themes is logical; citations and references very poorly handled	Poor writing standard; layout and format not too bad; hard to find logic in sequence of themes; citation and references very poorly handled

priorities, that the examiner has in mind when assessing an essay. Most students regard this as a useful aid to their understanding of what they actually need to do in order to achieve a high mark. The difference between these two figures is that the left-hand column in Table 4 clearly shows in advance what the examiners regard as important, rather than commenting on what he or she has found in the essay. We often see references to 'what the examiner is looking for'; well, this is it. It is also a good guide to 'what *not* to do'. Universities vary in their approaches to this but the principle is universal.

EXAMPLE OF AN ESSAY BRIEF

The following essay brief was issued to students on their second year of a BA (Hons) degree in Business Studies.

UNIVERSITY OF BELLCHESTER
ESSAY BRIEF

QUESTION:

What are the principal characteristics that differentiate *organic* and *mechanistic* organisational structures?

1 Draw up an essay plan of approximately 600 words containing (i) how you propose to approach the question; (ii) an introductory paragraph setting the question in context; (iii) a methodology showing how you will research the subject and why you have chosen those methods; (iv) a proposed reading list.
   The essay plan is to be submitted for assessment on the Tuesday of week 8.
2 When the essay plan has been approved, write an essay of not less than 2000 and no more than 2500 words and submit it to the Business School office on the Tuesday of Week 22.
3 In your answer you are expected to discuss how the level of environmental uncertainty may influence structure, employment policy and marketing strategy.

READING LIST

BURNS, T. and STALKER, G. M. (1961) *The Management of Innovation.* London: Tavistock.

HUCZYNSKI, A. and BUCHANAN, D. (2001) *Organisational Behaviour – an introductory text*, 4th edn. Harlow: Pearson Education.

JONES, G. R. (1994) *Organizational Theory – texts and cases.* Reading, MA: Addison-Wesley.

LAWRENCE, P. R. and LORSCH, J. W. (1967) *Organization and Environment.* Boston, MA: Harvard University, Graduate School of Business Administration.

You are expected to regard the above as an initial reading list – a starting point that will lead you to further reading.

ESSAY BRIEF: ASSESSMENT CRITERIA

In particular the examiner will be looking for:

- A literature review that is of sufficient breadth and depth; how it compares, contrasts and critically reviews what other writers have said about the subject and shows a clear link to the subject and the aims and objectives of the essay.
- A strong and convincing argument that supports your case; one that is feasible, logical, based on researched data and relevant to the question.
- Strong evidence to support your argument; sufficient evidence that is authoritative.
- How the information was collected, structured and presented.
- The general presentation, including writing standard, layout and format, sequence of themes, citations and references.

EXAMPLE OF AN ESSAY PLAN

The following is an example of an essay plan that might be submitted by a student who has been issued with the above essay brief. The title page will include the title of the essay and the student's name and other related details. The suggested title in the example is: *Environmental uncertainty's influence on strategy.*

What are the principal characteristics that differentiate *organic* and *mechanistic* organisational structures?

This essay plan outlines the approach to the above question, the methodology, including an explanation of and justification for the research methods to be used.

An initial literature search and review has been carried out, and a proposed reading list appears on the final page.

According to Jones (1994), the following figure demonstrates the relationship between environmental uncertainty and organisational structure.

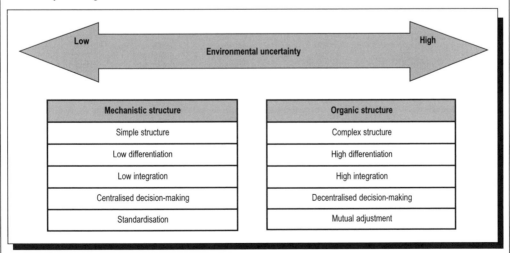

Figure 5 *Relationship between environmental uncertainty and organisational structure*

Since in this respect the structure of an organisation is influenced by the degree of uncertainty, this figure will be used to demonstrate the major differences between the reasoning behind having mechanistic or organic structures. It is anticipated, however, that further reading will lead to a discussion of other aspects, such as the effects on employment policy and marketing strategy.

For example, Burns and Stalker (1961), the originators of the mechanistic–organic concept, see it as a dimension, so that organisations are not distinctively mechanistic or distinctively organic. Organisations, they say, may be *more or less* mechanistic or *more or less* organic, depending on the stability or instability of the market in terms of demand.

Clearly, there is no 'one best way' to design and manage any organisation, since internally it needs to be capable of responding to external demands, the nature of which varies from one organisation to another and continues to change. In this respect, it seems from the literature that, in broad terms, mechanistic organisations serve stable markets while organic ones serve unstable markets. This, of course, has strong implications for so-called 'short', 'medium' and 'long-term' planning in that an organisation whose product/s have been in demand for many years with no indication that the market will change can afford long-term capital investment, since their confidence in the future of their standard product/s will ensure a return on their capital.

On the other hand, firms that are serving unstable markets, such as those in innovative products and services where rapid change is 'normal' need to respond quickly to the demands of their markets. Burns and Stalker (1961) maintain that it is unlikely that an organisation with a mechanistic structure would be able to do that effectively.

Another strong implication is that mechanistic and organic organisations are each likely to attract different kinds of employee. Mechanistically structured organisations tend to attract employees who are looking for long employment in a stable, unchanging work environment, whereas organically designed set-ups tend to attract people who are technical experts, who can innovate and communicate the technical aspects of their products.

There are further implications for employment policy, which include issues around leadership, loyalty and several further staff-related qualities, all of which will be addressed in the essay.

There is probably enough in the above to indicate the shape of the essay plan. The student will have explained his or her points of view further than I have in the above; and would have included a reading list.

SUMMARY

The purpose of an essay is to test your general knowledge of a subject and your skills in handling ideas and information in developing a convincing argument that supports the case for your point of view. It is also one of the means through which you learn, since you find new information through research. You start on the preparatory work by analysing the essay brief in order to clarifying your understanding of what you are expected to do. The essay brief sometimes contains the question; otherwise it will present the topic and require you to develop the question yourself. A clear grasp of the assessment strategy will give you a good understanding of the academic standard you are aiming to achieve. Some universities ask for an *essay plan*, which is often a first-year requirement that gives the tutor the opportunity to advise you on your approach to the topic.

CHECK YOUR UNDERSTANDING

1 What is an essay?

2 If you were approached by a worried colleague who said that he or she did not know where or how to start the essay, what would you tell them?

3 What are process words?

4 What is meant by the 'range of the topic'?

5 What are your most important sources of information when you are preparing an essay?

6 Why is it important for you to understand how your essay will be assessed?

7 What are the main features of a good essay title?

8 Why should you always 'aim for the top'?

9 What would you expect to find in an essay brief?

10 How should you regard the reading list you have been given?

FURTHER READING

BRAVERMAN, R. (1974) 'Degradation of Work in the Twentieth Century'. *Monthly Review Press* (New York), p36.

GHAURI, P. and GRONHAUG, K. (2002) *Research Methods in Business Studies: A practical guide*, 2nd edn. London: Paul Chapman.

HUCZYNSKI, A. and BUCHANAN, D. (2001) *Organisational Behaviour – an introductory text*, 4th edn. Harlow: Pearson Education.

JONES, G. R. (1994) *Organisational Theory – texts and cases.* Reading, MA: Addison Wesley.

RAIMOND, P. (1993) *Management Projects.* London: Chapman and Hall, in Saunders *et al* (2003).

SAUNDERS, M., LEWIS, P. and THORNHILL, A. (2003) *Research Methods for Business Students.* Harlow: Pearson Education.

Carrying out assignments

CHAPTER 5

> **CHAPTER OBJECTIVES**
>
> After studying this chapter you should:
>
> - understand the purposes of assignments as learning and assessment media
> - be able to analyse an assignment brief
> - be able to identify an organisational problem or issue that needs to be addressed
> - understand how assignments are assessed
> - be able to structure an assignment report

INTRODUCTION

Before we start it will be useful for you to understand that universities that offer professional courses will have been approved to do so by the relevant professional institutions, which provide universities with lead material describing the kind of course they would be likely to approve. This material covers, among other important aspects, the teaching, learning and assessment methods and the course content, which includes assignments. Clearly, therefore, the professional institute to which you aspire will have had a significant practical and academic input into your course. Variations between and among universities that offer professional courses, therefore, are fairly limited since they adhere to national standards.

DEFINITION: WRITTEN ASSIGNMENTS

Typically, an assignment is an item of organisationally based professional work in which the assigned student carries out an investigation into a problem or issue and produces a report outlining how it was approached, the research findings and a set of recommendations for action designed to resolve the problem or issue.

It is accepted that assignments take many forms (see Chapter 3), but the type that is defined above is the central focus of this section since it is used on most professional courses, such as those approved by the Chartered Institute of Personnel and Development (CIPD), the Chartered Institute of Marketing (CIM) and several financial and accounting professional bodies.

THE ASSIGNMENT BRIEF

The contents of the assignment brief will be related to the subject of your study unit and may contain any or all of the following:

- A description of the problem you are required to investigate, or a requirement for you to identify the problem
- Assignment proposal details (where applicable)

- An initial reading list (partly drawn from the reading list provided by the relevant professional institution)
- Details of the assessment strategy
- The date the work is due to be handed in
- The required length of the report.

There is an example of an assignment brief in the case study at the end of this chapter.

THE PROBLEM

There are several ways in which you may be presented with the problem, two of which are used frequently. The first of these outlines the problem in detail; perhaps by attaching a case study. Example 4 includes a case study and was given to second-year students on a CIM course.

EXAMPLE 4

Attached is a case study on how Celebrity Styles Limited launched a new product into the UK market. In the case, you will see that the launch failed. Your task is to analyse the case, identify the reasons for its failure and make recommendations for action designed to increase the likelihood that the organisation's future product launches will be successful.

In this example you are given the problem, since one has been identified in a particular area of marketing and written up as a case study for you to investigate.

Alternatively, the assignment brief might require you to identify a relevant problem in your own organisation, which is a version most likely to be issued to part-time students who are employed and, thereby, have an organisation to which they can relate their studies. Example 5 was given to second-year part-time students undertaking the CIPD course.

EXAMPLE 5

In your organisation, identify a problem in the area of training which, if resolved, would make a contribution to the achievement of the organisation's objectives. Investigate the cause of the problem and write a report not exceeding 2000 words. The report should outline how you approached the problem, the research findings and a set of recommendations for action designed to resolve it.

In this second example, the brief requires *you* to identify the problem to be investigated. You should bear in mind that the problem you identify should be fully related to the relevant study unit; that is, it has to be *clearly central* to one of the items on the study unit syllabus.

WHERE TO START

You start by analysing the assignment brief, which is the document that outlines precisely what you are expected to do. First, study the whole brief thoroughly and make sure that you have a clear understanding of the nature of the task. If there are any points you need to clear up, see your tutor. This is an important task, since it is your understanding of the requirement that determines everything you do from that point onwards, which includes: deciding on an approach to the problem, your research strategy and carrying out an initial literature search and review.

THE ASSIGNMENT PROPOSAL

This is not a requirement that is widespread among universities. Certainly where you are given the problem in the brief the requirement should be so clearly outlined as to dispense with the need for a proposal. It is, however, fairly frequently asked for when the brief requires you to identify the problem in your own organisation. If you are asked for a proposal, it is vital that you deal with it as early as possible, since you will have to submit it for approval well in advance of carrying out the main work. An assignment proposal is a document that contains:

- A clear description of the problem or issue you have identified
- An indication of your approach to the problem or issue, including the research methods you propose to use
- Details of possible findings (conclusions)
- Possible recommendations and an indication of the cost of implementation
- An initial reading list
- A proposed report title
- A proposed timescale for completing the assignment.

Some students regard the assignment proposal as a chore but, in fact, carried out properly it can be a very useful exercise. You should plan your work anyway, so I always urge my students to produce an assignment proposal. Students find that working in this way clarifies their thinking about their approach to the task while, at the same time, what they are actually doing is preparing for themselves a guide and a kind of checklist for the main work. It will force you to ask yourself the following questions:

1 Have I clarified my thoughts about the problem or issue, and have I defined it clearly?
2 Am I certain that the problem is centrally related to the subject of the relevant study unit, or does it need to be refined here and there?
3 Is my approach to the problem likely to lead me towards a solution?
4 Have I examined the texts on the reading list to check that they are likely to produce relevant information and will lead me to further literary sources to use in the assignment?
5 Are my possible findings and conclusions realistic, and could I defend them in a discussion?
6 Are my recommendations feasible and cost-effective?
7 Have I listed all of the physical resources I will need?
8 Have I included a timescale for the completion of the assignment?
9 Is the title sufficiently descriptive of the problem?

Finally, it is always wise to discuss your proposal first with your immediate boss. Show the brief to him or her, explain what you have to do and, you never know, your boss may even come up with an idea! If this does happen then you can be sure that it will be something that will benefit the organisation. Secondly, discuss it with your tutor and include the ground that you covered with your boss. Always makes notes as you go through these activities and then store them on your computer. They will stand well in your stead when you come to write up the proposal document. There is an example of an assignment proposal in the case study at the end of this chapter.

THE INITIAL READING LIST

At this point we will not go into great detail about reading lists and searching and reviewing literature, since they are discussed in chapter 6. However, when you embarked on your course you will have been provided with the standard course material, which should have included the reading list. You should always regard this as an *initial* rather than a *definitive* reading list. Really, the sources on the list are just a starting point because they will lead you to further sources (see Chapter 4). Finally, look through the list to see if it has been categorised, for example into *essential, recommended* and *supplementary* readings (see Chapter 4, p 37).

THE ASSIGNMENT REPORT

Assignment reports are sectionalised so that there is a visible distinction between the elements. The *assignment report* is the only means of assessment that the examiner has. When planning the report, there-fore, you should make allowances for the varying degrees of importance that the examiner attributes to each section, bearing in mind the limitations of the word count. Normally, the word count applies only to the *main sections* that are listed below. You need to develop an understanding of what you are expected to include in each of the sections, which run according to a logical sequence as follows:

1   Summary
2   Introduction
3   Definition of the problem
4   Methodology
5   Findings
6   Conclusions
7   Recommendations

Summary
This is a section that you cannot produce until the report is complete, since, as the word summary implies, it is a summary of the main points of the report and *not* a summary of all of the activities that led to its com-pletion. This includes a brief description of the problem and a very brief précis of the cardinal points of the main sections. In a report of 2000 words it is usually possible to get the summary on one page, depending on your writing skills. The purpose of the summary is to tell the reader what the report contains and why it was produced. The reader, therefore, who will be a tutor or an examiner, will know what to expect when they read on. In industry, if the report is picked up by a busy manager, he or she should be able to tell from the summary whether or not they need to spend time reading it or any part of it.

Introduction
This is an explanation of the type of organisation involved, the area or department in which the problem was identified and the effect it was having on people or other parts of the organisation; and it explains why the investigation was carried out. In other words, it sets the scene and puts the matter in context for the reader. It should be borne in mind that most professional institutions employ a selection of their senior mem-bers in the role of *external examiner* or *external moderator* (the titles vary). These people do not know you, your organisation or anything about the problem you are handling, but they are well-experienced pro-fessionals who know what makes a good report. The job of the introduction is to set the problem in an appropriate context so that they can understand it clearly.

Definition of the problem
You will have given an indication of the nature of the problem in your summary but here you describe the problem clearly and in detail. You should include where the problem exists in the organisation (the area, section or department, etc), what has caused it and the effect it is having, which could be an adverse effect on your department, the people working in it and/or those in other departments too.

Methodology

This section is about the research methods you employed to gather the information that enabled you to solve the problem. It is an explanation of how the investigation was carried out: what background literature was researched and reviewed; the theories that were considered; the type of primary research that was carried out: for example, how and where a questionnaire was used, how, where and with whom were particular types of interview or observational techniques applied and any pilot studies that were made. You should also justify your selection of the methods and techniques you used by explaining their relevance to the nature of the problem and how it may be resolved, and by explaining any other research methods that you considered and why you decided to discard them.

Findings

Here, you marshal and collate the information you gathered through your research. In other words, this is where you include the results of your research. In this section you will find yourself citing most of the sources of your information, such as the authors whose work you have read, website addresses, survey results and so forth. It is often one of the longest sections in the report and should lend authority to what you say in your conclusions and recommendations. If, for example, you make particular statements about good practice, you have to produce evidence in support of what you say. This is the section in which you compare, contrast and critically review the literature you identified as relevant to your investigation. Your literature review will add the authority of experts to the case you are making. Also, statements that purport to be facts should never be made without supporting evidence; otherwise they will be dismissed out of hand. It is vital, therefore, that you are especially careful over your research methodology in terms of the problem-related relevance of the primary methods chosen, and the accuracy of your subsequent analysis, calculations and statistical inferences. A report that contains information that is backed up by hard evidence can be extremely useful to the organisation and is likely to earn you a high mark from the examiner. You also need to be careful over the way in which you present the information; it should be attractive, appropriate to each research item, clear and concise. It is a good opportunity to demonstrate your IT skills but avoid unnecessary frills – they can look too flashy or amateurish

Conclusions

In this section you analyse and explain the conclusions you have drawn from the research-based information that you presented in your 'findings' section. You have to explain and justify the conclusions from the evidence gathered, including a discussion on the information gathered from your literature review. You also need to show how your conclusions relate to the problem or issue you identified in the first place. During the investigation, you may have identified several possible solutions to the problem, and these should be clearly stated, including an explanation of why, after due consideration, the solution you decided upon was the most logical choice.

Recommendations

This is where you make a set of recommendations for action that is designed to resolve the problem. The section also outlines how you would actually implement your recommendations and provide evidence to support the contention that the actions you have proposed will, indeed, be very likely to succeed. The recommendations have to be practicable, feasible and cost-effective. They also have to be realistic in the sense that implementation is actually possible. This section should include details of any physical, capital or human resources that would be needed to implement the recommendations and a calculated timescale to indicate the duration of implementation.

Table 3 Assessment criteria with percentage weightings, business/IT-related assignments

Element	Fail: 30% and below	Bare pass: 40–49%	Pass: 50–59%	Merit: 60–69%	Distinction: 70%+
Report summary and introduction: sets the scene for the reader. Outlines the major aspects of the report	Summarises the work rather than the report. Some aspects of the report are included	Sets the scene fairly well. Summary of the report insufficiently detailed	Summarises report well and sets the scene. Most of the major aspects included	Summary of report and scene-setting clear. All major aspects of the report are included	Good, clear summary. All major aspects of the report are included. Problem set in context
Problem definition: provides a definition of the problem, sets it in context and describes its effects	Unclear definition. Not set in organisational context. Effects are unimportant	Problem well-defined, but poorly set in context. Effects are fairly well-described	Clear problem definition. Shows fair grasp of its effects. Lacks context	Brief but clear problem definition. Shows good grasp of its effects. Not too clearly set in context	Problem defined in clear terms. Well set in context showing good grasp of its effects
Methodology: how the problem was approached. Methods of research used, explained and justified	Inappropriate research methods. Lacks sufficient explanation. Not justified. Little evidence of reading	Selected methods not totally relevant. Tenuous justification. Unimaginative general approach to problem	Selections of methods are appropriate to problem and justified. Application of primary method lacks respondent numbers	Methods selected are relevant and appropriate to the problem. Well-explained and justified	Relevant, appropriate methods selected. Well-explained, justified and skilfully applied
Findings/conclusions: research results and the conclusions drawn from them	Methods led to results that do not fully relate to problem	Dull. Unimaginative expression of findings	Findings show that more reading was needed, but are drawn from results	Well-related to problem and methods used. Seems well-planned	Clearly drawn from research results and related to problem
Recommendations: action designed to solve the problem. Practicality, feasibility, cost-effectiveness	Alternatives not considered. Lacks awareness of costs. Can be implemented but not problem-directed	Acceptable ideas. Lacks the product of adequate reading. Organisational awareness lacking. One alternative considered	Several alternatives considered. Good choice of one recommended. Practicable but costs are not considered	Practical recommendations. Costs shown are feasible. No serious quibbles with ideas. Several alternatives considered	Breadth and depth of research has produced practical, feasible and cost-effective recommendations
Citations/referencing: use of a recognised system. Clear distinction between own ideas and those of others	Citations and references do not completely match. Lacks ideas	Citations and references mostly match. Uses recognised system. Lacks own ideas	Citations and references mostly match. Makes proper use of system	All citations and references match. Uses recognised system	All citations and references match. Uses recognised system
Writing standard: includes spelling, grammar and punctuation	Writing lacks maturity. Spelling and grammar are acceptable	Poor writing standard, especially spelling and punctuation	Fair standard of writing. Poor grammar here and there. Lacks expression	Good standard of writing and grammar. Expressed well. Clear and legible	Excellent standard of writing throughout. Very well expressed
Presentation: general appearance, layout and format	Good presentation, layout and format. Good general appearance	Fair presentation, layout and format. Lacks title page	Good presentation, layout, format and general appearance	Quite attractive style of presentation. Layout and format a little dull	Attractive presentation, layout and format. Uses imagination

ASSESSMENT STRATEGY

It is vital for you to understand the expectations of the examiner in advance of carrying out any of the work, so study the assessment strategy very carefully. Notice in Table 5 the sequence of the first five elements in the left-hand column; this is the sequence of sections the examiner expects to find in the report (see Chapter 9).

If, in Table 5, you study the elements in the left-hand column and how the examiner's comments relative to how each one were handled by the student, you will begin to get a grasp of the standards you need to aim for. Also, notice in Table 6 how the marks are variously distributed to each element of the assignment. This demonstrates the importance that the examiner attributes to each of them.

Bearing in mind that the report is the examiner's only means of assessing an assignment, the approach shown in Table 6 provides an indication of the marks that are allocated to each element of the

Table 6 *Assessment guide: Allocation of marks and marks awarded for elements of Business and HR-related assignment report*

Element	Marks allocated	Mark awarded
Introduction and summary Sets the scene for the reader and outlines the major aspects of the report	5%	4%
Problem definition Provides a definition of the problem, sets it in context and describes its effects on people and other parts of the organisation	10%	7%
Methodology How the problem was approached. Explanation and justification of the research methods chosen; how well they were applied. Relevance to the investigation	20%	14%
Findings and discussion How research results are presented. Comparative, relevant and critical discussion of the findings from literature and other sources	20%	13%
Conclusions Conclusions drawn from the findings in relation to the problem in the organisation	15%	10%
Recommendations For action designed to resolve the problem, including feasibility, practicality and cost-effectiveness	15%	9%
Report presentation Including layout and format, writing standard, citations and references, general overall appearance	15%	7%
Final mark	**Out of 100%**	64%

assignment. When, for example, the examiner is assessing your introduction and summary, he or she will mark it out of 5. Your methodology, however, will be marked out of 20, and so on.

Table 6 is an example of an assessment sheet that has been marked. When carrying out this kind of assessment the examiner provides comments that justify the marks he or she has awarded, which are similar to the comments that appear in Table 5.

THE LENGTH OF THE REPORT

Plan to achieve the correct length, or thereabouts, in conjunction with the assessment strategy, especially the weightings given to each element of the assignment. When you are planning the report you need to ensure that you allocate appropriate study time and space in the report to each element. Notice that the higher allocations of marks go to the methodology, findings and discussion sections. It is, therefore, in your best interests to:

- Reserve an appropriate length of time studying the research options to ensure that the methods you eventually select are relevant to the problem. Here, you have to look ahead a little and ask yourself if the research methods you have chosen are likely to produce the kind of information that will contribute directly towards finding a solution to the problem.

- Analyse the research findings very carefully. Assignments present you with an opportunity to col- lect *primary data*, which are data that (i) do not exist in any other form or media because they are (ii) data that you collect directly from an original source, such as through a survey questionnaire or a series of structured or semi-structured interviews (see Chapter 8). You need, therefore, to develop the skills that will enable you to analyse and draw inferences from the analysis and present the data in an attractive and easy to understand format.

Writing to length is important. You might argue that quality, rather than length is the primary consideration, and you'd be right in general terms (Jankowicz 1995: 279). However, universities and professional institutions say that they doubt if the required breadth and depth of the work for an assignment could be achieved in less than a particular number of words, depending on the level of study and the complexity of the assignment brief. For a second-year student it is safe to say that an assignment report of less than, say, 1750 words and no more than 2250 would be ideal. Conversely, however, most professional institutions regard the report as, *inter alia,* an exercise in communication. They know that organisations expect their professional staff to be good communicators; and brevity, through word economy, is said to be one of the indicators of good communication. 'In doing an assignment, the effectiveness with which you communicate will affect your grade … because communication is an important aspect of management, you will be penalised if you show weakness in this area' (Cameron 2001: 224). It is a question of finding a balance between the various facets of the argument.

The important thing in terms of time and space allocation is that you realise that while the sections that carry the highest marks are important, do not allow them to use up your valuable study time at the expense of the other elements of the assignment. All of the elements carry marks you would not wish to lose, so it becomes a question of starting at an early stage and allocating your study time in a balanced way.

MEETING THE DEADLINE

You have to plan your way ahead. Make a note of the deadline date and work out a timescale that will ensure that you complete the work on time. Bear in mind, of course, that you also have assignments to carry out in respect of other concurrent study units for which you have to plan. Always allow a contingency period in your timescale (see Chapter 1).

BUILDING THE ASSIGNMENT

We have seen that when you are carrying out an assignment, you are solving a problem for an organisation. You are also making recommendations designed to solve that problem, but what you are actually doing is creating something that you hope the managers will be prepared to implement. Most managers are fully paid up members of the 'what's in it for us brigade', and that makes them pretty hard to convince; when it comes to allocating resources to tasks, especially human and financial resources, they do not make their decisions lightly. This means that you have to persuade them that the organisation will benefit from implementing your ideas, that a situation will be improved, made more efficient and effective, or that a problem or issue that you have studied will be resolved. In other words, you have to produce a report that will *sell* your recommendations to them. This will be impossible if you have not done a thorough job of carrying out the preparatory assignment work before you write the report. You have to build a convincing argument that will put you in a position to persuade these hard-bitten people that implementation is worth their while. At the same time, of course, you have to convince your tutor and the examiners.

Do not forget that you have been *assigned* to carry out an item of professional work; that is your assignment. The report is not your assignment. The report is the medium through which you tell your tutor, the examiner and your boss what you have done, how you went about doing it, the outcomes and the actions you are recommending.

You should build the report while you are doing the work by storing the information on your computer as and when you gather it, but it is the thoroughness with which you actually carry out the preparatory work that will determine the mark you get from the examiner and the boss's decision on implementation.

CASE STUDY

This case is about absenteeism, which is currently a worrying concern in industry and the public sector. The case will interest business students, particularly those undertaking HR degrees and the CIPD Professional Development Scheme (PDS).

Case study: Bellchester District Council

Following the completion of a national research programme that was carried out for central government, an order has been issued to all regional and local authorities to take steps to reduce their absenteeism by 6% by 2006 and by a further 4% by 2010.

Jenny Green works as an 'adviser' in the HR department of the council and has been asked by Margaret Browne, her boss, to investigate the causes of absenteeism in all departments and to report back with a set of recommendations designed to reduce it. Margaret has explained the government's concerns, given Jenny copies of the government report and has asked her to produce an action plan that will meet the 2006 and then the 2010 requirements. Margaret has told Jenny that her report should include a timescale for the implementation of her proposed programme.

Career-conscious Jenny has just embarked on the second year of her CIPD Professional Development Scheme (PDS) at Bellchester University and sees the absenteeism problem as a learning opportunity. She has been given an assignment brief for a study unit entitled Employment Practices and, having discussed the assignment with Margaret Browne, has now decided to see her tutor to discuss the possibility of making the absenteeism issue her assignment.

THE ASSIGNMENT BRIEF

UNIVERSITY OF BELLCHESTER – ASSIGNMENT BRIEF
TASKS

1   In your organisation, identify a problem which, if resolved, would make a meaningful contribution to the achievement of the organisation's objectives; **OR** identify a workplace issue which, if resolved, would produce greater efficiency and effectiveness in a particular situation.

2   Investigate the cause of the problem and write a report not exceeding 2000 words. The report should outline how you approached the problem, the research findings and a set of recommendations for action designed to resolve it.

3   The report is to be handed in to the Faculty Office between 9am and 5pm on the Tuesday of Week 10.

4   Draft an Assignment Proposal of not more than 600 words and hand it to your lecturer at the Week 6 seminar.

Study assistance may be obtained in the Library and Information Centre and on the University Intranet.

Note that if there are any points or issues that you wish to raise or if there is something in this assignment brief that you do not understand, please make an appointment to see me as soon as possible.

QUESTIONS

1   What issues do you think Jenny might wish to discuss with her tutor?
2   What do you think would be the tutor's main concerns?
3   What would be Jenny's immediate first priority?

Answers in Appendix 4

Obviously, the first page is the title page, not normally numbered, and might look something like the following:

Assignment Proposal

Absenteeism in a District Council

Jennifer Green

CIPD Course: Year 2

Figure 6   *Example of Jenny's assignment proposal*

The brevity of the proposal at 600 words dispenses with the need for a page listing the contents of the document. The next page, therefore, would contain the introduction, which tells the reader what the proposed assignment will be about and might look something like the following:

INTRODUCTION

Following the completion of a national research programme that was carried out for central government, an order has been issued to all regional and local authorities to take steps to reduce their absenteeism by 6% by 2006 and by a further 4% by 2010.

As an HR Adviser in Bellchester District Council, I have been assigned to identify the absenteeism figures, investigate the causes of absence and make recommendations for action designed to meet the government's requirements.

The council will implement the recommendations in the main assignment.

METHODOLOGY

Having studied the main issue, the approach decided upon was, first, to carry out an initial literature search and review, starting with the main texts on the reading list, in order to learn what other writers have said about unapproved absence and to sharpen my focus on the issue.

Secondly, a survey will be carried out within the council to establish reasons why employees take time off. The questionnaire, which will be anonymous and confidential, will be piloted in two small departments, which will not be included in the main survey. The main survey will include a representative cross section from all remaining departments. The questionnaire will be distributed as early as possible to give respondents ample time to complete and return it.

Finally, secondary research into the attendance and payroll records will be carried out to identify the cost of absenteeism within the council. The following formula will be used to calculate the absence rate as a percentage:

$$\text{Absenteeism} = \frac{\text{Number of employees absent}}{\text{Total number of employees}} \times 100$$

Notice that Jenny has written this in the *third person* and *future tense*. Nothing annoys an examiner more than 'I did this and I did that'. In any case, it is not very professional to write a business report in the first person. The reader knows that you carried out the work since your name will be on the title page. It is written in the future tense because Jenny is outlining something that *will be* done. Obviously, therefore, the main report will be written in the past tense, *after* it has been done (see Chapter 10). Depending on the nature of the problem or issue that is being investigated, the next page would outline possible findings, but in this case it would be virtually impossible to predict outcomes. The final page would be the reading list.

CHECK YOUR UNDERSTANDING

1 Why do you think the assessment strategy is included in the assignment brief?

2 When you have been issued with an assignment, what should be your first task?

3 Why is it a good idea to produce an assignment proposal, even if it is not a formal requirement?

4 When you identify a problem in your own organisation, with whom should you discuss it first and why?

5 How should you regard the main reading list?

6 Why is it important to deliver your assignment report on time?

7 Why is it important to arrange the sequence of the sections of a report in the recommended way?

8 In academic terms, what is the meaning of the word methodology?

9 What are primary data?

10 Why should you do a literature review when you are carrying out an assignment?

Answers in Appendix 4

SUMMARY

A written assignment is an item of professional work in which you are asked to define an organisational problem, use appropriate research methods to identify the causes and effects and to learn more about the nature of the problem itself. An assignment is also a means of learning about a specific subject and, for the tutor, assessing the work you have carried out. An assignment brief is a document that contains details of what you are expected to do. To clarify your thoughts about the task you should analyse the assignment brief carefully. When you identify a problem or issue in your workplace, you should ensure that it is centrally related to the study unit's syllabus and that the work to be carried out to resolve it meets the required academic level of the study unit. It is essential for you to understand how your assignment work is assessed. You need to know in advance what the examiner is looking for and you also need a clear perception of the required standards. Finally, it is important for you – in fact, for any aspiring or working professional – to develop good report writing standards.

FURTHER READING

CAMERON, S. (2001) *The MBA Handbook*, 4th edn. Harlow: Pearson Education.

JANKOWICZ, A. D. (1995) *Business Research Projects*, 2nd edn. London: Chapman and Hall.

Searching for relevant literature

INTRODUCTION

To succeed in carrying out any kind of research in a business or HR context, it is important for you to attain a good understanding firstly, of what other writers have said about your research subject (the existing knowledge) and secondly, of the data obtainable from other sources (see below). You attain this understanding by carrying out a *literature search*, which involves you in reading through, and learning from, the parts of the existing knowledge that are relevant to your topic.

> A literature search is an information-gathering process in which you select subject-specific data from authoritative sources.

This definition is a simple and a generalised one. It would be difficult to produce a comprehensive definition in the succinct terms that are characteristic of definitions, but hopefully, after reading on, you will develop a deeper understanding. The term itself precedes the advent of the computer and implies that you have to search through books and journals for information. To an important degree, that is still what you have to do. In recent years, however, the versatility of information technology has caused a significant, exponential growth in the number of data sources available, so that a 'literature search' now includes using an ever-widening variety of electronic sources, or e-data, such as e-journals and, of course, the Internet. You have, therefore, to be computer literate in order to carry out a full literature search.

Today's research environment is expanding continually and there is a massive increase in the amount of information being used. Initially, university libraries were set up mainly to classify and store text books to be accessed for academic purposes. Now, however, even though they have increased in size and added a broader and deeper range of expertise among their staff, university and public libraries are no longer capable of keeping all information on the premises, but they can still meet the needs of the researcher. 'Many academic libraries have become gateways to information rather than storehouses of knowledge' (Hart 1998).

Most new undergraduates have to develop the skills needed to carry out a successful literature search, after which they have to study the collected data, understand it, learn from it, assess its relevance to the research topic and then revisit the sources to collect more. Doing a thorough search is sometimes made difficult by the tight time spans that are often allowed between starting the work and submitting it. You need, therefore, to manage your time as effectively as you can (see Chapter 1).

THE PURPOSES OF THE LITERATURE SEARCH

You carry out a literature search for several reasons: firstly, it is a vital part of the need to gather the information that forms much of the basis of your research; secondly, when you are preparing your critical review, you need to analyse other writers' ideas; then you compare, contrast and critically review them in order to produce a reasoned argument in your final written work. Thirdly, since the literature you are using constitutes the main body of knowledge in your research subject, you can learn much from it and enhance your own knowledge.

Information technology significantly reduces the time needed to carry out research. However, when you discover a text or an item of data from whatever source you are using, you still have to carry out an evaluation of it to assess the degree to which it is relevant to your subject, which is a process that can be time-consuming. Regardless of the level at which you are studying, you will need to make several searches and evaluations of what you find. Such evaluations may amount to a kind of miniature 'review' of the data you have collected (see Chapter 7).

A WORD ABOUT THE LITERATURE REVIEW

It is logical to treat the literature search and review as components of the same concept, which is why the two chapters are placed together in this book. Your first aim is to demonstrate the degree to which you have identified relevant and appropriate literature in order to attain a comprehensive understanding of your subject (the literature search); your second aim is to review the information you have gathered in order to lend authority to, and provide evidence in support of, the arguments that you present in your final written work.

EFFECTIVE READING

When you carry out your literature search, you read the material you find so that you can assess its relevance to your research project. Your reading technique will have a significant influence on the quantity and, more importantly, the quality and relevance of what you finally select. One approach to collecting literary data efficiently is firstly, to *skim read* the material by running your eyes rapidly down the page/s to obtain a general impression of the content and style of the material. It is best to do this with the books before you take them out of the library, so that you are only carrying those that look promising.

Secondly, when you have taken the books out you might *scan read* them, which is similar to skimming but slightly more focused. This time, you are looking for specific information, and your eyes should latch on to *key words* (see later). Use the books when searching for answers to particular questions or to locate a reference.

Thirdly, *reading for learning* requires you to consider the full meaning and implications of the material and the context in which it was written, and will generally require you to reread certain sections and take notes. This does not necessarily mean that you need to read slowly. When you are reading in order to learn and understand, with a view to possibly including the material in your literature review, you should regard, say, 200 words a minute as good. It has been said that you can speed things up by ignoring irrelevant material but, of course, you have to give such material a little more than a cursory glance in order to assess its relevance. If you adopt a logical and consistent approach to your reading you should harvest some useful stuff. Reading like this is all part of the narrowing-down process in which you prioritise what you find and, eventually, put aside what you think you may not use so that you are left with the cream of what you set out to find in the first place.

WHAT TO LOOK FOR

If you have collated the data logically, you should be able to identify and assess the differences between various authors' approaches to the topic. In this part of the exercise, bear in mind that each writer's approach will have been influenced by the purpose of his or her research. Normally, therefore, there will be variations between each writer's treatment of the topic, and you should be able to observe any contradictions. In the first instance, you are looking for data relevant to your purposes. In this respect, when scanning data, you need to:

1   Look at the introduction to identify the aims and approach taken by the writer
2   Look at the conclusion to see what he or she hopes to have established
3   Use the signposts you identified in your initial scan, carefully read and reread the relevant text, examining it carefully to try and identify:
    i   the main points of the passage
    ii whether it is convincing in terms of the argument presented
    iii references to supporting and conflicting material
    iv whether it answers the questions you started out with
    v whether it raises further issues you will have to resolve yourself.

Retracing your steps

All of this can be a time-consuming process, and you will not get it all done in a single session. When you stop for a rest, therefore, always leave the gate open for when you need to access the material again. You can do this by taking notes as you go along, referencing them to page, paragraph or even line number, which will make it easier for you to pick up the threads when you go back to it and, if you need to, recheck any of the material you have already covered, although you are not advised to mark the copy itself (see below 'Managing your notes'). When you feel that you understand what the material is saying, you can summarise it in expanded note form. As we said earlier, this writing process will help to clarify your thoughts and will provide you with a good solid record for rereading and revising.

Managing your notes

You should regard all of your notes as the core material for your literature review, which, of course, will form a large proportion of the final total write-up. When you are considering and re-examining your notes, try to avoid highlighting or underlining the parts you favour mostly for use in the review. Remember the analogy in Chapter 4 entitled 'the gift shop window'? The principle expressed there also applies here. If you have marked out by highlighting or underlining what you regarded as your most important notes, you will tend to concentrate on those and, perhaps, miss once more something you missed previously. You have to hold on to your objectivity and try to reread the notes as if you have never seen them before. It has been argued that if you leave such traces on your notes it will help you to tune back into the thoughts you had when you first drafted them. If that is what you wish to do, fine. But is that *really* what you wish to do; or would you rather review your notes objectively; with a fresh eye? Marking your notes may well help you to tune back into your previous thoughts, but it can also inhibit the thoroughness with which you review them and may prevent you from viewing the material in a different light and from a different angle. After all, the main purpose of this kind of research is to find things out, examine what you find critically, compare and contrast the work of others, draw conclusions about your own findings and then share those findings with others by writing them up. You can only do that by holding on to your objectivity.

Include direct quotes where they are relevant. You need to do this anyway as preparation for the citations you are going to include in your text, but at this stage, do not allow these to become a substitute for your own ideas. How *you* have interpreted the material is of prime importance.

Setting targets

Many people set themselves *reading time targets* in which they decide to read a certain number of pages in any one session and then plod on regardless of the content. Indeed, some academic writers say that they 'reserve blocks of time' in which to write. Truly, it is a relative thing, since the amount of time for which individuals are able to sustain concentration varies from one person to another. An approach that may help you to achieve more is one in which you first decide what you would like to learn from your reading and then stop when you have learned it. Obviously, there is no point at all in reading unless you understand thoroughly what you are reading and even then you need to allow yourself sufficient *soak time.*

ANALOGY: 'SOAK TIME'

In one sense, part-time (employed) students have a distinct advantage over the full-timers because their sessions are more spaced out. They take in, say, an afternoon and/or an evening session and then the tutors do not see them again for another week. Obviously, if they are employed, the course may add to their time pressures, but despite this it does seem as if their brains have been working on their behalf because when they come back they have a good grasp of what they have learned and are loaded with questions.

What has actually happened during that time is that they have been actively considering and reflecting upon what they have learned. Learning, therefore, is more effective when the sessions are further apart in time. *Soak time* refers to the longer time spaces, when more is retained than when, for example, the student has 'end-on' classes to attend. When lectures and seminars are run one after the other in quick succession for the same students, the amount of learning that is retained from the earlier sessions can be severely limited. If you find that is a problem, the answer may be to ensure that you take plentiful rereadable notes.

The point of the above analogy is that the same principle applies to reading. You may learn more in four separate sessions of 30 minutes each than in a straight two-hour session, especially if the material is complex. There is more to reading than simply allowing a lot of words to pass before your eyes, which is what will happen if you try to concentrate for too long a period of time. Keep your mind on the *purpose* of your reading. Reading has several purposes, some of which are to:

- Learn, by having your questions answered by a variety of experts
- Gather information and ideas
- Observe how current thinking is analysed and expressed
- Test hypotheses and develop your thoughts.

Sometimes you will achieve this from the detailed reading of a single piece of work. At other times you may gain more by dipping in and out of several texts in order to broaden your general knowledge of the subject. What you gain is determined by *why* you are reading, so remember to keep *your* purpose in mind.

Keeping the purpose in mind may aid your concentration. If, for example, you are actively looking for an answer to a question, or a subject word, you somehow seem to find that you are able to focus quite sharply on your reading – a little like looking in a dictionary for the meaning of a word. On the other hand, the time will come when you suddenly realise that you have turned over a couple of pages without really taking anything in. This should not worry you; it happens to everybody. It is very common for the brain to go into 'automatic pilot' sometimes even within half a minute of picking up a textbook. Keep in mind the reason why you are reading that particular text and you will find yourself in control again.

A COUPLE OF TIPS

- Keep a dictionary at your elbow. If you ignore a word because you are uncertain of its meaning you put yourself in danger of misinterpreting the whole point that the writer is trying the make

- Avoid the temptation to photocopy an article after you have only skimmed through it, thinking that you have read it. You have not; moreover, you certainly have not learned from it.

DEALING WITH 'READER'S BLOCK'

We have all heard of, and sometimes experienced this. Reader's block is sometimes erroneously referred to as 'word-blindness', which in fact, is a symptom of dyslexia. Here we are talking about that phenomenon that occurs when you seem to have been stripped of your ability to concentrate. You look at a word or a phrase – it may be a technical word or perhaps just an everyday expression – the meaning of which you would normally take for granted. This time, however, it means absolutely nothing to you no matter how long you sit and stare at it. So, what can you do about it? One answer is to get up and leave what you are doing. Go and make yourself a cup of tea and think about something else. Use distractions such as watching television, listening to the radio or reading the newspaper.

I know that your time is precious and that you have deadlines to consider, but you will be wasting your time if you try to force yourself to continue. Try going back to your serious reading after about 20 minutes (the amount of time needed varies from one individual to another), and change your attitude towards the text. Look more critically at what you were reading *before* the block occurred, skip the part where the block did occur, and read and try to understand what follows it; then go back to the blocked area. You should find that it slots nicely into position.

SECONDARY DATA

The search also includes the results of research work undertaken by others, such as those found in other researchers' dissertations, theses and major projects; government statistics; in-company documents containing statistics and a very wide variety of company records. We refer to these as *secondary data*.

> We have all seen the word *data* used to describe a single item of information. In fact *data* is the plural, which is why we write about *them* in the plural.

Cameron (2001: 318) says that by using secondary data you will have access to far more information than you could possibly collect yourself, and much more rapidly. She does, however, go on to warn that you may not know how much reliance you can place upon it (see below). Most of the secondary data that you identify will have been collected for purposes other than your own. Principally, it is the *results* of the search, or data items in records, that you are really interested in, which is why reliability and validity are particularly important here.

Secondary data may be *qualitative* or *quantitative*. Qualitative data may be found in the form of opinions given at interviews, notes made during focus group discussions, or managers' verbal assessments of staff's performance. Quantitative data comes in the form of figures, such as statistical data that have been arrived at from, say, the analysis of questionnaires or structured interviews, or statistics that are in public records (see Chapter 8).

Data taken from company records, such as productivity figures, need to be checked for reliability. You can do this by going back to the source to see if there were any organisational pressures that might have influenced the veracity of the data. In considering whether to check the data in this way, you would have to assess its importance to your research against the amount of time the checking will take; bear in mind that in your report you are going to base your ultimate findings, conclusions and recommendation on *all* of the data you collected.

EXAMPLE 6

For an assignment, you are researching into the company's health and safety record with a view to making recommendations for action designed to reduce the rate at which accidents are occurring. You have interviewed the relevant managers to gather their comments on the causes of accidents in the past.

Now you are going to examine the company's accident records and compare what you find with what the managers have told you.

USING SECONDARY DATA

The data that you use may be *raw* data, where there has been little if any processing, or *compiled data* that have received some form of selection or summarising (Kervin 1999). You may use secondary data by:

- examining the objectives of the original researcher and comparing them to the findings, which will enable you to assess their relevance to your research

- analysing the data that were collected to identify *how* they were used and to see if they could be legitimately reworked to suit your purposes. For example, could the data be integrated with your own primary research?

- analysing how the original researcher used the data, assessing their usefulness to your research and then deciding if there is anything there that would justify reviewing any aspect of your own research.

Mini-case: The effects of change

Leo works for a firm of management consultants and is undertaking a part-time degree in business studies. Now in the final year, he has entitled his dissertation: *The effects of restructuring on internal communication.* He has found that much of the literature cites a variety of causes of the demand for change, including competition, markets, and customers; and, in the overall context, the need to survive. His search also revealed cases in which internal communication had been adversely affected by restructuring, especially that which had included *downsizing* and *rightsizing*; this had been attributed to the change being mishandled. Leo's reading included articles from journals in which change strategies were advocated.

He still feels, however, that he needs to collect data that would provide insight into the experiences of real organisations that had recently undergone change.

DISCUSSION QUESTIONS

1 What kind/s of data do you think Leo has in mind?
2 What would be the principal uses of the data he collects?

PREPARING YOUR LITERATURE SEARCH

Getting ready to carry out a literature search appears to be a random process and, indeed, parts of it are. Students who are not experienced in this area find it difficult to make a start. You can begin by adopting a structured approach to your search. If you know where you are going you are more likely to get there, which means that you need to have a purpose-driven sense of direction. In that context, a strategy that will enable you to attain a sense of direction is the *literature search cycle* (LSC). The cycle breaks the search down into six phases (see Figure 7).

In this way, the literature search becomes a systematic process. It provides you with a structure to work to, but you do need to develop within yourself the ability to use specific techniques, such as those required for generating key words and knowing how to get the best from books. Business and HR tutors normally offer guidance on how to gather information from literature. If you are doing a higher degree, the university may require you to take a course on research skills, and you will be allocated a project tutor (see Chapter 9). There are usually fixed sessions for undergraduates so you may find yourself learning the techniques in the classroom. Additionally, you can attend your study skills department or consult a librarian.

Guidance on using the techniques follows next. If we take the six stages in order, we may proceed as follows.

STAGE 1: ANALYSE THE PROBLEM

Firstly, consider the subject you are researching and how you intend to approach it. Think about all the angles that need to be covered in your research. Your aim is to develop a clear understanding of what you have to do and to gain an appreciation of the *kind* of information you need to gather and *where* to look for it. Then you can develop a time-related plan that leads to the completion of the task. Until you have done

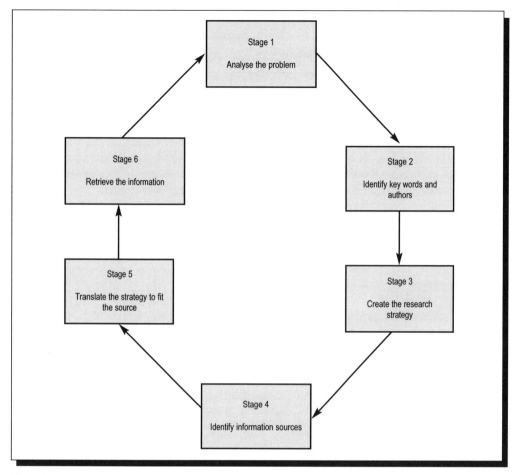

Figure 7   *Literature search cycle (LSC)*

all this there is obviously no point in starting to look for information, since you need to know in advance precisely what you are looking for. Where an item of work has been issued to you as part of a course, the best approach to developing this understanding is to analyse the brief (see Chapters 4 and 5).

Q: Note the deadline and your other commitments; have you allowed enough time for everything in your plan?

STAGE 2: IDENTIFY KEY WORDS AND AUTHORS

Now that you have a clear understanding of your subject or question, you can take steps to identify key words, which are the words you will ask a search engine to find and which you will need to drive your search of the various databases and indexes. The identification of *key words* or *search* terms is the most important part of planning your search for relevant literature (Bell 1999). There are several techniques for generating key words, which include:

- Utilising parent disciplines
- Using dictionaries, encyclopaedia and thesauri
- Using lecture notes and classroom handouts

- Having discussions with tutors and librarians (by appointment!)
- Accessing recognised professional and academic journals and studying review articles on your subject
- Studying the work of the relevant authors from your reading list
- Brainstorming ideas, alone or with student colleagues, and collecting terms and concepts that could possibly have anything to do with your search
- Using *relevance trees.*

In the process of using these techniques, you will come across further words that you may regard as prospective key words; make a note of them. You may not need all of the words you collect, but it is better to have to discard a few than to start hunting around again for new ones. Do not forget to store your ideas on your computer at every stage; later, you will need to revisit your sources.

Utilising parent disciplines

One initial approach to generating key words is to access the general area in which your research subject resides; for example, your research subject may be: *recruitment, performance management, absenteeism, production systems, merchandising, organisational change,* etc. You can get to these subjects by identifying 'parent disciplines'.

A parent discipline is a hierarchically superior discipline that contains a structure of sub-disciplines.

You may, for example, be on an HR degree or the CIPD professional course, in which one of the main subjects is *human resource planning* (HRP). Your research, therefore, could be on some aspect of selection interviewing. In such a case you would use HRP as the parent discipline, to which one of the sub-disciplines would be recruitment. Then, under recruitment you will find, among other related disciplines, *selection interviewing.* Likewise, 'marketing' is the parent discipline of, *inter alia,* selling, marketing research, merchandising, distribution and customer care (see Figure 8).

The arrows in Figure 8 show the path that your search might take, eventually arriving at 'interviewing'. From there you can start to generate a list of further key words, such as occupational testing, questioning techniques, etc, all of which you can use to direct and refine your search.

ACTIVITY 7

You have been asked to research the most frequently found effects that mergers have on the cultures of the merged organisations. Identify the parent discipline and develop at least six key words to start driving your research.

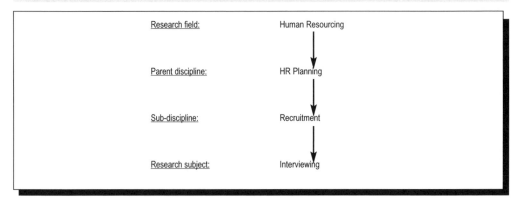

Figure 8   *Identifying parent disciplines: example for researching an HR subject*

Using dictionaries, encyclopaedia and thesauri

These are fine for finding obvious, generic meanings of words and terms, but there is a word of caution. Be careful with your use of dictionaries, encyclopaedia and thesauri. In many scientific disciplines some words have their own special meanings, and the meanings are not always the same as those defined in a normal dictionary. If you are in any doubt, consult a *technical dictionary,* a *subject directory* or a relevant textbook. You can see your librarian for advice on these. Take, for example the word triangulation. According to the *Oxford English Dictionary*, 'to triangulate' means (i) to divide into triangles or (ii) to measure or map out (an area) in surveying by means of calculations based on a network of triangles. However, according to Saunders *et al* 2003: 492, it is 'the use of two or more independent sources of data or data collection methods within one study in order to help ensure that the data are telling you what you think they are telling you'.

Using lecture notes and classroom handouts

Trawl through your lecture notes and classroom handouts and select words and terms that you think are possible key words; note them down as you go. If you find something you are uncertain about, discuss it with your tutor.

Having discussions with tutors and librarians

As a student, of course, you are supposed to do the work, but most tutors and librarians are only too happy to help you to identify key words. Be ready to explain the precise nature of your research and to discuss your intended approach to the subject. The more precise you are in your explanations the more they will be able to help. Oh, and by the way, the tutor is more likely to show you how to generate your key words, rather than do the job for you!

Accessing journals and studying review articles

In particular *recent* review articles can be useful, since they contain the latest thinking and the most up to date knowledge on the subject. Identify the subject-specific words that the writers have used and note them down as possible key words.

Studying the work of the relevant authors from your reading list

Study their work and take note of subject-specific words they use that you think might be key words for you; note them down, along with the titles of their articles.

Brainstorming ideas

Brainstorming is based on random and spontaneous thinking with a particular purpose and/or subject in mind. How do you do it? Keeping your subject in mind, try to think of all of the words and phrases that may be associated with it. No matter how irrelevant some of the words may seem at the time, write them down; you can always eliminate them later; provided, of course, they have not acquired some extra meaning or relevance after the brainstorming process! Experience shows that brainstorming is more productive when carried out in groups, so if you arrange sessions with your colleagues you can help each other in this way.

Using relevance trees

You can build a relevance tree by starting with a central concept, which may be your parent discipline, your research subject or even the subject of your course or study unit. Relevance trees are a particular type of diagram, which can be used as a device for generating research topics or for focusing your interest in a research topic (Collis and Hussey 2003). They can, however, also be used in searching literature when you already have a topic. Hierarchical in form, they are made up of headings and sub-headings, which you generate by starting from the central concept (see Figure 9). The headings and sub-headings may be key words that you can use to drive your search. You can also use a relevance tree to record your key words. Relevance trees are often constructed after brainstorming (Jankowicz 2000). Obviously, one could add to this diagram with further words and terms, such as the name of authors, and so forth.

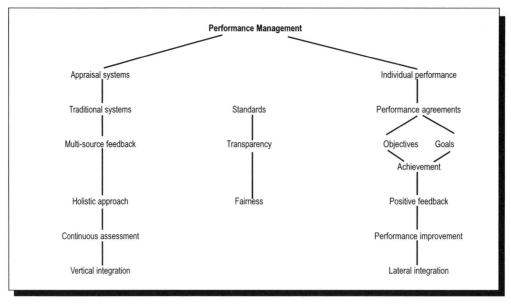

Figure 9 *Relevance tree: Parent discipline: Performance Management*

EXAMPLE 7: CHOOSING KEY WORDS

James was in the second year of a business studies degree. His essay question was: 'What is the advantage of strategic alliances as a way of exchanging resources?' James needed to identify key words for his initial literature search. From his lecture notes he saw that strategic alliances had been included in a lecture on 'resource dependency theory' (RDT), so he decided to try that as the parent discipline. In his initial search he found a definition of RDT and several cases in which companies had formed alliances. Then, after a brainstorming session he developed an initial set of key words:

> Contracts – symbiosis – resources – exchanging – sharing – alliances – joint ventures – networks – minority ownerships – formality – long-term contracts – new business opportunities.

After his first search, he eliminated several key words. His final choices were:

> Contracts – symbiosis – alliances – networks – joint ventures – minority ownerships – long-term contracts

James used these key words to search the literature sources.

ACTIVITY 8

By carrying out a brief, superficial trawl of the literature you can check your key words to assess the likelihood that they will get you into the required area and produce the kind of information you seek. This means discarding the ineffective key words, and may also mean renewing your search for new ones. Still, if you have maintained a record of your sources, this task will be eased considerably.

Q: Have you identified all key words and authors and written them down?

STAGE 3: CREATE THE RESEARCH STRATEGY

Defining your search area

At an early stage, you need to identify the type of area you should search. Is it predominantly academic data that you need, perhaps for an essay or dissertation? Or is what you are doing organisationally related, as it would be if you have been asked to carry out an investigation into a work-related problem? If it is academic data, then you need to search for texts that are written specifically about the subject or data that are academically orientated. If it is organisationally related, then you need to search not only the literature but the relevant area of the business sector such as manufacturing, banking, pharmaceuticals or whatever is the nature of your organisation's business.

Do you only need to study literature that was produced over a particular period of time? How far back in time you need/wish to search: five years? Ten? 100 years? The historical time span you need for your research is dependent on your aims and objectives, the nature of the research subject and how you intend to handle it.

USING THE WORLD WIDE WEB

Searching the World Wide Web without some guidance can positively devour time, and produce results ranging from amazingly good to worthless (Cameron 2001: 24). Mature students, however, are much more likely to enjoy a debate over a pint or a gin and tonic and, arguably, far more information changes hands in such encounters than in any formal lecturing situation. Nevertheless, as a student, you have a serious job to do in the university, which involves collecting data. The fact has to be faced that the Internet is the greatest source of information the world has ever seen and it should, therefore, figure prominently in your search strategy.

There is a considerable amount of information freely available on the Internet, and you can access data from worldwide sources, including many internationally reputed universities. Most students are already accustomed to using the Internet when they join a course, but the few who are not can usually obtain advice and assistance from the information librarian. Good hands-on guidance will increase the rate at which you search and raise the quality of what your search produces, but there is no substitute for experience, and there certainly is a strong element of experiential learning in using the Internet. Also, universities normally offer their students free short courses on various uses of the computer, which include guidance on how to make the best use of the Internet. Your library will be on the university website, and the obvious starting point is the homepage. There you will find pointers to search engines, the library catalogue and the subject pages.

ACTIVATING THE SEARCH

When making their first attempt at a literature search, some first-year students worry that they will not be able to do it or that their efforts will be unproductive. You could ask an information librarian to sit with you to ensure that you will get somewhere with it. But why not just dip your toe in and see what happens?

Boolean logic

This is a technique in which you can link your key words together in order to control the results of your search. Applying the technique may be loosely compared to carrying out a mini-scientific experiment in which you manipulate your key words *(the independent variables)*; use them to drive your search *(the process)*; and then examine the results of your search *(the dependent variables)*. What you are actually

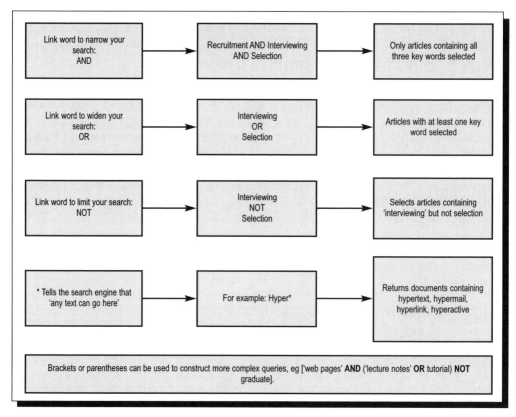

Figure 10 *Using Boolean logic*

doing is linking your key words together with *conjunctions* or *link words*, such as AND, OR, NOT and several other board keys such as asterisks and brackets. Conjunctions or link words are words that join other words together in order to give a specific command or a meaning to a particular input. It is a well-known technique, and the appropriate librarian should be able to help you. Let us return to our research on interviewing with a guide that demonstrates Boolean logic (see Figure 10).

To clarify: Boolean operators are terms that allow you to link key words in specific ways: **AND** tells the search engine to find documents that contain all the key words you input; **OR** tells the search engine to find documents that contain any of the key words you input; **NOT** tells the search engine to find documents that do contain the term before the 'not' but do not contain the term after the 'not' [eg tutorial NOT graduate] – some search engines do this with plus and minus signs [+tutorial –graduate]; *Wildcard tells the search engine that 'any text can go here' – so, for example, 'hyper*' returns documents containing hypertext, hypermail, hyperlink, hyperactive.

The syntax for advanced searching like this can vary. Make sure that you have read the 'Frequently Asked Questions (FAQs) or your help page for a specific search engine before using these operators. Don't expect instant success. You may well get thousands of hits and have to narrow down your search with a second or third attempt. Alternatively, you may get none. If the search results are not what you expected, try different forms of each key word or substitute synonyms. Different search engines allow different kinds of query, and these are changing all the time, so do make use of the help page to widen your repertoire. Remember to focus the search in your mind, looking for something that uniquely identifies your target.

All search engines do key word searches against a database, but factors such as size of the database, frequency of update, search design (how crawlers actually read and classify html documents), geographical bias and speed all produce amazingly different results. Do not worry, you will soon find your own favourite 'portal' on the Web. Those most frequently used are listed in Appendix A to this chapter.

Search indices or gateways
Unlike search engines that are indexed automatically, search indices and gateways are catalogued and categorised by real people. By far the best known and most extensive are Yahoo! and Google, but there are many subject-specific indices that are ideal for research (see Appendix B to this chapter). These are often subject to some kind of peer review, which means that sites included are likely to be highly relevant and of good quality. However, the human labour involved in this task makes it inevitable that some sites will slip through the net.

Meta search engines
These promise to index the indexes for you and so can lead to extensive (but localised) resources. To find out how they work, try Metacrawler (http://www.go2net.com/search.html), Inference Find (http://www. inference.com/infind) or SavvySearch (http://guaraldi.cs.colostate.edu:2000/form).

Evaluating Web resources. Finally, when you have found some relevant resources, how can you tell whether they are any good? Obviously, this will depend largely upon whether they are appropriate to your own learning and to the aims and objectives of your research. However, websites do need to be assessed using rather different criteria from, say, textbooks or student essays and dissertations. There are a number of general tools to help you to do this (see Appendix C to this chapter).

Lastly, a word about language. In your readings, and elsewhere, you must have noticed the differences between English and American spelling; and, indeed, the fact that sometimes the actual words used are different. This is important when you are searching databases. In America, cars are *automobiles,* lifts are *elevators* and pavements are *sidewalks;* and the company chairperson is the *president.* Of particular importance when you are using key words are the different spellings, such as behaviour and *behavior,* centre and *center.*

Q: Have you discussed your search strategy with your tutor and the relevant librarian?

STAGE 4: IDENTIFY INFORMATION SOURCES
The vital key to carrying out this important task is to get to know your university library very well. Develop and internalise a mental map of where everything is and get to know the specific expertise of the various members of the staff. Then you will be able to go directly to the resources you need to use and/or consult the appropriate library staff member about, say, additional or alternative sources of information. Always keep notes of the details of all your sources; ultimately, you may not use all of them, but it is easier and less time-consuming to discard a few than it is to go hunting again when drafting references. The library can help you in many ways:

- If the library does not have the book, journal or paper you need, it may be obtainable from another library through the Inter-Library Loans Scheme
- Books, journals and full-text CD-ROMS will be held there
- Access to information sources not held in your library may be gained through indexing CD-ROMS, online databases, online catalogues, or the Internet
- Usually, there are staff on hand to help you to use the various facilities and databases.

Most universities offer a service in which you can make an appointment with your *information librarian* for specialist help in your subject area. It is worth noting that specialist librarians are usually very busy people, so it would be unwise to imagine that you can just 'drop in' for a consultation. Make that appointment; the library staff are only too happy to help.

LIBRARY FACILITIES AND SOURCES

Libraries in today's educational institutions have computerised library catalogues listing all the books and other materials that are in stock and accessible from the library's terminals. Usually, the catalogue is also accessible from the university's own intranet, or on the Internet. The homepage of most libraries also has a link to a page listing other library catalogues and the British Library Catalogue.

There are also CD-ROM databases that list books in print. *Bookfind* covers publications from the UK and other parts of the world. *BNB* is the British National Bibliography on disk and goes back to 1950. Remember too that there are online bookshops such as Amazon and Blackwell. If you are on a professional course and are a student member of the professional institution, it will have its own library, website and specialised information bank from which you can obtain a wealth of information.

JOURNAL ARTICLES

Your university library will also have abstracting and indexing services that allow you to find journal articles using a *subject search.* Some of these give just enough information to enable you to trace the article; others also give an abstract of the article. There are an increasing number of databases that contain the full text of articles.

DISSERTATIONS, RESEARCH AND CONFERENCES

There are publications that specialise in publishing theses, research reports and conference proceedings; and some offer translations of reports that have their origins overseas. Your need to access these in the early years of your studies will be limited, but it is as well to know about them now. Examples of such publications are:

- British Reports Translations and Theses
- Index of Conference Proceedings
- Current Research in Britain
- Index to Theses (CD-ROM).

STATISTICS

The Office for National Statistics' Guide to Official Statistics and Warwick University's *Sources of Unofficial Statistics* are useful guides. Consult your information librarian on how and where to access these.

DATABASES

There are literally thousands of databases. You will probably find that your university stocks several hundreds, and lists them under three main categories:

1 Indexing and abstracting databases, which are short references to articles
2 Full-text databases, which usually contain complete articles, but without graphics
3 Multimedia databases, which contain text, pictures and animations.

HOW FAR DO I HAVE TO GO?

Students usually want to know: 'how many references do I have to have on my list?' This depends on several factors. Firstly, since the academic standard increases as you progress from one stage of a course to the next, you are expected to study at a progressively increasing breadth and depth in order to match or exceed the standard at that level (see Chapter 5). What is expected of you, therefore, is partly determined by the stage or level of your current studies. Secondly, 'the closer you move to the academic end of the spectrum, the more substantial will be the expected literature review part of your dissertation' (Cameron 2001: 314). Here, Cameron was referring to postgraduate or at least, third-year degree work, but the same principle applies to first- and second-year undergraduate and professional studies work.

You may, for example, be a second-year undergraduate writing essays, which, as you will appreciate, are predominantly academic by nature. When writing an essay you are answering an academic question and, therefore, you need to carry out a literature search that elicits enough relevant *academic* information of an appropriate breadth and depth to provide support for the arguments you make in your answer to the question. The more you read the more you will develop and deepen your understanding of the subject, which in turn, will enable you to strengthen your argument and make it more convincing. If you get to a point at which you think you have enough data relevant to your subject and closely related to your argument, then you have probably got enough.

On the other hand, you may be on the second stage of a professional course, in which case you will be carrying out investigative assignments. Unlike an essay, in which you answer a question, carrying out an assignment involves you in trying to solve a problem, which is usually a workplace problem. While this opens the door for you to gather *primary data* directly from the area in which the problem exists, you still need to search literature to find out what others have said about the problem because you need to deepen your knowledge of the type of problem in terms of the organisational subject area in which it exists; is it, for example, a market research problem; an absence management problem or a problem with policy?

Through reading, you are also advancing your knowledge, thereby putting yourself in a position from which you can cite the work of relevant authors in a way that will lend authority to the arguments you present, which should be based upon *all* of your research findings. However, with supporting evidence from primary sources, your literature search may not need to be quite as extensive as that needed for an essay.

Q: Have you identified all relevant sources?

STAGE 5: TRANSLATE THE STRATEGY TO FIT THE SOURCE

Consider the nature of the source you are about to search. For example, if it is a newspaper it will have been written for general public consumption using non-technical language. On the other hand, if it is a specialist database, the language will be much more technical and contain the special terminology and technical vocabulary related to your subject area. This means that you have to choose your sources carefully, since specialised and technical databases, regardless of similarities between their nature and your subject, may or may not be useful to you. It depends upon the degree to which they are compatible with what *you propose to do* with the subject.

Q: Have your chosen sources produced data that is relevant to your aims and objectives?

Case study

Susan has just started her second year as a student on the Chartered Institute of Marketing course and has been issued with the following case-based assignment.

Medsun Tours Limited is setting up a tour operating company to sell tour breaks mainly to Mediterranean resorts. Write a 2000-word report laying out the developmental and marketing plans for the enterprise and deliver it to the Faculty Office during Week 11.

Questions

1   How should she start her research?

2   What parent disciplines would lead her to her key words?

3   Which data sources would you expect her to use?

4   How might researching into case studies help her?

STAGE 6: RETRIEVE THE INFORMATION

Using the various databases to retrieve the information, consider what you have got and assess its level of relevance to your subject-related aims and objectives and the approach you have chosen to adopt. Re-examine and analyse your task again to ensure that the information contributes directly to the way in which you wish to answer the question or solve the problem.

This is a good point at which to review and reflect upon the depth of the knowledge and understanding of the subject you have developed through studying the information you have gathered. In fact, at this stage, you will probably be pleasantly surprised at how your understanding of the subject matter has grown.

Now return to stage 1 and consider your question, problem and your original aims and objectives in the light of the information you have gathered

KEEPING RECORDS

At all stages of the literature search, remember to note and store details of where and how you accessed your sources and whether or not you actually used them. This will help if you find that you need to go back to a reference. If you list them in a 'reference style', such as the Harvard System (see Appendix 1), you will ultimately have a comprehensive list of your sources of information, which is essential for the bibliographical details you cite in your report.

START EARLY

What is said above may seem daunting to the student who has never carried out a literature search. It looks as if you have to go to considerable trouble to obtain a large number of minor items of information, but that is not the case. Gathering information should not present many difficulties. The key is to give yourself sufficient time, particularly to find out where it all is. If you leave things until the last minute you may not get all of the information you need, so it is important to start the work as early as possible. Take notes while you are reading. When you recognise something that is truly relevant to your aims and objectives concerning your topic, write it down immediately, including the date and the source, ready for storage in your computer.

> **TIP**
>
> If at any time you get an idea, write it down as soon as possible. I always carry a notebook and keep it on my bedside table overnight. If you do not write down your idea you are almost certain to forget it.

INFORMATION HANDLING

Technically, what you have gathered is data. '*Data* consists of the basic building blocks ... *Information* is data arranged into meaningful patterns ... *knowledge* is the application and productive use of information' (Armstrong 1999). '... information is data endowed with meaning and purpose' (Drucker 1988).

Taken literally, these statements could mean that a library is full of data, which means that your task is to scan the data until you find items that have meaning for the nature of the work you are doing. It is when you can see that the data you have gathered are relevant to your work that it becomes meaningful to you; in other words, that is when the data become information.

COLLATING INFORMATION

Assignment and project work always produces a demand for several different kinds of information. HR students, for example, may find themselves carrying out a training assignment, which might say: 'You are to produce a one-day training course for managers who become involved in the employment selection process.' To complete this task, the HR student will need to gather information on the subject matter of the course, such as preparing for the interview, handling the documentation, employment selection techniques, the law on discrimination, the implications of occupational test results and making the employment decision. Furthermore, the student will need to make decisions about the training techniques to be used, such as the sequence in which the subjects should appear, how much training time should be allocated to each subject and the methods and media through which the trainees may best be developed on a course of this nature. All of these different sets of information have to be collated and stored separately.

Alternatively, marketing students may be given a case study and asked to prepare a marketing plan for the launch of a new product. Accountancy students may be asked to produce an advisory document on budgetary control for managers, or on how to draft a cost benefit analysis. A glance at these examples tells us that you will find yourself handling several different categories of information.

You may have noticed that the categories of information cited here in respect of the training assignment, although different from each other, are interrelated. It is possible to find all of them in a single text, such as a book on employee development, but authors are not always in agreement with each other, so it is wise to gather from a selection of sources; then what is said in one text may be compared and contrasted with another. Also, some texts may be more relevant than others to your specific item of work. The information in each category, therefore, will have been gathered from several sources, and when storing and collating them care needs to be taken to keep them separate.

INFORMATION STORAGE AND RETRIEVAL

This is a job for you and your computer. There are various ways in which data can be stored, and it is important to point out the advantages of storing the information you gather in an organised way that is safe, secure and easy to retrieve.

A simple approach is to create a folder to which you give a name and in which you store each item of data in its own separate file, then give each file a name that is indicative of its content. The folder will automatically list the items in alphabetic order; or alternatively, you can have them appear as icons displayed across the screen. Most users prefer to list the items, especially if there are a lot of them. This method lends itself easily to e-mailing, cut and paste, etc, which you will find handy when it comes to reviewing the literature and writing it all up.

One cannot stress too often or too strongly the importance of backing up the file on a floppy or compact disk (depending on the volume of the data). As we said above, if the volume of data is high and/or complex, it is a good idea to double the back-up. Having seen why and how a literature search is carried out we have to discuss what we do with the information now that we have got it (see Chapter 7).

CONCLUDING NOTE

Finally, it is worth mentioning that when you read the kinds of professional and academic journals mentioned above, you will notice that the same writers' names keep appearing. These are usually the recognised authorities on the subject; when you have their names, of course, you can track down any academic textbooks they may have written. It is important to note that the names that keep cropping up are the names the examiners will expect to see cited in your text and on your list of references when they are assessing your work.

CHECK YOUR UNDERSTANDING
Questions

1 Why is it important to find relevant and appropriate literature for your research project?
2 How would you define/describe a literature search?
3 In what ways has the Internet influenced research activity?
4 How do data and information differ in meaning?
5 How would you go about identifying key words?
6 What is a relevance tree and why would you create one?
7 Define/describe Boolean logic
8 In addition to storing and backing up the data you collect, what further information would you treat in the same way and why?
9 What is the vital key to identifying information sources?
10 How many literature searches might you have carried out after you have completed the research project?

Answers in Appendix 4

FURTHER READING

ARMSTRONG, M. (1999) *A Handbook of Human Resource Management Practice*, 7th edn. London: Kogan Page.

BELL, J. (1999) *Doing your Research Project*, 3rd edn. Buckingham: Open University Press.

CAMERON, S. (2001) *The MBA Handbook*, 4th edn. Harlow: Pearson Education.

COLLIS, J. and HUSSEY, R. (2003) *Business Research*. Basingstoke: Palgrave Macmillan.

DRUCKER, P. (1988) *People and Performance: The best of Peter Drucker on Management*. London: Heinemann.

HART, C. (1998) *Doing a Literature Review*. London: Sage Publications.

JANKOWICZ, A. D. (2000) *Business Research Projects*, 3rd edn. London: Chapman and Hall.

KERVIN, J. B. (1999) *Methods for Business Research*, 2nd edn. New York: HarperCollins.

SAUNDERS, M., LEWIS, P. and THORNHILL, A. (2003) *Research Methods for Business Students*. Harlow: Pearson Education.

APPENDIX A: THE MOST FREQUENTLY USED SEARCH ENGINES

Alta Vista (http://altavista.digital.com) is one of the largest and most comprehensive search engines available. It searches the entire html file and also gives the option for searching Usenet discussion groups.

Excite (http://www.excite.com) has a feature called 'more like this' that can be helpful, and 'channels' that offer news and reviews of other sites.

HotBot (http://www.hotbot.com) has some unique search features that make this a very useful search engine, including sorting results by date or media type.

Infoseek (http://www.infoseek.com) can narrow your search by subject area and geographical location.

Lycos (http://www.lycos.com) is one of the oldest search tools on the Internet, but keeps up to date with a variety of query options.

Northern Light (http://www.northernlight.com) is one of the newest, with extensive content and a feature for classifying hits into custom search folders.

WebCrawler (http://webcrawler.com) is a good place to start for identifying major resources and mainstream sites, and for those new to key word searching.

APPENDIX B: LIST OF SEARCH INDICES OR GATEWAYS

For general gateways (see page 69), try: **Yahoo!** (http://www.yahoo.com); **Look Smart** (http://www.looksmart.com); **Magellan** (http://www.mckinley.com); or **Snap!** (http://home.snap.com)

For HE subject-specific gateways, a good place to start is the relevant CTI Centre website. A range of UK HE gateways are also listed on the central CTI website at http://www.cti.ac.uk/links/t&l/info.html

APPENDIX C: TUTORIALS AND 'HOW-TO' SITES

How to be a Web Hound: http://www.mcli.dist.maricopa.edu/webhound/index.html

What a Site!: http://www.mcli.dist.maricopa.edu/show/what/ start.html

World Wide Web FAQ: http://www.boutell.com/faq/oldfaq/index. html#intro

Choosing the right tools and search engines: http://www.kcpl. lib.mo.us/search/srchengines.htm http://www.lib.berkeley.edu/TeachingLib/Guides/Internet/ToolsTables.html#Choosing

Evaluating Web resources for student: use Internet Detective at the University of Bristol: http://sosig.ac.uk/desire/internet-detective.html

Assessing Net Worth: http://cee.indiana.edu/interact/

Preparing the literature review

CHAPTER 7

CHAPTER OBJECTIVES

After studying this chapter you should:

- regard both the literature search and the review as integral components of the same concept
- be able to evaluate data in terms of relevance to your subject and your research objectives
- be able to structure and organise data and decide where they can be integrated into your argument
- recognise the meaning of scholarship and practise it in your work
- have confidence in your own ability to evaluate the work of others and place it within the context of your work

INTRODUCTION

In Chapter 6 we said that the literature search and the literature review are regarded as integral components of the same concept. We also outlined the principal tools and techniques that may be used in your search. In this chapter we turn your attention to a sequence of steps you may take in preparation for drafting the critical review.

1 Firstly, you need to study and understand what the data say so that you can evaluate this in terms of relevance to your subject and research objectives.
2 Secondly, you turn to critically comparing and contrasting the various authors' approaches so that you can demonstrate how the data stand in relation to your own arguments.
3 Thirdly, you will then be in a position to draft extended notes and passages, which are intended for inclusion in the final version of the literature review itself.

EVALUATING DATA FOR RELEVANCE

All the data you have gathered needs to be evaluated. At this stage, you are not critically analysing the data; you are assessing the degree to which it is relevant to your research objectives.

SO, HOW DO I KNOW IF IT IS RELEVANT?

When you first collected the data you must have thought that they were at least *related* in some way to your objectives and/or your research question/s; otherwise you would have passed them by. You may also have noticed that the various items of data relate to different aspects of your topic. Now, you are looking more closely at what you have got, and you have to use your judgement to evaluate relevance. You have to ask yourself how each particular item of data will help you to achieve your research objectives and help you to answer your research questions.

'How much data do I have to collect?' is one of the most frequently asked questions from students. Another is: 'How many references do I have to have on my list?', which really amounts to the same query. We discussed these questions in Chapter 6, but they are matters that concern this discussion too, because when you are assessing the value of what you have collected, you also have to ask yourself if you think you have enough evidence to support your argument. If a further search does not reveal any more relevant data, then you have probably collected enough.

Hopefully, you will have found your research interesting. Evaluating the data, however, can be a tedious task, but it is one that simply has to be carried out. To relieve at least some of the tedium and, more importantly, to assist your judgement, there is a useful checklist that you can use to provide a structure to what you are doing.

The idea is to evaluate each data item against the questions on the checklist while at the same time asking yourself: is this data item of sufficient relevance to include in the critical review? If so, how will it help me to answer my research questions, and how will it fit into the case I am making in my argument? The aim of Table 7 is to explain the questions it asks and to suggest how you might get the best from using the checklist.

The process of evaluating the data for relevance may reduce your stock of data because you will discard some of them, perhaps on the grounds that while they were *related* to the research subject, they were not sufficiently relevant to feature in the argument that is related to your research question/s. It does mean, however, that what you are left with is data that you can use effectively.

When you are carrying out this kind of work, you cannot tell yourself, 'Whew! Now that I have completed the search, I can get on with this', since your literature search cannot be regarded as complete until you have finished writing up your critical review. This is because as soon as you start to write, you start thinking again, 'is that what I *really* want to say?' and then, 'what is the best way to say it?'

Most of the academics who write about and teach research and study skills say that writing reactivates your thinking and clarifies and refines your thoughts about how you might approach your topic. In a sense, when you are at the keyboard, it is almost as if you are thinking through the ends of your fingers. You start to rethink what you are trying to achieve and, perhaps, amend something you have said and how you have said it, which in turn, may lead to the need for more data, which of course, takes you back to your literature search. As we said earlier, the search continues and runs concurrently with the review.

SCHOLARSHIP

Chris Hart paints a poignant picture of the scholar: 'Scholarship is often thought to be something academic high-brow types do. We are all familiar with the popular image of the scholar as one of an ageing bespec-tacled man with unkempt hair, dressed shabbily in corduroy, with a thick old leather-bound book in hand' (Hart 1998: 8).

Wilhelm Wundt, physiologist and pioneer of modern experimental psychology, was the German version of Hart's excellent vignette. Below average height and thin in stature, Wundt always wore a white bell-shaped school smock, crumpled trousers and clogs. He would appear in the classroom carrying reams of lecture notes, clatter across the wooden floor, dropping some of his notes on his way to the raised lectern from which he would hold forth. He never needed to consult his notes. Everyone knew that everything he said had been thoroughly tested and supported by evidence. His students and his colleagues had a great deal of affection for him, but in serious terms he was highly regarded and certainly thought of as a true scholar.

Table 7   *Checklist for evaluating the relevance of literature*

Question	Guidance
1. How recent is the item?	This question does not mean that all of your data should be recent. You are expected to demonstrate your awareness of up-to-date thinking, but this is not to say that you should ignore older sources purely because of their age. There are theories and expert opinions that are still valid after many years.
2. Is the item likely to have been superseded?	To find out, compare the item with other similar items of data, note the dates and assess the degree to which they all match up. If the item is the oldest, does not match up *and* other theories may be taken as modern alternatives to those in the item, then the likelihood is that it has been superseded.
3. Is the context sufficiently different to make it marginal to your research question/s and objectives?	Evaluate the degree to which the item is central to your research objectives. 'The literature that is most likely to cause problems is that which is less closely related' (Gall *et al* 1996). Hold on to the item for now – its marginal status may not imply unimportance in respect of your subject, and you will have to decide if it can/should feature in your argument.
4. Have you seen references to this item (or its author) in other items that were useful?	If you have, then study those other items to see if this one should be integrated with them. How does it relate to them? Is the item strong enough to justify inclusion? At this stage it is not advisable to discard marginal material. If you list your data in order of importance, any marginal material will still be there if you need it.
5. Does the item support or contradict your arguments? For either, it will probably be worth reading!	If the item supports your argument, and is central to your research questions, it will serve as evidence for your case. If it is contrary, you may still decide to use it when you are comparing and contrasting what others have said.
6. Does the item appear to be biased? Even if it does, it may still be relevant to your critical review!	While not all published material provides a balanced view of the subject, what is said may be relevant to the questions you are answering. You have to decide if it fits into your argument and, if so, where.
7. What are the methodological omissions from the work? Even if there are many, it may still be of relevance!	Does the item include sufficient evidence to support what is being said? Should the researcher have used different research methods and, perhaps, further methods so that the data could be cross-checked? How valuable is it to your research objectives?
8. Is the precision sufficient? Even if it is imprecise it may be the only item you can find, and so still is of relevance.	Lack of precision may have occurred in the application of the data gathering and analytic techniques. Before you use imprecise data, you have to check their validity. If you decide to use something you should point out where you think the imprecision lies. If it is the only item you could find when you did the search, try searching further.

Sources: The left-hand column is adapted from Bell (1999); Jankowicz (2000); McNeill (1990). The right-hand column is based on the author's experience.

Mini-case

Sailesh, a student in the third year of his marketing degree, was in difficulties. He was working on his dissertation and had started to write up the notes for his literature review when he suddenly realised that while all the data he had finally collated was relevant to his subject, most of it was in agreement, or at least not sufficiently opposed to, the argument he intended to put forward. He had revisited all of the sources he had used but still failed to find data that opposed what he felt he had to say. Sensibly, he decided not to sit around worrying about it, but to try to do something about it.

Questions
What can Sailesh do to progress his literature review notes? Try to think of at least three steps he could take to rescue his dissertation from disaster.

Answer in Appendix 4

Many universities, on their assessment criteria sheets, refer to the word scholarship as something that they expect to see demonstrated in the students' work. Jankowicz (1995: 52) says that 'all institutions expect this (scholarship) of you, and though they don't necessarily think about it in the same words, so do all employers involved in project work. It's a word of the finest pedigree: but what does it mean? The primary meaning is quite clear:

- Careful and accurate use of evidence
- Care in the discovery and attribution of sources
- Thoroughness in the coverage of subject-matter
- Respect for truth and the validity of data and assertions.'

Clearly, therefore, when we refer to searching literature, categorising and storing information, and retrieving it for use in support of our argument, we were not referring to scholarship. Scholarship is demonstrated by the way in which you go about these tasks. It is the intellectual capacity to learn the subject; it is the careful way in which you analyse what others have said; the care and honesty with which you separate your own ideas from those of the writers whose ideas and concepts you are using; your knowledge of the subject and the intelligence with which you interpret the work of others, compare and contrast it and use it to support the argument you are presenting. All of this, along with the thoroughness with which you validate the data and the assertions you make, is scholarship.

A GENTLE WORD OF WARNING

Cheating
All universities have a strict policy, a set of regulations and a systematic procedure for handling allegations of cheating. In the section on scholarship, we referred to the care and honesty with which one separates one's own ideas from those of the writers whose ideas and concepts you are using. It is vitally important for all students to understand that when you use the work of others, you should always advise the reader of the source of the information by citing it in your text and including the full bibliographical details in your reference list. Any student who fails to follow these rules will be deemed to have cheated.

Plagiarism
If in any of the work that is submitted for assessment, a student incorporates another person's or body's work by unacknowledged quotation or by paraphrasing it or presenting it in any way that suggests that it is his or her own original work, then he or she will have committed *plagiarism*.

Collusion

This occurs when, without official approval, two or more students (or student/s and a non-student) collaborate in the presentation of work that is submitted for assessment as the work of a single student. Collusion also occurs when a student or number of students allow their work to be incorporated in, or represented as, the work of another student.

Falsification

This is where the content of any assessed work has been invented or falsely presented by student/s as their own work.

Replication

This is where a student submits the same or similar piece of work on more than one occasion for assessment to gain academic credit.

The list of these offences can be expanded to include taking unauthorised notes into an examination; obtaining an unauthorised copy of an examination paper; communicating, or trying to communicate, with another student during an examination and being party to impersonation in relation to an examination.

Those who break these rules are taking an enormous risk because if you study the nature of the offences, you will see that they are almost certain to be found out. With regard to cheating and plagiarism, for example, the likelihood that the tutor who is marking an item of work will recognise the work that the student is passing off as his or her own is very high indeed. This is because the examiner who is assigned to mark the work will be very familiar with the subject; he or she do actually read the books they recommend and keep themselves up to date with new developments.

Penalties

Depending on the gravity of the case, the penalties range from being failed in (i) the assessment; (ii) the whole study unit; (iii) that particular academic year. In very serious cases, the student may be required to withdraw from the course.

DIGGING DEEP

Some subjects have been studied from time immemorial and successive theories about them have evolved across time. Many such theories have a history that has developed a kind of folklore leading to sets of assumptions or so-called scientific judgement. Researchers attempt to challenge these judgements, and their findings are reported in what we call *refereed* journals, which exist at scientific and professional levels. The lesson here, then, is to search not just books but scientific and professional journals and the many further sources that are mentioned earlier in this chapter and in Chapter 4, since that is where the most up-to-date theory is found.

Even the current year's books may be a little out of date, especially those on law and professional practices, which are changing continuously. This is because it may have taken as much as two to three years to write them, added to which is the time it takes to publish them. Journals, therefore, often contain research findings that supersede theories and new ways of thinking about developments in professional practice.

REFLECTION

This is an important aspect of learning, and time should be reserved to practise it in respect of the learning you achieve from the literature. Reflection is the active process of mentally summarising what you have learned from an experience, such as a seminar, a lecture, a discussion with a tutor or, of course, reading as part of your research. If you are a part-time student and you are employed, then you may also reflect upon what you have learned from your workplace experiences.

Some writers believe that reflection should take place at specific times, such as once a day or once a week. It is true that if you do that, it will occur more easily because your brain becomes accustomed to the regularity of when you do it. On the other hand, you may prefer to do it immediately afterwards, while the details of the experience are still fresh in your mind. The purpose of reflection is to reinforce and retain what you have learned so that you grow psychologically from each experience. The way in which *you* choose to do it is probably the right way, since all individuals have different learning styles, which means that there is no blueprint for the process. If you are a full-time student, it might be possible for you to practise reflection immediately after an experience. On the other hand, if you are a busy manager and have just successfully dealt with a workplace crisis, then, like most managers, you will go on to the next task as a matter of course, rather than reflect on what you may have learned from what you have just done. You could, however, try to reflect upon the experience at the next available opportunity, beginning by asking yourself where, when and how you acquired the knowledge and skills that enabled you to deal with such a crisis and, of course, what you actually learned from the crisis itself.

As a student, you will attend your lectures and seminars in the company of your student colleagues. By reflecting with them you will hear their understanding of the experience; the perceptions and views of others are always useful, even when you disagree with them. Mind you, you may find that not all of your colleagues are equally motivated to do it.

Carrying out this kind of activity is an important part of your self-development, which may continue after your formal studies are finished. The CIPD promotes *continuing professional development* (CPD), which is akin to *lifelong learning.* Most of those who advocate lifelong learning recommend that you make notes about your learning experiences in a *learning diary.* Cameron says that we should make 'tacit knowledge' (things that we know, but have not yet put into words, even for ourselves) explicit. This knowledge can then be more easily retained and shared (Cameron 2001: 334). There is no doubt at all that writing something down aids knowledge retention; not only is it then clearer in our minds, but we retain it for longer; if it is recorded in a *learning diary*, then we can see it within the whole context of our previous learning.

ACTIVITY 9

Start a learning diary now. Learning is a continuous process but sometimes we learn and forget, so write it down. Having a record of your knowledge and skills will help you enormously when you go job hunting. 'What can you do?' This is a frequent question asked by prospective employers, who will show interest in your degree but chiefly they want to know what you learned from it in terms of knowledge and skill.

DRAFTING NOTES FOR YOUR CRITICAL REVIEW

One of your chief aims now is to check that you have an adequate record of the main sources of the information you have gathered; that you understand the ideas of the authors who are recognised authorities on your topic – how they expressed current thinking and discussed the issues and main theories.

You should now be ready to retrieve enough of the kind of information that will enable you to make a start on drafting expanded notes for inclusion in your critical review of the literature. One useful tip is that when you have drafted copy for your literature review, read it aloud to yourself. It is surprising how this will help you to sort out any clumsy, ill-written or muddled phrasing.

THE PURPOSES OF THE LITERATURE REVIEW

When you are preparing to draft copy for your literature review, try to keep in mind the *purposes* of what you are doing. All of the preparatory steps you take should be purpose-driven. There are several *basic* purposes that remain constant, and the literature review should:

- provide a context for the research
- justify the research
- ensure the research hasn't been done before (or if it is repeated, that it is marked as a 'replication study')
- show where the research fits in to the existing body of knowledge
- enable you to learn from previous theory on the subject
- illustrate how the subject has been treated previously
- highlight flaws and gaps in previous research
- show that the work is adding to the understanding and knowledge of the field
- help to refine, refocus or even change the topic (see Ward 2003).

WHAT THE EXAMINERS WANT

A further important purpose is to keep in mind that the examiners will expect you to have made yourself aware of what is already known about your subject by searching for, finding, studying and critically analysing the literature that is relevant to your research subject. That is a minimum requirement. The literature review itself demonstrates to the examiners how you analysed the information you gathered, critically compared and contrasted what others have said and demonstrated why you think the information you have selected is relevant to your subject and to the aims and objectives of your research project.

LAST-MINUTE SCRAMBLES

Too often I have read research reports in which the so-called literature review amounts to nothing more than a list that reiterates what well-known writers have said about the topic. Obviously, there is much more to it than that. In writing the literature review, the purpose is to convey to the reader what knowledge and ideas have been established on a topic, and what their strengths and weaknesses are. The literature review must be defined by a guiding concept (eg your research objective, the problem or issue you are discussing or your argumentative thesis). It is not just a descriptive list of the materials available, or a set of summaries (McKillup *et al* 2003).

One of the purposes of reviewing the literature is to learn as much as you possibly can about your topic. If your sources produce relevant information, then the literature you are searching constitutes the main body of knowledge in your subject. Combined, the literature search and review represent the degree to which you have identified relevant literature in order to attain a comprehensive understanding of your subject. You should also ensure that the data you have collected lend themselves to the approach you intend to adopt, in that they can be interpreted in a way that will support the arguments you wish to present in your text. Handled with insight, therefore, your literature review should allow you to:

- Demonstrate your familiarity with the subject
- Show where your research fits into the main body of knowledge
- Demonstrate that you are sufficiently intelligent to select and abstract literary items that are relevant to what you wish to achieve

- Provide evidence in support of the arguments you present
- Make statements backed up by evidence from authoritative sources.

Hart defines the literature review as: the selection of available documents (both published and unpublished) on the topic, which contain information, ideas, data and evidence written from a particular standpoint to fulfil certain aims or express certain views on the nature of the topic and how it is to be investigated, and the effective evaluation of these documents in relation to the research being proposed (Hart 1998: 13).

A literature review places your work within the wider context of what constitutes the existing body of knowledge gained from research in the particular area of your study. Given the choice, you will have selected a subject that you enjoy and it is likely that you already know something about it, but critically reviewing the literature on it is a very important element of writing up any piece of academic work from essays to PhD theses and everything in between.

No matter how much you already know about your subject, your reading will add to that knowledge, influence the ways in which you regard the subject and enrich your perception of it. Developing your own learning like this will enable you to use the literature in a way that will strengthen the arguments you present, not only in your literature review section, but in the rest of the text too. If you examine the assessment criteria you will find that they always require you to show that you are aware of the current, and sometimes historic, body of knowledge on your subject. The examiners, therefore, will expect you to have:

1 Identified and studied literature that is relevant to your subject and to the aims and objectives of your research
2 Analysed what other writers have said in terms of their approach to the subject
3 Critically compared and contrasted what they have said
4 Shown how your analysis and critical review of their work relates to your approach to the subject
5 Demonstrated how your research fits into the reputed knowledge of the subject.

WHAT DO YOU MEAN: CRITICAL?

We should deal with a particular worry that is experienced by students who are new to carrying out this kind of work. It is to do with the word 'critical'. The literature review may alternatively be referred to as a 'critical review' or as a 'critical analysis of the literature'. Students become concerned about their ability, or even their right to *criticise* the work of experienced academic writers: 'Here am I, a raw beginner, yet I am expected to criticise the work of highly qualified and long experienced experts.' If you see it in that way, of course, the task may at least cause you to be reluctant to do it, even be daunted by it, but this is a ghost that really should be put to rest.

THE DIFFERENCE BETWEEN *CRITICISM* AND *CRITICAL ANALYSIS*

Criticism means looking for faults and passing critical comments. Criticism is a negative process whereby one tries to find fault or pass judgement on something. *Critical analysis,* on the other hand, is a positive process involving reflection and evaluation in order to determine the truth or merit of something.

When you write any piece of academic work, not only are you *allowed* to use your informed judgement to evaluate the work of others, you are *required* to do it. The work you are doing is important; it is something you are doing because you have something to say for yourself about your chosen subject.

Authors are not gods; they are usually researchers who are trying to share their findings with others, which is the whole point of scientific research, and they are well accustomed to having their work critically discussed; indeed, it is extremely disappointing for them if their work is ignored! If you *read critically, purposefully* and *actively* in the first place, you will begin to reformulate and modify your views as you concentrate on what has been written.

CRITICAL ANALYSIS OF DATA

In our context, being critical means to draw your reader's attention to the strengths and weaknesses of the work of other writers whose work is relevant to your topic and your approach to the topic. As we have seen, reading *critically* does not mean finding fault with what has been written; you have to think of it as a mechanism by which you may substantiate the validity of an argument. By testing the data you are collecting, your understanding of the subject will be enhanced and, thereby, you will be able to present a more convincing argument when you write up your project.

Primary materials are first-hand accounts, reflections and statements. They are not based on other written works. They are in their original form, without having been arranged or interpreted by anyone else.

SO, HOW DO I ANALYSE DATA?

1 Consider the type of data you are reviewing

2 Identify the assertions being made

3 Examine the evidence that is presented in support of the assertions

4 Consider all-round appropriateness

5 Identify any ambiguities or biases

   i *Type of data.* Are you reviewing primary or secondary source material? (see Chapter 8). You will be able to identify this from the following:

   Official documents, diaries and letters are the best examples of primary sources (original catalogues, photographs and newsreel footage also fall into this category). Secondary sources – by far the larger group – discuss primary sources. They consist of works which select, edit and interpret this raw material (Berry 1994: 19).

   ii *The assertions being made.* Here, you have to determine what the author *states* as opposed to what he/she *implies,* so that you can separate fact from opinion. You also have to identify what the author *assumes.* You can do this first, by testing the statement in terms of how it relates to, and depends upon, his/her foregoing statements and secondly, by ensuring that it is not supported by evidence. Finally, examine what the author rejects. Is the rejection justified by the strength of the author's argument? We discuss this in the following items.

   iii *The evidence.* Is it logical? Is it supported by research results? If there are tables, graphs, maps or charts, how relevant and how useful are they? Does the evidence fully support the author's interpretation? Could other interpretations be placed on the evidence? Is the raw data included for you to interpret for yourself? Is the argument reflected consistently in a variety of sources?

   iv *Appropriateness.* This refers to the appropriateness of the methodology, the choice of references and citations and the measures of reliability used to test the hypothesis being presented.

   v *Ambiguity and bias.* Are there conflicting statements or ideas within the text or between this text and others on the same subject? What is the author's interest in the subject? Are there competing interests, eg economic, social ecological or personal? You must try to remain objective and detached and be careful to place your own biases to one side.

Finally, record your findings carefully and cross-reference information to highlight the strengths and weaknesses of the argument.

At this stage, on the threshold of writing your literature review, you will already have evaluated the relevance of the data (see Table 7). Now the data need to be collated and prioritised in terms of the degree to which they are the most promising for inclusion in your literary review. This involves examining the data and writing brief comments on each data item about:

1 the degree of its relevance to your research
2 where it may be integrated into your argument
3 the degree to which it may help you to answer your research question/s.

Then you can categorise the data into sections according to their intended purpose in your review. This seems like a lot of work to gain a little, but once you get started, you will find that it is not difficult, and you will feel the benefit of having done it when you come to draft the literature review itself.

The next step is to draft extended notes about each item, and, bearing your own study in mind, draw attention to the strengths and weaknesses of the arguments that others have presented; make evaluative comments about other studies; and comment on the main theories that you discovered in your literature search. Drafting extended notes means that you have started to create your literature review.

Some writers maintain that in a *literature* review it might be acceptable just to report on the various assertions, findings and conclusions of the various authors on the subject. The same writers, however, say that in a *critical* review you have to try and explain why there might be different interpretations of the same material. In writing up your text, you should attempt an explanation of divergent theories to show that you have engaged with the material you have read. Merely reporting the facts is not enough. You need to demonstrate that you have explored the arguments and that you also have an opinion. If your objective is merely to prove to the assessor that you have 'done your reading', don't fool yourself. The assessor will not assume that you have read everything that appears on your reference list; he or she will be looking in the main body of your text for real evidence of the knowledge you have gained from your reading and how you have handled the data in respect of your argument.

To summarise: the professional approach to comparing and contrasting is an evaluative one. You have to *critically evaluate* what was said by one writer, analyse and *critically* evaluate what was said by others, compare and contrast them and then write *your own* evaluation, not only of what they have said, but how it all relates to and integrates with your topic and leads to the achievement of your research objectives. You have to think deeply about what you are doing and find your own insights. It is at this stage that you begin to realise what you have learned from the reading you have done.

DEVELOPING YOUR ARGUMENT

You will have noticed my frequent reference to 'your argument'. It is appropriate at this point to provide an explanation of what I mean by 'argument'.

An argument involves putting forward reasons to influence someone's belief that what you are proposing is the case (Hinderer 1992).

Used in this context, your argument resides in the statements you made about the aims and objectives of the item of academic work you are doing. In a proposal for a dissertation or major project (see Chapter 9), you will include a section outlining the findings and conclusions you are likely to reach on the basis of the data you intend to collect. This implies that as you were making the decision about the topic you wished to investigate, the basis of your argument was already formulating in your mind. Then as you worked on, collecting and evaluating the related data, your argument clarified further and you were able to target data with a particular purpose in mind – your argument. It is difficult to write about constructing an argument without making it sound as if all of my students are going to make earth-shattering discoveries. In fact, 'new ground' is seldom broken in undergraduates' projects, although you may find yourself investigating a problem from a new perspective or drawing upon evidence that has not previously been applied to such a problem.

CREATING THE REVIEW

The quality of your literature review is determined by your ability to analyse, and, in a professional, scholarly and mature way, critically compare and contrast what other writers have said. Many students think that when they have arrived at the stage at which they have all of the necessary information at their fingertips, they can just sit down and produce the report in one sitting, which is why many usually leave it too late. There is little that is worse than submitting your work and then remembering that you meant to change something, or having to bear the stress of struggling to meet an impossible deadline and, in the process, accepting the fact that in the end you have to submit an inferior product. Give yourself enough time to prepare in the way that is discussed in this chapter. Start early and give yourself a chance to do what you set out to do. This will enable you to look objectively and critically at your own work and amend it where necessary. Don't be afraid of chopping and changing; your second, third or even fourth efforts are usually the best, and more accurate and in line with what you meant to say. Ernest Hemingway's Nobel Prize-winning book *For Whom the Bell Tolls* contains 80,000 words, but Hemingway, at a party after receiving the award, remarked that with chopping and changing he must have written about a million words before he was finally satisfied with what he had done.

EXAMPLE 8: JIT PURCHASING

Frank is in the final year of a part-time business degree and is working on his dissertation. Following the completion of an expansion programme, his own sponsoring organisation is experiencing a storage problem with the inventory, which, in an attempt to save money, had been excluded from the original planning.

Conscious of the costs involved in storing inventory, Frank, in his quest for a solution, has carried out a literature search. When he used 'inventory' as a key word, he was led to the subject of 'just-in-time management' (JIT), which he then pursued as a possible solution to his company's problem.

He then carried out primary and secondary research by interviewing the managers to gain their views on possible solutions and studying the original expansion plans and other relevant company planning documents. Finally, he carried out interviews with managers in other companies that had experienced a similar problem in order to discover how they had tackled it and what were the outcomes.

Having evaluated all of his data, he has started to draft his literature review. His approach is to critically compare and contrast the work of other writers and then compare what they have said with the findings from his own primary and secondary research.

Frank now has sufficient evidence to support his argument in favour of introducing 'JIT purchasing', in which raw materials and components, which make up the inventory, are delivered just when they are needed. His company's alternative would have been to become involved in an expensive building programme to accommodate the inventory.

CHECK YOUR UNDERSTANDING
Questions

1 What are the purposes of the literature review?
2 At what stage can your literature search be regarded as completed?
3 What happens to your perception of the work you have done when you start to write it up?
4 What do we mean by the term *narrowing down*?
5 What do we mean by *critically* reviewing literature?
6 How would you assess the relevance of the data you have collected?
7 Why should you not highlight or underline your notes?
8 What is *soak time* and what are the benefits of it?
9 Why is it important to reflect upon an experience?
10 What do you understand by the term scholarship?

Answers in Appendix 4

SUMMARY

1 Always keep in mind the main purposes of the literature review. When you are writing up your preparatory notes, be open-minded and think holistically, visualising the subject in its total breadth and depth. In this way you can see the whole picture and will be able to demonstrate where your research, your contribution to the body of knowledge, fits in.

2 Learn to accept that the act of writing influences your perception of your aims and objectives and, thereby, of your main argument.

3 Prepare your review by breaking it down into thematic sections and treat each of those sections as a mini-review.

4 Summarise (in writing) each paper you read, and you will find that it helps you to sharpen your focus upon what the writer is saying.

5 Practise reflection, it is an important technique that help you to retain what you have learned.

Writing a good literature review is an indication of scholarship, of knowledge of the subject and of professional maturity. It involves the use of particular skills, which develop within you as you encounter each element of the total task. These include:

1 Improving your reading skills, particularly in the development of reading critically
2 Improving your writing skills. The language of writing is different from the language of speaking and this is especially true of academic writing
3 Learning to place your subject within its appropriate academic framework
4 Learning to regard your stock of relevant data holistically
5 Learning to analyse, assess and evaluate the work of others.

FURTHER READING

BELL, J. (1999) *Doing Your Research Project*, 3rd edn. Buckingham: Open University Press.

BERRY, R. (1994) *The Research Project: How to write it,* 3rd edn. London: Routledge.

BUZAN, T. (1980) *Use Your Head.* London: BBC Publications.

CAMERON, S. (2001) *The MBA Handbook*, 4th edn. Harlow: Pearson Education.

COLLIS, J. and HUSSEY, R. (2003) *Business Research*, 2nd edn. Basingstoke: Palgrave Macmillan.

DINGWALL, R. (1983) *The Management of Stress.* Budleigh Salterton, Devon: The Granary Press.

DREW, S. and BINGHAM, R. (1997) *The Student Skills Guide.* Aldershot: Gower Publishing.

GALL, M. D., BORG, W. R. and GALL, J. P. (1996) *Educational Research: An Introduction*, 6th edn. New York: Longman. (In Saunders, M., Lewis, P. and Thornhill, A. (2003) *Research Methods for Business Students.* Harlow: Pearson Education.)

HART, C. (1998) *Doing a Literature Review.* London: Sage.

HINDERER, D. E. (1992) *Building Arguments.* Belmont, CA: Wadsworth.

JANKOWICZ, A. D. (1995) *Business Research Projects*, 2nd edn. London: Chapman and Hall.

JANKOWICZ, A. D. (2000) *Business Research Projects*, 3rd edn. London: Chapman and Hall.

McNEILL, P. (1990) *Research Methods,* 2nd edn. London: Routledge.

NORTHEDGE, A. (1990) *The Good Study Guide.* Milton Keynes: Open University Press.

WILLIAMS, K. (1989) *Study Skills.* Basingstoke: Macmillan Press.

WEBSITES

MCKILLUP, S., WEBSTER, B. and WARD, T. (2003) *Why do a Literature Review?* www.library.cqu.edu.au/litreviewpages/

SCOWN, B. (2003) *What is a Literature Review?* http//www.library.cqu.edu.au/litreviewpages/tips.htm

WARD, T. (2003) *Why do a Literature Review?* http://www.library.cqu.edu.au/litreviewpages/why.htm

Collecting primary data

INTRODUCTION

This chapter sets out to explain what primary data are, to examine the main approaches that are used to collect primary data and to discuss the nature of the data collected through the use of each approach. The aim of all of this is to provide you with a basic understanding of the methods and techniques that are available for you to use when you wish to collect particular types of primary data. We also discuss and explain the common uses of each method. As you will see, there are three main techniques, and the application of these is explained and discussed separately in the main sections of the chapter.

DEFINITIONS

Primary research is research that produces data that are only obtainable directly from an original source. In certain types of primary research, the researcher has direct contact with the original source of the data.

Primary data are data that were previously unknown and which have been obtained directly by the researcher for a particular research project.

Primary information is primary data to which meaning has been added; in other words, the data have been analysed, inferences have been drawn from them and, thereby, meaning has been added.

THE NEED FOR PRIMARY INFORMATION

The decision to collect primary data for your research project is influenced by the kind of research you are carrying out. The need for primary information is far more frequently related to the practical, rather than the academic aspects of study. For example, part-time students on professional courses are required to carry out investigative assignment and project work that is related to real organisations, usually their own sponsoring organisations. Primary data is less frequently needed for essays, which, by their nature, are traditional features of degree courses. A third-year dissertation or a thesis for a higher degree such as an MBA, however, very often includes primary information.

You carry out primary research when the data you need is not available from published sources. For example, if you are carrying out an assignment, a major project or a degree dissertation, you may need information that is only available from key individuals, such as managers, a group of employees in an organisation, customers or other members of the public. Conversely, you may need to know how groups and individuals react to particular situations and ideas, or how they behave when they are carrying out their jobs.

THREE PRIMARY METHODS

There are three main methods you can use to collect primary data, and the method/s that you decide upon are determined by the type/s of data you need. The methods are:

- The survey method
- The interview method
- The observational method.

In a sense, the interview method is also a survey, but the word survey has become most frequently associated with questionnaires, so that when someone says 'I'm carrying out a survey', it is generally assumed that there is a questionnaire involved. The objectives when carrying out interviews are more or less the same as those when using questionnaires; Arnold *et al* (1991) say that the interview is, in effect, often used as a 'talking questionnaire'. However, the techniques used are different for each of the two approaches, so we will refer to them as *questionnaire* and *interview* techniques.

Unlike questionnaires or interviews, the observational method does not put questions to respondents; it collects data about behaviour. The researcher observes and records behaviour that is relevant to his or her research.

DEVELOPING A RESEARCH STRATEGY

When you are formulating your primary research strategy, you have to decide which of these approaches you think would be the most appropriate in terms of the kind of data you wish to collect. In the large majority of cases the decision is to employ more than one primary method (see below: *triangulation*). It is also important for you to understand and develop skills in the application of the techniques you may use when employing a particular method. Perhaps at this stage we should distinguish between what we mean by *method* and what we mean by *technique*. 'In our context, a method is *a systematic and orderly approach taken towards the collection of data so that information can be obtained from those data* ... Techniques, in contrast, are *particular, step-by-step procedures which you can follow in order to gather data, and analyse them for the information they contain*' (Jankowicz 1995).

THE 'METHOD EFFECT'

The choice of a particular method or methods is a very important decision in assignment and project work, since it is *what* we are doing and the *kind of data* that we need that determines how we should go about collecting it. According to Saunders *et al,* 'there is an inevitable relationship between the data collection method you employ and the results you obtain. In short, the results will be affected by the method used. The problem here is that it is impossible to ascertain the nature of that effect. Since all different methods will have different effects, it makes sense to use different methods to cancel out the "method effect". That will lead to greater confidence being placed in your conclusions' (Saunders *et al* 2003: 99).

TRIANGULATION

This is the term used to describe combining several methods in the same single study. When setting your strategy, you may, for example, consider the possibility that relying on a single method may adversely affect the reliability and validity of the results – bear in mind that the ultimate conclusions you draw and the recommendations you make in your report will be based on your research results. In that context, it is certainly advisable to use at least one extra method in order to compare the two sets of results and cross-check the data. Lingering doubts may lead you to base your conclusions and recommendations on several methods, including *secondary research,* in which you can rework the findings from a set of data that has been collected for some other research purpose (see Figure 11).

Kane represents an archival review, questionnaires, interviews and participant observation as potentially overlapping in scope (Jankowicz 1995):

> If you had to stake your life on which of these is likely to represent the accurate, complete research information, you would choose the centre [of the overlap] in which you got the information through interviews and questionnaires, reinforced it by observation, and checked it through documentary analysis (secondary information) …. Here you are getting not only what people say they do and what you see them doing, but also, what they are recorded as doing (Kane 1985: 51)

Kane's 'belt and braces' approach is not meant to imply that you should use as many of the techniques as you possibly can in order to sharpen up the quality of the results you get. Ideally, you should select

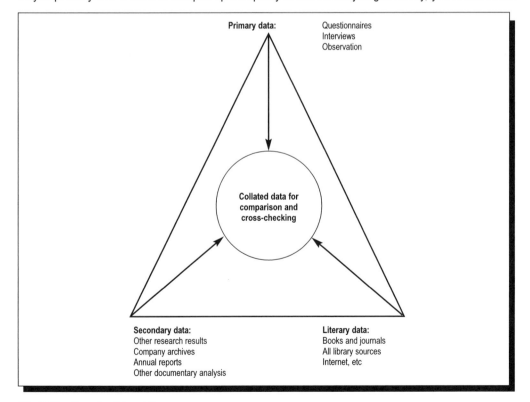

Figure 11 *Example of triangulation*

the techniques that will allow you to cross-check the data and use one set of results to corroborate another. Try not to overburden yourself unnecessarily with too many sets of results. It will not look impressive in your methodology section, not to mention the amount of time it will all take.

KEEP YOUR EYE ON THE BALL

When you are using any one particular method, you should ensure that your desire to demonstrate skill in choosing and using it does not allow it to take precedence over the reason why you needed it in the first place. Truly, you will earn extra 'brownie points' for demonstrating good research skills, but it is the

---

Case study

Christine is the assistant HR manager in an insurance company in Bellchester, which is in the south of England. She has enrolled in a part-time MBA at the local university and at present is trying to identify a topic for her project.

The company directors have expressed concern about how employee performance is being managed. According to the records, the average performance has been teetering around the minimum standard. Last year's performance audit indicated that progress was expected, but now, there is a discernible lack of zest and commitment in the internal environment.

It is generally accepted that the accumulative performance of any workforce is the main influence on the performance of the whole organisation. The present situation, therefore, has led the board to ask Julios, the HR manager, to have an investigation carried out and report back with an explanation and recommendations for a performance improvement programme. Julios has delegated the task to Christine, who is delighted, since she regards it as the answer to her search for a topic.

Christine has a fair understanding of performance management, but since most of her career so far has been spent in recruitment and selection, she knows that she now needs to learn as much as she possibly can about it, especially in terms of recent theory and developments in practice.

Drafting the methodology section of her proposal, she is now considering her research strategy. Obviously, she has to carry out a literature search and review in order to learn more about performance management and to understand what other writers have said about her topic.

She can also see, however, that she will also need to collect a considerable amount of data from within the company. She will have to examine performance records; talk to the senior managers to identify their attitudes towards and ideas about how performance should be managed; and talk to the middle managers to understand how it actually is managed. Also, she will need to gather data from the employees themselves, in order to assess why they think their performance has been suffering recently.

Try to answer this question:
What would you expect to see included in Christine's research strategy?

Answer in Appendix 4

---

relevance and quality of the data you collect, as well as the methods you used to collect it, that will gather in most of the brownie points.

One cannot overemphasise the importance of thinking things through in advance of implementing the techniques. At first you may have thought that you needed to use just one primary technique, along with your literature review and any secondary data you may have collected. However, if you think deeply about your data collection objectives, you will find yourself using two, or even all three primary approaches. If you are doing your major project, a dissertation or an MBA project, you will have to include your research strategy in the methodology section of your proposal; you will need this to be as close a representation as possible to what you actually do, since one of the final assessment criteria may be the strength of the relationship between what you proposed and what you actually did.

QUALITATIVE AND QUANTITATIVE DATA

Some approaches to researching a particular phenomenon produce *qualitative data,* while other approaches produce *quantitative data.* Qualitative data are data that have not been quantified, although that is not to say that they have not been *analysed.* Qualitative analysis is carried out when, for example, during and after interviewing someone, you formulate an understanding of the meanings that can be attributed to their responses to your questions. You assess the value of the responses, the degree to which they are meaningful to your research objectives and their prospective usefulness in lending support to your arguments. By nature, qualitative information is subjective since it is the product of the respondent's personal opinions, values, attitudes towards and perceptions of the subject of the interview conversation. You collect qualitative data when you need the perceptions and opinions of key people as individuals, which inevitably means that you collect it from small groups.

Quantitative data are specific and, obviously, are data that have been quantified, such as when the data that are obtained from an occupational selection test are analysed using psychometric techniques, or when the results of a large-scale survey are analysed and quantified.

Distinctions between qualitative and quantitative data are drawn on several grounds because it is clear that different approaches to gathering data are specifically designed to produce *either* qualitative *or* quantitative data – for example, interviewing (qualitative) versus large-scale surveying (quantitative). Firstly, qualitative data tend to be obtained from small groups, such as a group of interviewees or a focus group, while quantitative data are obtained from large groups, such as a representative cross-section from the employees of a large organisation or from a large group of consumers. Secondly, there are variations in the reliability and validity of both types of data. Qualitative data tend to be high on validity and low on reliability, while the reverse is true for quantitative data. (For more detailed explanations of qualitative and quantitative data, see Saunders *et al* 2003; Jankowicz 2000; and Hart 1998: 53.)

The purpose of these explanations is to help to guide your decision-making when you are preparing your research strategy. Remember that collecting primary data is part of your total research strategy, and it is worth bearing in mind, therefore, that the data you collect should bear a strong relationship to the data you collected from your literature search, which, combined with your primary information should lend support to the main arguments you intend to present.

TECHNIQUES

It is vital to the success of your project that you develop the skills that will enable you to apply the methods you adopt. Techniques are there to guide you through this kind of research work; applied correctly and imaginatively, they take you through the process of using the methods. They are the practical means that we adopt, the actual steps that we take in order to get the research work done. In short, techniques tell us how to use the methods. Next in this chapter, we explain and discuss the techniques involved when we employ the main methods of collecting primary data.

THE SURVEY TECHNIQUE

In this section we use several words that are commonly found in surveying. Let us describe and define their meanings before we start.

- A *survey* is a technique in which a *sample* of prospective respondents is selected from a *population.* The sample is then studied with a view to drawing inferences from their responses to the statements in a questionnaire, or the questions in a series of interviews.

- *Population* is the term we use to describe the main group of people from which a sample is drawn. A population, therefore, may be an organisation's workforce, a management group or a group of customers.

- A *sample* is a representative cross-section of people drawn from a population so that their responses may be studied.

The sizes of the samples and the structures of the surveys are determined by the kind of data that needs to be collected and from whom.

QUESTIONNAIRES

Most people are familiar with questionnaires. We see them being administered for a variety of reasons in many walks of life. TV companies use them to assess their programmes and viewing figures; marketing researchers use them to obtain people's opinions of their products and services; and psephologists, who are briefed by the media and political parties, use them to obtain data about trends and habits in voting.

Occasionally, however, we receive questionnaires in the workplace asking our opinions of say, the pension scheme, or the organisation's policies on health and safety, pay, holiday entitlement or promotion. The purposes of surveys that are carried out in organisations usually set out to:

- Identify employees' attitudes towards something
- Elicit employees' opinions of something
- Obtain data about employees' characteristics
- Ask employees about their behaviour
- Obtain information about their perceptions of something in particular, such as the cause of a continuing problem.

At first glance, some of these purposes may seem similar, but there are subtle differences which, if ignored, could affect the quality of the data you ultimately collect. An *opinion,* for example, is an unproven belief or judgement about something such as the effects of mobile telephone masts on people's health, whereas an *attitude* may be a disposition to act for or against something or a predisposition to respond consistently in a positive or negative way to some person, object or situation. An attitude, however, is not actual behaviour, but attitudes do cause people to behave in the way they do. Individual *perception* is a mental *process.* It is the process that gives us the ability to make sense of things in the world around us. Truly, these words are used conversationally and different meanings are attributed to them. In scientific terms, however, the true, non-colloquial differences are of paramount importance when we come to construct the question items for a questionnaire or for a series of interviews, since it is the precise wording of the questions that determines the relevance and types of responses we obtain. This brings us back to considering the kind of data we wish to collect. Do you, for example, want people's opinions of some event, object, policy or idea? Or do you want to elicit their *attitudes* towards it? If you consider the meanings of these words as they are stated above, you should be able to see how they influence the way you formulate your questions.

TYPES OF QUESTIONNAIRE

There are several different designs for survey questionnaires. Each design is governed by the purpose of the survey and the kind of data that the researcher seeks. All designs, however, must meet certain criteria. These include to:

- Measure what they are supposed to measure
- Be distributed to a random sample of people to whom the subject of the survey is relevant
- Be structured carefully so that the questions or statements are unambiguous and likely to elicit the data needed.

'The survey method has both advantages and disadvantages. It can be used with people directly involved in the issues to be investigated. It can investigate their experiences in their day-to-day setting. It is relatively easy to conduct and makes relatively low demands on people's time' (Arnold *et al* 1991: 37). By using a survey questionnaire, you are not disturbing or controlling the normal routines of a setting.

One of the disadvantages of using a questionnaire, however, is that it keeps the researcher at a distance from the respondents, so that opportunities to probe, to go back to check an answer or have an answer explained further are denied. This is yet another reason for constructing the questions carefully in order to ensure that the quality of the responses meets with your expectations.

DESIGNING THE QUESTIONNAIRE

The questionnaire is the most widely used technique for collecting primary data. Depending on the nature of the data you are looking for, the form may ask questions, make statements, or do both. If you choose to use questions, always use closed questions, which are questions to which there is only one answer. If you are looking for answers to specific questions, then you need somehow to ensure that the answers you get are brief and to the point; otherwise, the subsequent task of analysis is going to be difficult. The questionnaire should be designed to head off such a problem. The design of a questionnaire includes:

1   The general layout of the questionnaire form
2   A statement of the purpose of the survey
3   The number of questions or statements
4   How the questions or statements are worded
5   The response system, eg tick boxes or a measured scale, and the conditions of response, such as the return date, anonymity and whether or not all questions should be answered.

It is critically important to get the design right since it affects:

1   The kind of data you collect
2   The number of responses you receive
3   The reliability and validity of the data
4   The quality of the responses.

When you use a questionnaire, all those in the sample are asked to respond to the same set of questions or statements. You cannot just sit down and draft a meaningful questionnaire in an arbitrary fashion. You need to think very carefully about the exact nature of the data you wish to collect before you start to frame your questions or statements. Do not fall into the trap of thinking that this is an easy task; it isn't.

QUESTIONING TECHNIQUES

The most frequent question I am asked by students who wish to design a questionnaire is 'where do I start?' I always advise them to start by drafting the questions. It is the most difficult task in questionnaire design, but how the questions are asked does determine the rest of the design. One approach to this task is to brainstorm ideas about the questions that need to be answered and write them down. It is a random process, but the questions you come up with can be modified and placed in order afterwards. Doing it this way, you will probably finish up with too many questions, some that you can immediately reject. After discarding the obvious ones, check the remainder to see if you can improve the wording with a view to achieving exact and unambiguous meanings. You may still have too many – a large number of questions will reduce your response rate – but you should not discard questions arbitrarily. Again, study each question separately and carefully to see if it needs to be amended. There are criteria to help you to make such decisions in respect of each question. Czaja and Blair (1996) proposed a checklist for eliminating questions (see Figure 12).

When you have developed all of the questions you can, list them in a logical sequence and carry out a pilot study on a group and people who understand the subject of your research and your objectives. Show them to your tutor, who might have some suggestions for further questions or for amending the ones you do have. Remember that you have been deeply absorbed in the task, and to have someone look at the questions with an objective eye is usually very useful.

THE ATTITUDE SURVEY

A frequently used questionnaire in organisations is one that is designed to measure people's attitude towards something. You may, for example, need to find out what the employees think of the design of the work system or the communication style of the managers. There are several techniques for this, one of which is the *self report questionnaire* in which respondents are asked to report their feelings, beliefs and behaviour towards the subject of the survey.

1   Does the question relate directly to some aspect of your research?

2   Will the content of the question convey the right information?
    (If the answer is NO to both 1 and 2, drop the question; if YES to 1 and NO to 2, rewrite the question.)

3   Will all respondents understand the question in the same way?
    (If NO, revise or drop; if YES, retain.)

4   Will all respondents have information to answer it?
    (If NO, drop; if YES, retain.)

5   Will most respondents be willing to answer it?
    (If NO, drop; if YES, retain.)

6   Is other information needed to analyse this question?
    (If NO, retain; if YES, retain only if required information is available.)

7   Should this question be asked of all respondents, or only a subset?
    (If only a subset, retain only if the subset is identifiable beforehand or through questions in an interview.)

Figure 12   *Checklist for eliminating questions*
Source: Adapted from Czaja and Blair (1996: 61). In: Collis and Hussey (2003)

Semantic differences

When you place a numerical rating scale against a number of questions, the difference between the num-bers on the scale is usually equal; for example, if you take a five-point scale: **1 2 3 4 5,** the difference between the numbers is 1. This, therefore, is an *equal interval scale.* However, when you look at statements that range from highly positive to highly negative, you will see that the difference in value between the values of the statements is not exactly equal. The trick, therefore, is to get the value difference between the numbers to match that of the statements. Obviously, you cannot amend the statements for this purpose, since that would affect the quality of the data you collect from them, so you have to change the numbers.

THE THURSTONE APPROACH

The Thurstone approach attempts to overcome this problem. Here the researcher develops a large number of potential questionnaire statements, ranging from highly favourable to highly unfavourable in terms of the respondents' attitudes towards the *object.*

> People, situations, events and ideas towards which people have attitudes are referred to as the attitude object. Thus, when considering my attitudes towards, say, the Prime Minister, then the PM is the attitude object. This means that I have feelings and beliefs about the PM, which may be positive or negative and which will determine my behaviour towards him (Currie 1997).

The researcher takes the potential questionnaire statements to a subset of the sample and asks them to rate the statements on an 11-point equal interval rating scale. Using these responses, the researcher discards some of the questions on the grounds that the subset respondents could not agree on them. The discarding process is continued until the researcher is left with about 20 statements, although it is normal practice to have 11 questions on a Thurstone scale. From Figure 13, you can see how the numbers have been manipulated to reflect the value differences between the statements.

The next step is to arrange the statements randomly on the questionnaire form. As you will see from the figure, the respondents are asked to tick against every statement with which they agree. An individual's attitude is the mean (average) of the numerical values of all of the ticked statements. If, therefore, a respondent had ticked statements 5, 6 and 8 in Figure 13, the attitude score of that respondent would be 6.87, which would have been calculated thus:

$$\frac{8.50 + 7.00 + 5.10}{3} = 6.87$$

To calculate the accumulative attitude of the whole sample, simply summate the individual score and divide by the number of valid responses.

It is claimed that compared to other, simpler systems, the Thurstone rating scale produces a very accurate reflection of attitudes. Figure 13 represents the researcher's master copy of the questionnaire. The numbers in the right-hand column are not included in the questionnaire that is distributed; instead, the right-hand column is used for the tick-box responses.

The company is considering reorganising the IT service and before making a final decision would like to hear your opinion of the service as it is now.

We would be grateful, therefore, if you would take the time to complete the attached questionnaire and return it through the internal mail in the envelope provided.

Important: this is an anonymous survey of your true opinions and you are asked not to include your name so that we can respect confidentiality.

Statements	Numerical value
1 The organisation's IT service is excellent in all respects	11.00
2 All aspects of the IT service are very good	10.80
3 Most of what IT does for us is very good	9.30
4 Most of the time our IT service is very good	8.90
5 I like the way our IT service operates	8.50
6 Our IT service is probably as good as any other	7.00
7 Our IT service is not too bad	6.50
8 Our IT service could be better organised	5.10
9 Our IT service is somewhat disorganised	3.90
10 Our IT service could be considerably improved	2.30
11 Our IT service is a mess	0.50

Thank you for taking the time to complete this questionnaire.

Figure 13 *An example of a Thurstone rating scale to measure employee attitudes towards the quality of the organisation's IT service*

THE LIKERT APPROACH

This is another of the most commonly used rating scales, sometimes referred to as the *summated scale*. It is one in which you ask the respondent to tick a box or circle a number that appears against the statement that most accurately reflects their feelings and beliefs about an attitude object. As in the Thurstone approach, the researcher develops a large number of statements, which should be clearly for or against the attitude object. The Likert technique can employ a rating scale of four, five, six or seven points. Using the longest scale, the data is more accurate and refined, but they do take longer to analyse. There have been several approaches to the steps to be taken before reaching the final set of statements, although the basic principles are the same. Firstly, a panel of judges or a subset of the sample is asked to indicate their agreement or disagreement with each statement. Secondly, you compare the responses and select only those statements that are similar in the way in which they were responded to and those which drew the same responses on at least two occasions. Thirdly, you write up your final list.

Writers vary over how many statements you should aim to include in the final list. In making this decision, you should try to strike a balance between two main factors. Clearly, your data collection objectives must come first, but you should also bear in mind that a list that is too long can reduce the response rate. An additional inhibiting factor is the length of the rating scale. If, for example, you were to draft a questionnaire containing too many statements *and*, say, a seven- or nine-point scale, your response rate would be reduced considerably. These are factors that affect both the response rate and the accuracy and refinement of the data you ultimately collect. To ease your understanding, in the example that follows (Figure 14) I have used only 10 statements and a five-point scale. The respondents are asked to rate the degree to which the intrinsic design of their jobs motivates them to become involved.

Another approach to questionnaire design using the Likert scale is to place each statement above the scale itself and show the respondents the extent to which they are being asked their opinion. The

Please circle the number that most accurately reflects your feelings

I have enough responsibility	1 2 3 4 5	I have too much responsibility
I have enough authority	1 2 3 4 5	I have too much authority
My job is a complete task	1 2 3 4 5	I only do part of a total job
I can demonstrate my skills	1 2 3 4 5	Too much of the job is automated
The job is interesting	1 2 3 4 5	The job is boring
Others benefit from what I do	1 2 3 4 5	My job does not benefit others
I can make my own decisions	1 2 3 4 5	I have to follow strict routines
I know how well I am doing	1 2 3 4 5	I get no feedback from the job
My work is highly valued	1 2 3 4 5	My work is taken for granted
I have total discretion	1 2 3 4 5	I have to stick to the rules

(The statements in the figure are based on the Hackman and Oldham (1976) Job Characteristics Survey in which the *intrinsic factors* of a job are said to generate *job involvement,* as opposed to the *extrinsic factors,* which are said to generate *job satisfaction.*)

Figure 14   *An example of a Likert questionnaire using a five-point scale and 10 statements*

respondent is asked to circle the number against the statement that most closely reflects his or her opinion. For example:

I have too much responsibility

1	**2**	**3**	**4**	**5**
strongly disagree	disagree	don't know	agree	strongly agree

Within this scale the 'don't know' option is given to those who (i) do not have enough information about the attitude object to justify expressing an opinion; (ii) they are indifferent to the attitude object; (iii) they are ambivalent, in the sense that they think that the good and bad points about their jobs are about equal.

Notice that in all questionnaires, there is only one attitude object and only one aspect of that object in each question or statement. You cannot measure people's attitudes towards several objects on the same questionnaire.

COLLECTING DATA THROUGH INTERVIEWING

The interview has been called 'a conversation with a purpose', and more formally 'a purposeful discussion between two or more people' (Kahn and Cannell 1957). You can collect data using *structured, semi-structured* or *unstructured* interviews.

Definitions

1   A *structured interview* is one in which the interviewer simply reads out a set of closed questions in a particular order and notes the interviewee's responses. Structured interviews are sometimes referred to as *standardised interviews* (Healey and Rawlinson 1994).

2   A *semi-structured* interview is one in which the interviewer has a pre-set type and order of questions, but is prepared to add to the number of questions, vary the theme of the interview and the order in which the questions are asked if doing so is of benefit to the research objectives.

3   An *unstructured interview* is one in which the interviewer starts with a single theme; some questions may be written down, but the whole ambience is one of informality, so that the interviewer may explore the several aspects of a complex issue in depth by asking *open questions*, which are questions designed to invite explanatory or detailed answers. In some unstructured interviews there is more than one interviewee, depending on the areas you wish to explore and the different expertise that may be required.

Semi-structured and unstructured interviews are sometimes referred to as *non-standardised interviews* (Healey and Rawlinson 1994).

STRUCTURED INTERVIEWS

When you are stopped in the street by researchers carrying clipboards, they usually want to ask you questions about last evening's TV, a product, a recent event or a proposed action, such as the building of a new road that would affect the immediate locality. In the clipboard, they have a list of set questions, and if you agree to answer them, they will simply read them out from the list and note your responses. Everyone who cooperates is asked the same set of questions, which means that the interviewer is conducting a *structured interview.* The process of carrying out the structured interview sounds simple, but the whole business of interviewing involves considerable skill. Just as when you are constructing a questionnaire, care has to be taken over formulating the questions and the order in which they are asked. Also, when you are face to face with the respondent, *how* the questions are asked is also important, including your visible manner and any emphasis you may deliberately or inadvertently place on particular words or phrases in the question. Unlike the *distributed* questionnaire, therefore, you do have a strong element of control over the situation in which the questions and responses are dealt with. For the same reasons, you would have the same degree of control conducting a series of structured interviews among managers or small group of other key people in an organisation.

SEMI-STRUCTURED INTERVIEWS

Unlike the structured, the *semi-structured interview* does allow the respondent to talk freely, expand upon answers and even change the theme of the interview. That is fine as long as the interviewee (i) does not digress to the extent that they depart from your research subject, and (ii) is contributing to the kind of data you are trying to collect.

UNSTRUCTURED INTERVIEWS

When you are carrying out an *unstructured interview,* you are playing the role of moderator or the chair of a meeting, and to elicit any meaningful data from such meetings, you need to develop appropriate skills. The main advantage of unstructured interviews is that they allow you to probe in a greater depth than you can when you are limited to the confines of a set of predetermined questions. Saunders *et al* (2003: 247) refer to unstructured interviews as *in-depth interviews.*

The advantages of semi-structured and unstructured interviews are firstly, that you hear different views expressed about the same topic or issue as you progress from one interview to the next. Secondly, when you are summarising and collating the data you have collected and find something that needs expansion or explanation, you can go back to the interviewee to obtain such clarifications.

USES OF INTERVIEWS

It is clear from what is said above that the decision about the most appropriate type of interview is a critically important one; in fact, your research may include more than one type. You may, for example, decide to collect both qualitative and quantitative data. When you conduct unstructured interviews, clearly, you are collecting qualitative information, which you glean from the flow of conversation. On the quantitative front, however, you may also use such probing, in-depth interviews to identify the variables you will need in order to design your survey questionnaire or list of questions for a fully structured interview.

FOCUS GROUPS

Alternatively, you could organise a focus group consisting of just a few people and in which you, the researcher, may loosely lead the meeting. Because of your role, the focus group is, in effect, an unstructured interview because your role is to guide the conversation and keep it to the central theme, or at least to a theme that, when discussed, is likely to produce data that would contribute to your research. Keeping control of the general conversation is a skilled social activity, and researchers vary in their ability to do this effectively. You have to recognise when to allow the conversation to flow and when to steer it towards a new direction. The objective is to make the best possible use of the knowledge and expertise of people in the group. What they say during the conversation may give rise to further questions that you think need to be answered. Always plan the duration of the meeting. Put together a number of questions that you think can be discussed, conclusions reached and useful data obtained. The more complex the questions are, the greater the amount of time the meeting will take.

TELEPHONE INTERVIEWS

The quality of the data that you can collect on the telephone is determined primarily by your own telephone skills. Table 8 provides you with some indication of the effectiveness of using the telephone to conduct particular types of interview.

The effectiveness of the interview may also be reduced by distractions at the other end. You are in a good position to control things at your end, but if you are telephoning, say, a busy manager you have no way of knowing what is going on at the other end.

Table 8   *The effectiveness of telephone interviewing*

Interview type	Effectiveness
Structured	Effective, depending on telephone skills at both ends. A prolonged interview may reduce effectiveness Advice: Adopt the method when convenient to both sides
Semi-structured	Fairly effective. Lacks the influence of face-to-face contact, which could inhibit breadth and depth of exploration of subject Advice: Adopt the method only when face-to-face cannot be achieved
Unstructured	Least effective. Lacks the influence of face-to-face contact Can only talk on a one-to-one basis Lacks the required conversational flow Advice: Avoid where possible

The point should also be made that cost is also a factor. You may think that you are saving time and money by not travelling, but the likelihood that you will be making the call during business hours is very high, and that, of course, is exactly when the telephone companies charge their highest rates.

NOTE-TAKING AND RECORDING

In this section, we are mostly concerned with note-taking and vocalised recording of conversations in semi-structured and unstructured interviews. Normally, in a structured interview, people expect you to take notes. Such notes are normally brief and to the point, and the design of the form on which you have your interview questions listed should also include a space for the responses next to each question (see Table 9).

From the table you can see that the notes you are taking are answers to closed questions and, therefore, do not take long to write down.

The time you spend interviewing people at semi-structured and unstructured interviews is very precious, but it is time wasted if you fail to make accurate records of the data made available to you during the event. It can be difficult to hold a reasonable conversation with someone, let alone control the meeting, if concurrently you are trying to keep abreast of what is being said by writing continuously. Also, if you sit there making copious notes, you will inhibit the free flow of conversation and, indeed, may even lose valuable data that would have come out instead of those embarrassing silences.

It is the foresight and the skill with which you plan the event that determines how smoothly the interviews run. I use the word 'foresight' because it is worth taking a little time to think about all of the administrative tasks you can carry out before the event. You know the theme/s you are going to be handling and the questions to which you need answers. One approach to handling this is to set up a document that will enable you to make a comprehensive record of the event. Do one page for each interviewee and divide it into sections (see Figure 15).

There is more writing space than the figure indicates since it represents a whole page. Alternatively, you could use a landscape page set-up.

Using a system like this, you can fill in sections 1 to 4 in advance of the interview. During the interview, all you will appear to be doing is making the occasional note without interrupting or inhibiting others and allowing you to listen and participate. Figure 15 is just an example. Depending on the kind of data you expect to collect, you may decide to divide the page into a greater or smaller number of sections with appropriate headings. Having it there in front of you during the interview means that you do not need to make any preparatory entries; you will have a concise record of who said what, and the section headings will remind you to draw out the main points and the various facets of any argument. It will give a routine to your note-taking, and as you build on your interviewing experience, you will become more adept at using it.

Table 9 *Abstract from a typical structured interview form*

Questions	Responses
1. Excluding overtime, how many hours are there in your normal working week?	Normally I work 40 hours
2. Do you work any overtime?	Yes

1. Interviewee name	2. Date........................

3. Main theme/s:

4. Questions:	5. Responses:

6. Main points made:

7. New information:

Figure 15 *A standardised page layout for taking interview notes*

VERBAL RECORDING MACHINES

Some people react negatively to the prospect of having their conversation recorded. For ethical reasons and as a common courtesy, you need to obtain their permission to use a recording device, which is something you can do in advance of the interview. The interviewee should be given some control over the use of the machine. For example, the answers to some of the questions you ask may be politically sensitive, but the interviewee may be prepared to answer your question if the machine is switched off while he or she is speaking.

Advantages and disadvantages
The advantages and disadvantages of using a recording device are related to the type of interview you are conducting, ie semi-structured or unstructured, one-to-one, one-to-several, and people's reactions to the machine itself.

Obviously, a recorder will hold the most precise and unbiased account of a one-to-one interview, but with several participants, as there are in some unstructured interviews and focus groups, it is sometimes difficult to identify who said what when you are reviewing the interview at a later stage, although you may ask the participants to state their names before they speak. A group of interviewees will normally react more positively to the use of a recorder, but in a one-to-one interview the interviewee's awareness of it may make it difficult to establish a good rapport. One further problem is that the interviewee's awareness of the machine may cause them to divide their attention between you and it, especially at the beginning of the interview.

If you borrow a recorder that your great grand-parents have had for many years, you may find it cumbersome, difficult to operate and inefficient. Always use a free-standing battery-driven machine that

Table 10 *Advantages and disadvantages of using a recording device*

Advantages	Disadvantages
Records a precise and unbiased account of the interview	May disrupt rapport, especially at the beginning of the interview
Several people being interviewed concurrently usually react more positively to it	After the interview it is sometimes difficult to identify who said what when there were several interviewees
Allows interviewer to concentrate, listen and participate more fully	Technical problems, such as expiring battery interrupting flow
Allows for a more confident review of the interview conversation	Transcribing a recording can be very time-consuming
Provides a permanent record of exactly what was said	May cause interviewee to divide his/her attention between you and the machine

you can place on a surface that is within your reach, but not too close to the speaker/s; after a while they tend to forget that it is there. Check the capacity of the tape to ensure that it is large enough to keep recording for the total duration of the session; you can get tapes that will last up to four hours. Finally, it is embarrassing if the battery runs out so take a spare.

Using a modern recorder will help to head off some of these problems. You may decide to use a digital recorder, most of which are quite small and unobtrusive; furthermore there is no tape to expire, and you can use long-life batteries. In most models, the storage capacity in terms of time is three hours, which is fine for most interviews, but in some models it is longer than that. You can also get them with a remote microphone facility, but now we are talking real money. These advantages and disadvantages may be summarised (see Table 10).

THE TIME FACTOR

Many students underestimate the amount of time they should allow for interviews. The position of a prospective interviewee in the organisation and the likely demands upon his or her time should be considered. The time factor is an issue that should be considered carefully, and you should refer to it during your first contact with the prospective interviewee.

Depending on the nature and complexity of the subject, interviews can take anything from one to three hours. Key people in organisations, for example, often cannot afford so much time. They may, however, agree to a shorter interview; especially if the subject of your research has excited their interest. It is a good idea to make an estimate before you make contact and add a 10 per cent contingency time allowance so that the prospective interviewee can reserve sufficient time for you. You may not need that extra time, and if you do not, at least it will make you look efficient.

Another possibility is that they may agree to two or even three shorter interviews so that the subject can be dealt with thoroughly. This means, however, that your notes and/or vocal recordings have to be labelled and stored carefully in order to ease the task of picking up the threads from where you left off. An advantage that is worth mentioning, however, is that the time between interviews may turn into 'soak' time (see Chapter 6), in which the interviewees reflect upon what was said in one interview and come to the next one armed with further questions and ideas for discussion, which can only improve the quality of the data you collect.

When you are making these arrangements, you usually do it on the telephone. You may find yourself talking to someone whom you regard as important. So here you are, a mere student, talking, perhaps, to a senior company manager. I know from personal experience that many students feel this way, but you have to sound confident and be relaxed; what you are doing is also important. You have to find a balance between sounding respectful (which you must) and obsequious (look it up!), which you mustn't. If you achieve the right balance you will instil his or her confidence in you. If they refuse to be interviewed, remain respectful and just accept it.

USING OBSERVATIONAL METHODS

There are two approaches to collecting primary data through the use of observational methods. The first is *structured observation*, in which the researcher simply observes and records behaviour. The second is *participant observation*, in which the researcher actually takes part in the behaviour being studied.

STRUCTURED OBSERVATIONAL TECHNIQUES

We are all familiar with the old-fashioned *work study practitioners* who, with their clipboards, stopwatches, pens and pads stood and observed people working. They were using *structured observational methods*, which are quantitative. They may have wanted to know how many times a person carried out a cycle of work activity within a particular period of time; and if a different method of working would improve productivity.

Unlike the data gathered from an interview, this kind of observation records irrefutable *facts* about people's behaviour. However, structured observation is quite a 'cold' exercise in that it tells us little about the subject's emotions – their reactions to what they have to do and their thoughts and feelings about it. Those being observed are usually aware of what you are doing and, for ethical reasons, they should be told anyway. Exceptionally, when there is no alternative and when the observation subject is sufficiently important to justify it, covert observation takes place. Obviously, this raises ethical issues. Researchers do not normally set out to deceive people. On the other hand, the transparency of the observation creates a dilemma because in certain circumstances the probability of collecting accurate data is reduced markedly since those being observed seldom behave in the way they would normally. Undoubtedly, behaviour departs from the norm when people are aware that they are being watched; this is a phenomenon that was observed during the Hawthorne studies in Chicago in the 1920s. Another form of deception takes place when as part of an ostensibly overt observation exercise, such as participant observation (see below), the behaviour that is being observed by the researcher may be outside the limits of his or her stated intentions.

PARTICIPANT OBSERVATIONAL TECHNIQUES

By nature, *participant observation* is qualitative. As a generalisation, it is safe that say that everyone is a participant observer. If you are a member of a group such as a sports club or a political party, you are in a good position to observe the values, motives and behaviour of your fellow members and to share with them the experience of being a member. All of these are characteristic features of formal participant observation in which you gather such information about those within the group. In the formal research situation, however, you become fully involved with them and their activities, and they usually know why you are there.

It is important to understand that the *situations* being described here are *natural settings* in which you are unable to exercise any control over the variables. This is not meant to imply that you would wish to exercise control over the variables, because the whole point of participant observation is to observe people in their natural settings. A natural setting as opposed to a *laboratory setting* is 'a research environment that would have existed had researchers never studied it' (Vogt 1993: 150).

Some writers say that because you cannot control the variables in a natural setting, you may observe the behaviour in a second, or even a third, natural setting and then draw comparisons. This, however, assumes that the environment, which plays a significant role in determining people's behaviour, is the same in all settings. In fact, there is no such thing as identical settings, since the people in them are different and so will be their behaviour, which means that you would not be comparing like with like. One approach to solving this problem may be to use two observers concurrently in the same setting, which has the additional benefit of reducing the chance of something being missed or misinterpreted.

PROBLEMS WITH OBSERVATIONAL TECHNIQUES

Two problems associated with observational techniques are *response bias* and *observer bias.* Response bias occurs when someone who knows that he or she is under observation behaves in ways that are designed to provide the researcher with information that the person observed thinks the observer seeks (in an effort to 'help' science). If this goes undetected, it may contaminate the data.

Observer bias occurs when two observers place different interpretation on some item of behaviour. Obviously, no two interpretations are ever exactly the same, but when they are markedly different, we have to either reach a compromise about the meaning of the behaviour, or simply agree to differ. It could, of course, be behaviour that is normally repeated, in which case both observers could be on hand to observe it concurrently and then reach an agreement.

While observational methods are used less frequently than surveys and interviews, they are always worth considering for your total research strategy, depending, of course, on the nature of what you are researching. It is worth repeating that the reliability and validity of data is increased by the evidential corroboration and cross-checking that the use of more than one method of data collection provides.

CHECK YOUR UNDERSTANDING
Questions

1 Define primary data

2 What are the three main methods of collecting primary data?

3 What do we mean by *triangulation*?

4 What is the difference between *methods* and *techniques*?

5 Give two examples of techniques that produce quantifiable data and two that produce qualitative data

6 (Read question 7 before you answer this one.) How might interviews be categorised?

7 List and qualify at least three ways in which interviews may be conducted

8 What are the five main points of questionnaire design?

9 What are the main disadvantages of using a recording device?

10 What would you gain from carrying out a pilot study of a questionnaire?

Answers in Appendix 4

FURTHER READING

ARNOLD, J., ROBERTSON, I. T. and COOPER, C. L. (1991) *Work Psychology*. London: Pitman.

COLLIS, J. and HUSSEY, R. (2003) *Business Research*. Basingstoke: Palgrave Macmillan.

CURRIE, D. (1997) *Personnel in Practice*. Oxford: Blackwell Publishing.

CZAJA, R. and BLAIR, J. (1996) *Designing Surveys: A guide to decisions and procedures.* Thousand Oaks, CA: Pine Forge Press.

HACKMAN, J. R. and OLDHAM, G. R. (1976) 'Motivation through the design of work: Test of a theory'. *Organisational Behaviour and Human Performance*, 16: 250–79.

HART, C. (1998) *Doing a Literature Review*. London: Sage.

HEALEY, M. J. and RAWLINSON, M. B. (1994) 'Interviewing techniques in business and management research', in Saunders *et al* (2003).

JANKOWICZ, A. D. (1995) *Business Research Projects*, 2nd edn. London: Chapman and Hall.

JANKOWICZ, A. D. (2000) *Business Research Projects*, 3rd edn. London: Chapman and Hall.

KAHN, R. and CANNELL, C. (1957) *The Dynamics of Interviewing*. Chichester: Wiley.

KANE, E. (1985) *Doing Your Own Research: Basic descriptive research in the social sciences and humanities.* London: Marion Boyars.

SAUNDERS, M., LEWIS, P. and THORNHILL, A. (2003) *Research Methods for Business Students*. Harlow: Pearson Education.

VOGT, W. P. (1993) *Dictionary of Statistics and Methodology*. Newbury Park: Sage.

Dissertations and management reports

CHAPTER OBJECTIVES

After studying this chapter you should be able to:

■ understand the nature of dissertations and major projects

■ understand the role of your dissertation or project tutor

■ choose a topic for your dissertation or report

■ draft a proposal for a dissertation or management report

■ structure your dissertation or report in a logical sequence

■ structure separate management reports for (i) assessment and (ii) the organisation

INTRODUCTION

The discussions in this chapter will be useful to students in their final year of a degree or professional course, and those who are contemplating or actually working on a higher degree, such as an MBA. The prospect of having to produce an extended piece of work is sometimes daunting, not only to undergraduates but to those on higher degrees; and, indeed, to the academics too! Most of the anxieties are related to the required approximate word count, the sufficiency and relevance of the data they have collected and the time factor. There are a variety of factors that can interfere with your progress and the only way to clear your mind is to attend to them.

THE NATURE OF DISSERTATIONS AND MANAGEMENT REPORTS

There is a pretty even balance of similarities and differences between dissertations and management reports. Dissertations tend to be more academic in that they are traditionally associated with the work of undergraduates in their final year and those on taught master's degrees. A management report, on the other hand, is a document in which students on professional courses who have carried out a work-related major project report on what they did, how they did it and the outcome. It is also true, however, that dissertations are often problem-driven, and students undertaking business and HR degrees are expected to demonstrate the application of theoretical perspectives to practical business issues. This, in a sense, draws the nature of the dissertation a little closer to that of the management report. Where it is appropriate we will separate the aspects of our discussions that relate exclusively to one or the other type of work.

THE ROLE OF YOUR TUTOR

In formal terms, the tutor is assigned to supervise your work and to offer guidance and advice whenever it is appropriate. It is important for you to establish a friendly but businesslike relationship with your tutor. He or she can be of enormous help to you, but you have to bear in mind that it is *your* work that ultimately will be assessed, and not that of the tutor.

Your tutor will be someone who is well versed in the subject you have chosen. This means that you have to choose your topic *before* a tutor can be assigned to you. In some universities, you are not assigned a tutor until after you have submitted your proposal (see later). Under this system, your chosen topic is noted and an appropriate tutor is then assigned to you; your proposal becomes the discussion document for your first meeting.

Once you have been given the name and contact details of your tutor, the onus is upon you to seek his or her help and advice as and when it is required. In the first instance, it is normal to meet and chat about your topic and how it might be approached. After that you should try to keep in regular contact. E-mailing between you and your tutor is sometimes a feasible alternative to face-to-face meetings and will also produce evidence that the contact has actually occurred. Normally, you will find that contact will be at its most frequent in the final stages.

Your tutor can help you from the beginning. Since s/he will be well versed in your subject, s/he can guide you with your choice of topic and how it might be approached; an objective eye can provide valuable insights into the *feasibility* of what you are proposing and the *potential problems* you may encounter in its implementation. Also, s/he will be able to advise you on your preliminary literature search and other research aspects of your proposed methodology.

RAISING YOUR GAME

Dissertations and management reports are, of course, more substantial in size than essays and assignments, and this is a reflection of the breadth and depth of the study you are about to undertake. Depending on the type of course you are on you may be asked to produce a document of between 8000 and 20,000 words. Table 11 shows the typical length of dissertations and reports.

If you are in your final year of a degree or professional course, you will see from what is said above and from the table that what you are about to embark upon is probably the most complex and important piece of academic work you have ever carried out.

The experience you gained in your previous academic years will stand to your credit in this task. In that context, your tutor is entitled to assume that, at this level, you have developed and internalised a good understanding of, and the ability to apply, the study skills required to do a good job (see 'activity' below). Now is the time to show the tutor and – where relevant – your employer just how good you are! You have to raise the level of your performance to a new standard. In this chapter I hope the guidance offered will help you to do that. Choosing the right topic is the key. Ideally, it will be something that greatly attracts your interest; something you will enjoy researching and something that invokes excitement within you.

Table 11   *Typical length of dissertations and management reports*

Types of study	Typical lengths
Undergraduate dissertation	10,000–20,000 words
Management report	5000–10,000 words
Taught master's dissertation	Approximately 20,000 words

ACTIVITY 10

Carry out a review of the study skills you have developed and used in the earlier parts of your course. Are there any further skills you need to develop for the greater breadth and depth of study that you need to achieve?

CHOOSING A TOPIC

This is your first and most important step. Everything you do, from deciding on your approach to the type of data you collect, is determined by the nature of the topic you choose. You will have known long in advance that this major task was coming, and ideas may have occurred to you. If you already have an idea, you might like to test it against the criteria given in Table 12.

APPROACHES TO MAKING THE TOPIC DECISION

For some students, trying to identify something that is relevant, feasible, interesting, exciting, researchable and likely to enable them to meet the required standards can be difficult. There are, however, several ways of approaching this important task.

Rational approach

1   With the contents of Table 12 in mind, go through your lecture and seminar notes looking in particular for things that you found interesting, but try to avoid the danger of selecting something that amounts to nothing more than an extension of something you have already done. When you have found something you think is worth looking at, ask yourself about the 'range of the topic' (see Chapter 4). Consider the breadth and depth of the research you need to carry out. Has your initial research shown that there is enough in the topic to justify its selection? How does it match up to the above criteria?

ACTIVITY 11

Do an initial trawl of the literature to check firstly, that the topic is researchable and secondly, to check that there is enough substance in the topic to justify its selection.

2   *Talk it over with your colleagues.* Students are usually interested in what others are doing for their final piece of work anyway. Perhaps you could organise a small-group session with them to discuss ideas. Do not forget to write down the ideas as they emerge.

3   *Examine past dissertations and projects.* Have a look at the dissertations and projects that students have completed in the recent past. For your purposes, the best idea is to peruse the list of titles because what you are principally looking for are ideas. Always check that the subject that you are examining is still current. If it is and you think that the idea might be a good one, remember that it is what *you* wish to do with it that counts. You may access past dissertations and projects through the library.

Creative approach

1   *Keep a notebook* of all of the ideas you get. Like most writers, I keep a pen and pad on my bedside table, just in case I wake up with an idea!

2   *Use relevance trees.* Relevance trees have several uses. For example, they can be used for developing

Table 12 *Criteria for choosing a topic*

1 *Relevance.* Is the subject relevant to a discipline that is within the main syllabus of your course? In any case, it makes sense to choose from a subject that you have been studying for the past three years.

2 *Interest.* Did you choose to undertake the course you are on because you were drawn to its main interest, such as marketing, HR or general business studies? In the same vein, if you have chosen to undertake a particular type of taught master's degree, then you will have done so because of the interest and enjoyment you experience in that subject and its sub-disciplines.

3 *Familiarity.* Did you choose a topic with which you are already familiar? This is fine as long you have not made the choice because you think it will give you an easy ride. There are advantages to already having a fair understanding of the subject; at least you will be aware of the basic elements, especially if you handled the subject earlier in your course, but you still have to achieve the breadth and depth of analysis required at this level. To develop knowledge and skills that are really valuable you may have to assess, in advance of finalising your choice, that there is a wide enough gap between what you know now and what you will know when you finally emerge from the experience. In terms of learning, the gap needs to be wide enough to justify the choice of topic.

4 *Researchable.* Before you make your final decision, do a trawl of the literature and look on the Internet to identify the breadth and depth of the available relevant reading. The amount and type of available data is critically important for your research. If you intend to carry out primary and secondary research, ensure that you will be able to gain access to the sources, especially if the sources are within organisations. Even if your proposed sources are not organisational – it may be, for example, that you intend to carry out a structured street survey – you would be wise to check with the relevant local authorities that you will be allowed to do it.

5 *Standards.* When you are wrestling with the problem of deciding on a topic, bear in mind that you have to meet or exceed the required standards. Most students become so preoccupied with the problem of deciding on a topic that they forget about standards. 'It's my suspicion that weak projects are often unsuccessful because the issue of standards was scarcely considered …' (Jankowicz 1995). Three of the factors that will determine the degree to which you may meet the standards are:

   i   The level of study skills you have developed
   ii   The degree to which you are motivated to do well; this will be reflected in the amount of effort you are prepared to put in
   iii The topic itself, which, by its nature, may not lend itself to high achievement.

6 *Capability.* First and foremost, consider if you think you have the necessary study skills to see it through. Is it likely that you will need to enhance the skills that you have used so far in order to achieve the required breadth and depth of research? If there is a particular skill requirement that you feel is beyond your reach in the time available, then you might decide to modify your intentions.

7 *Feasibility.* Is it actually *possible* for your research plan to be implemented? 'However coherent your ideas and exciting your research plan, it counts for little if what you are planning to do is simply not possible' (Saunders *et al* 2003). This brings us back to the value, indeed the *necessity*, of talking it over with your tutor in advance. If you are investigating an organisational problem with a view to making recommendations for a solution, then it will also be advisable to talk it over with the employer. Things that are *possible* are not always *feasible*; costs, for example, may outweigh the benefits.

key words when searching literature (see Chapter 4), but they can also be used to generate ideas for a research topic.

3 *Brainstorming.* Back to your group of colleagues again. You could try this alone, but experience shows that the best ideas are generated by groups.

Refining your research idea

When you finally do come up with an idea, it may need to be refined. You can get pretty excited when you first think that you have 'cracked it'! When you look at it the next day, however, you begin to have doubts about it in its present form, and your objectivity fails you because you have been immured in its creation for too long. You decide to send for the cavalry again in the form of your student colleagues.

GROUP TECHNIQUES

Hopefully, your colleagues are a group of good friends who all enjoy helping each other, especially when it is fun to do so and there is a useful outcome at the end.

The Delphi technique

This time you are going to ask them, as a group, to help you to develop your idea further; you want it to be clearer and more specific (Robson 2002). The *Delphi technique* is one that has been used for many years in industry to tackle problems and to generate and refine business ideas.

POINT OF INTEREST?

Delphi, an ancient Greek city on the southern slopes of Mount Parnassus, was the site of the most famous oracle of Apollo, which often gave out obscure and enigmatic prophecies. It is thought that the technique we are discussing was named after this.

The Delphi technique is one of a trio of types of *problem-tackling* groups. These include the *interactive group* and the *nominal group.* A particular advantage of nominal groups is that independent thinking in a group situation is cultivated, unlike the circumstances in an interactive group (McKenna 1994: 325). The original Delphi groups never met face to face. Instead, the group members were advised of the problem and asked to provide a solution. This was done through the use of a structured questionnaire, which was completed independently by each member and returned anonymously. The members then received back a tabulation of all of the results, in the light of which they were asked to provide a second solution to the original problem. This process was repeated until a consensus was reached.

Today, Delphi groups are more akin to interactive groups in that the members are often together as a group and they do interact, although some independent thinking is normally encouraged.

Creative problem-solving groups

These can be used effectively if we treat the need to develop and refine an idea for a topic as a problem. One criticism of this type of group is the amount of time it takes. You will see why in the procedure given in Table 13.

The explanation of this concept may seem complex, but it is fairly easy to operate, especially after a dry run. The advantage is that the problem (refining your topic) has been studied by several people who were thinking independently and modifying each other's ideas.

I first saw this kind of cooperation between students on part-time professional courses, when they invited me to attend one of their meetings as an observer and adviser. They had been meeting in the evenings

Table 13   *Using a creative problem-solving group to refine a research idea*

1   The group, usually not more than six people, are seated around a table in the style of having a meeting. They are asked *not to communicate* with each other.

2   Each member is given an A4 pad, with the problem outlined at the top of the first page and a set of instructions.

3   Individuals in the group are given time to study and write down their solutions to the problem. The time allocated depends on the complexity of the problem.

4   The members are then asked to pass their written solutions to the right.

5   Each reads the solution, tries to improve it and then passes it to the right. It is important to note that the task is to study the given solution and try to improve that solution; it is not to impose one's own answer.

6   The process (at 4 and 5) is repeated until all of the original and subsequent solutions have been read and have received improvement. At this point everyone will have had his or her original solution returned with the improvements attached.

7   Interaction is necessary at this stage. All of the final solutions are collated and a consensus is reached in open discussion.

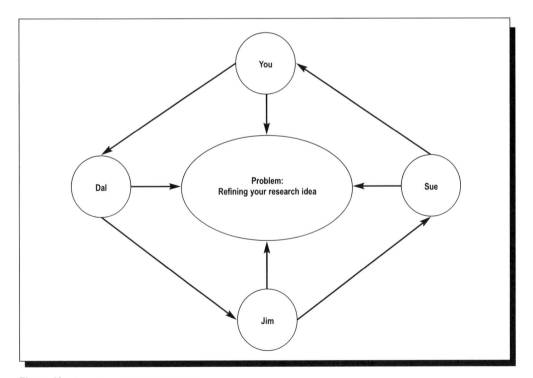

Figure 16   *A creative problem-solving group*

in each other's houses, but for this particular session I found an empty interview room. They told me that they had felt a little hesitant about asking for a room since they had heard that accommodation was hard to get. Teaching accommodation is carefully planned and full-time students, who are usually in the majority, occupy the classroom during the day, which eases such problems for the evenings.

Whichever method you use to refine your research idea, your next step is to discuss it with your tutor. He or she may suggest that you modify it even a little further; perhaps it is thought that you are being a little too ambitious or that the research possibilities that you had envisaged are not what you thought they were. Having reached an agreement with your tutor, you now have to submit a formal proposal, or resubmit a modified version of the one you submitted in the first place, depending on the system used by your university.

EXAMPLE 9: TREATING THE IDEA AS A PROBLEM

Oliver and his colleagues made a group of five. The problem he had written down was that he wanted to research the reason for the increasing size of the gap between the earnings of senior executives and those of ordinary workers. They worked as a creative problem-solving group (CPSG).

On completion of the cycle, it was obvious that all members of the group thought that the idea was too ambitious. The following, more specific ideas emerged:

- The effects of the pay gap on the culture of the organisations concerned
- A comparative study on the pay gap in the UK and other countries
- The roles of the trade unions and shareholders in controlling the pay gap
- The criteria against which the value of industrial high performers is assessed.

The group then discussed all of these ideas, after which Oliver carried out a preliminary trawl of the literature. With the agreement and help of his colleagues at a second meeting, he decided to research into:

- The effectiveness of trade unions compared to that of shareholders in controlling the pay gap.

ORGANISATIONAL PROBLEMS AS TOPICS

If you are a doing a part-time master's degree, or are in the final year of a part-time professional course, it is likely that your own sponsoring organisation will be the base for your research. This should ease the task of finding a topic because your familiarity with the organisation's strategy, systems, policies and procedures will enable you to identify problems and issues that need to be resolved.

As an employee, you are more likely to be given access to the people and places that hold the information you will need in your research. This is quite a significant bonus, although you should always check this with your employer as soon as you get the idea, and certainly before you approach your tutor with it. A further bonus is the value of your own work experience and what you have learned from it.

Starting off with a good knowledge of the topic, however, is not always an advantage; over-familiarity with the topic can close your mind to the ideas of others. Also, you should take advantage of the work as a learning opportunity. Choosing a topic which is made up of something you do every day or every week implies that you already possess the required knowledge and skills, which means that you will finish up learning nothing, or least very little. (Whenever possible, a good manager will delegate projects to people who will learn from them.)

IN-COMPANY DELEGATION AS A TOPIC

The idea of your employer providing you with a problem for research and resolution could in itself produce a problem for you. Firstly, you may already have what you regard as a good idea for your project and do not want to be burdened with a chore. Secondly, it may be something in which you are not avidly interested, and if your motivation to work on it is not all that it should be, then the likelihood that you will do a good job is reduced. You should, however, study the project you have been offered. It may be possible to improve and refine the idea and make it more interesting in the process.

Alternatively, it may be possible to abstract and refine a part of it to use as your project. If you did this you would have to plan your time very carefully, because you would have to carry out the whole project for your employer and then write a separate report on the abstracted section to hand in at the university. Even if you had accepted the whole of your employer's project in the first place, you would still have had to write two reports, because the kind of report required by your employer would be different from that required by your university.

PREPARING YOUR PROPOSAL

While the dissertation or major project proposal usually represents 10–15 per cent of the marks available for the work, you should really think of it as a planning exercise, rather than just a piece of work to submit. Your proposal, which is really a framework for the main work, tells your tutor what you wish to do and how you intend to do it.

This is a crucial stage in your dissertation or major project. In alluding to the proposal earlier, I said that it may serve as a discussion document for the first meeting with your tutor. You should come away from that meeting aware of any changes that are necessary to turn it into a feasible prospect, feeling that you have a clearer perception of what you are about to do and that this has given you a clear sense of direction.

Structure of the proposal. The proposal should have a logical structure and be brief and to the point, so that you can explain what you are proposing in about 1500–2000 words. For a taught master's degree it may be slightly longer. Table 14 overleaf suggests a structure.

It is important to note that the structure given below applies only to the *proposal*. The structures for the main dissertation or project report are discussed later in this chapter.

Table 14 *Suggested structure for a dissertation/major project proposal*

Section	Suggested contents
Summary or abstract	A summary of the contents of the *proposal document.* This includes the topic, your approach to it, a brief outline of your proposed methodology, the context in which the study is set and the research questions that need to be answered. It is best to write this up after you have completed the rest of the document.
Introduction	Identification of the topic or organisational problem and a brief overview of the context in which it is set. Provides enough background for the reader to understand why the topic was chosen and the context in which it is set. Concludes with the aims and objectives of the study.
Literature review	A brief outline of the relevant literature including quotations and citations. Includes a *mini-critical review* of the main relevant work. Gives an idea of your approach to the literature.
Methodology	This is a brief and simple statement of the research methods you are planning to use; it is your explanation of *how* you will tackle the study. It also provides a rationale justifying the use of the particular methods you have chosen in relation to the *purpose* of the study. It is the means through which you intend to achieve your objectives.
Potential conclusions	These should follow naturally. Also, the evidence you have provided in the foregoing sections provides some justification for predicting the conclusions you are likely to draw.
Time and resources	If the research is based in your sponsoring organisation, you will need to provide an indication of the likely cost of what you propose to do and how long it is likely to take. This should include the resources (human, financial and material) that will be needed and, where possible, an indication of the cost of your time and that of others when you carry out the research. At this stage it would be impracticable to indicate the cost of implementing the recommendations.
References and bibliography	A list of the full bibliographical details of the sources you have cited in the document.
Appendices	Material that, because of its length (full explanations, etc) or design (graphics) would clutter the body of the text or would otherwise be inappropriate.

PUTTING IT ALL TOGETHER

This is where the perennial problem of *getting started* rears its head again. Your target is to finish up with a logically sequenced proposal document that carries a full account of what you wish to do.

TRY THIS!

Put about 10 sheets of paper between two pieces of A4 card, puncture them and put them into a plastic file. In the same order as that given in Table 14, label the top of each page with the section headings. Under the section headings, start to fill in sub-headings and notes that are appropriate to each particular section. In this way, your proposal becomes a tangible document that you can carry about with you. Eventually, of course, you will turn the whole thing into a file on your computer. When you do, you will be able to drop in any tables or diagrams as you think necessary.

The more you think about the nature of what you are doing, the more ideas you will get; jot them down on the appropriate pages. As you continue to work on the proposal, you will import more data, and your thoughts about it will clarify further (the magic of writing!). You almost certainly will need to amend some of the headings and the text that you have placed under them.

Synthesis
The next step is to synthesise everything you have got so far. You do this by:

- checking that the material you have gathered is on its right page
- collating it
- writing it up in narrative form
- amending your earlier notes where necessary.

In this way you are demonstrating how the elements of your proposal fit together harmoniously. You will see that what you have written has started to make sense and your proposal has begun to take a logical shape.

Looking at Table 14, you may have noticed that I have used the future tense and you may decide to write up your proposal in the same way. While there are no set rules about this, it makes sense because you are saying something you *propose* to do. Likewise, when you write up the main dissertation or project report, it makes sense to use the past tense throughout, since then you are writing about something you have done. This may seem obvious, but a surprising number of students continue with the future tense in their main work, probably because they have a copy of their approved proposal handy while they are working on it.

EXAMPLE 10: A PROJECT PROPOSAL

Sarah works as an HR planner in a pharmaceutical company and is in the final year of the CIPD professional course. Her proposed project concerns the link between employee commitment and individual and team performance.

Her company believes there is a lack of employee commitment, evidenced by rising absenteeism and disappointing results in performance assessment.

Title: The influence of managerial style on employee commitment.

INTRODUCTION

Encouraging employees to show commitment to the aims and objectives of the organisation has become widespread in Europe in recent years. The advent of human resource management (HRM) popularised this in the belief that it enhances performance, although from the data collected so far, this seems to be based more on assumption rather than evidence. Nevertheless it has attracted considerable attention in UK companies.

It is important to note that there are also strong implications here for the `management of change' (from control/compliance to the commitment model) but a project such as this does not allow the time or space to discuss this issue.

Commitment in this context means commitment to the organisation, its aims, values and objectives. First, however, the employee has to be able to understand the aims and objectives, which assumes a level of knowledge of company affairs that some employees may not possess. Communication, therefore, has a significant role, especially in the style and content of communication between managers and their staff. Managers have to learn to portray the spirit of the 'commitment model' and adopt a style of communication that elicits commitment and motivates their staff to learn the aims and objectives.

I intend to demonstrate in this project report that lack of commitment adversely affects attendance and performance and that if steps are taken to elicit commitment, the attendance and performance problems in the company will be moderated and performance will be enhanced.

LITERATURE

The literature on this topic began with Walton's (1991) article in the *Harvard Business Review* in which he asserted that, 'At the centre of this philosophy is a belief that eliciting employee will lead to enhanced performance. This belief is well founded.' For Walton, 'commitment' represents the latest stage in the evolution of managerial practice (Goss, 1995). Goss goes on to describe the change from the control/compliance model of managerial practice to models of commitment and involvement. Clearly, action in this respect would have to include a culture change and this will involve studying such authors as Oliver and Low (1991), Deal and Kennedy (1988), Armstrong (2000) and Maund (2001). Walton, R. (1991) 'From control to commitment in the workplace', in Steers and Porter (eds) (1991) *Motivation and Work Behavior,* New York: McGraw-Hill.

METHODOLOGY

To study the assumption that commitment enhances performance and search for data that indicates supporting evidence.

To carry out a review of the literature on human resource management, employee commitment, involvement and the shift from control/compliance to the 'commitment model'.

To review the literature on attendance management and absence control to identify the most frequent reasons given for absenteeism.

To collect from within the company, (i) primary data to identify the reasons for poor attendance and (ii) secondary data to gain an understanding of company policy on attendance and to examine the procedure for controlling absence and to collect data on the attendance records to establish actual attendance.

This will help me to further develop my hypothesis that a lack of commitment and poor attendance adversely affects performance.

POTENTIAL CONCLUSIONS

It is anticipated that the data will lead to the conclusion that if employee commitment is elicited, the absenteeism will reduce and performance will be enhanced.

TIMESCALE – 2005–2006

November:	review the literature
January:	develop, pilot and modify questionnaire for internal survey
February:	distribute questionnaire and draft literature review
March:	Draft interview questions and agree access to managers for interviews. Interview managers and collect questionnaires
April:	Analyse primary and secondary research results and write them up
May:	Draft report

RESOURCES

I have to take up executive time for the interviews. I will need access to company resources such as archives for research, and the use of company hardware and software. All of this has been agreed by my employer.

This example of a proposal is given mostly for the content. In terms of the format and layout of a proposal, universities vary in their styles and you may have been given an advisory handbook on what is required of you in terms of your dissertation or management report.

We said earlier that the proposal may account for 10 to 15 per cent of your total marks for the work. Normally, you will submit your proposal to your tutor who will assess it and then discuss it with you, explaining any modifications he or she thinks you need to make. If you have left yourself a margin of time before the hand-in date and wish to show someone what you have done to ask them what they think, you may decide instead to get on to an *expert system* such as Peer Review Emulator. This software is available either on its own or as part of the Methodologist's Toolchest suite of programs. It asks you a series of questions about your proposed research. The programme then critiques these answers to ensure that common research standards are achieved (Scholari Sage, 2002).

ACTIVITY 12

Draw up the main elements of a structure for your dissertation or project proposal using Table 14 as a framework.

STRUCTURING DISSERTATIONS AND PROJECT REPORTS

Now that you have completed your proposal and your plans have been approved, you can start on your main work. At this stage, having had several discussions with your tutor, you will have embarked on the work anyway. We discuss writing it all up in Chapter 10; here we are principally concerned with structures; although at this stage you should have drafted your literature review and research findings. Dissertations and management reports differ in their structure; for example, dissertations are not always problem driven and, therefore, it may not be necessary to include a chapter entitled 'recommendations'. On the other hand, management reports are always problem driven and drawing up a set of recommendations designed to resolve the problem are not only expected by the tutor, they should also attract the interest of your employer for very practical reasons. As Anderson (2004) points out: your study centre may have particular requirements for the structure of the report, although most allow for some variation where it is appropriate to the nature of the topic and the research approach that has been utilised. Here, Anderson was writing about projects reports, but the principles she outlines are the same for dissertations.

When I refer to 'structure' in this respect, I mean the sequence in which the sections or chapters appear and the logic that underlies that sequence. What follows includes the total sequence of sections and provides brief descriptions of their content. It also makes allowances for the differences between dissertations and project reports, including those for taught master's degrees.

ORGANISING YOURSELF FOR ACTION

Before you start, work out a plan of action. If you do this you will save yourself a considerable amount of revision work afterwards. Clearly, you can only work on one section at a time and when you do this, there is a tendency to isolate it in your mind from the rest of the report, whereas you should be thinking holistically. This means that when you are working on a section, you are writing it within the context of the total study. You can achieve this by studying the structure described above. Note that it breaks the whole study down into its sections and since they are comparatively small, they are easy to manage. You can arrange these into a framework as shown in Figure 17.

The figure below is a small outline of the idea. If you use a sheet of A4, you will have space to write into each pod the main themes of the sections/chapters. Having a framework such as this at your elbow while you are working on a section will help you to think holistically (see Chapter 10 for more detailed guidance on writing it all up).

Table 15 *Structure and content of a major study*

Front cover often referred to as the *title page,* includes the title of the report, your name and, where required, your student number, the course title and submission date.

Contents page. Ideally, this will list the section titles down the left side of the page, with the appropriate page numbers listed opposite on the right side of the page. The important sub-headings in the sections may also be included by indenting them under each section title.

Summary. A brief overview of the whole dissertation. Its purpose is to inform the reader of the issue or problem that has been investigated, the context in which it is set and the approach that was taken. It finishes with a précis of the main findings, conclusions and, where appropriate recommendations. It is unlikely to occupy more than a single side of A4.

Introduction. This sets the scene for readers and should be designed to draw them further into the document. It provides an introduction to the topic or issue and should provide enough background information for the reader to understand the context of the study. It should explain the aims and the research objectives, the terms of reference or the hypothesis to be examined.

Literature review. This is where your study is placed within the context of the main body of knowledge about the topic or issue and indicates how your study builds upon what is already known. You have to make it clear that the literature you have critically reviewed in this section is (i) relevant to your topic, (ii) has helped you to answer your research questions, (iii) has helped you to decide on the approach you adopted and (iv) has built considerably on your knowledge of the topic. In *critically* reviewing the literature you point out the strengths and weaknesses of the arguments you found, including those of your own argument (see Chapter 7 for more about what you have to include here).

Methodology. This is where you state the methods you used to carry out the research, including the literature you selected and reviewed. You also analyse and provide a rationale for the approach you adopted and the direction of your argument. You also *describe* the methods and techniques you used in order to collect and analyse the data, such as interviews and surveys and their pilot studies, the observational techniques you employed and whether or not you triangulated your methods in order to achieve the greatest possible reliability and validity of the data.

Findings and analysis. For some research projects you may decide to divide this into two sections. If this is the case for you, then you simply present the data you collected in an attractive and easy to understand form and save your analysis and interpretation of the data for the 'analysis' section. Basically, it is a presentation of the data you collected. There cannot be a specific format for this because how you interpret and present the data will be determined by the approach you adopted and the nature of the data you collected.

Conclusions. Conclusions are drawn on the basis of the evidence you set out in your earlier section/s. Neither the introduction of new evidence nor your opinions have a place in this section. It is a summary of the main features of the analysis and the implications of it for both theory and practice (Anderson, 2004). For a major project, you will have written a management report and it is usual to include here conclusions about the resolution of a problem. The implication here is that you have identified several possible alternative solutions to the problem or issue, but you save the one you are recommending for the next section.

Table 15 *continued*

Recommendations. For dissertations, it is not always appropriate to make recommendations. This is where you outline your recommendations for action designed to resolve the problem or issue that you investigated and it is, therefore, where you present the solution selected from the alternatives that you presented in the previous section. You have to include a rationale to justify your selection of this alternative and demonstrate why, above the other alternatives, this would be the best way forward. You should indicate the timescale within which implementation may be completed, along with an estimate of the costs involved, the resources required (including the human resource) and the involvement of any external assistance.

References. This is a list of the full bibliographical details of the sources you have cited in the body of the report. You may also include a 'bibliography' which is a list of sources that you have consulted but not necessarily cited in your text. Beware of trying to impress with a separate bibliography. The examiners are well acquainted with the literature and will look for evidence that implies the use of these sources (see Appendix 1 for further guidance on references and bibliography).

Appendices. If, in your main sections, you need to include an explanatory item that would clutter the text and interrupt the reader's flow, put it in as an appendix. This applies particularly to the 'findings and analysis' section in which you present the data. The idea is to allow the reader to go through the document smoothly without being bored or tired. You could lose brownie points by trying to use appendices as a means of meeting the word count.

Annexes. Sometimes it is necessary to include a company document such as a written policy or part of a report. In order be clear about whose wrote what, I ask my students to treat appendices as described above, as long as it is their *own work* and to include any company documents, etc, as annexes. This separates the student's work from that of others.

Section 1
Introduction

Front cover
List of Contents
Summary

Section 2
Literature Review

Section 3
Methodology

Section 4
Findings and analysis

Section 5
Conclusions

Section 6
Recommendation

Figure 17 *Outline framework of a dissertation/management report*

CHECK YOUR UNDERSTANDING
Questions

1 Can you think of four ways in which your tutor can help you?

2 Describe four of the criteria that your chosen topic should meet?

3 What would you do if your manager gave you a company topic?

4 Explain the differences between three types of problem solving group

5 Write down three of main purposes that your project proposal may serve

6 Name three of the factors that will determine the degree to which you will meet the required standards

7 Differentiate between the *rational* and *creative* approaches to generating ideas for your dissertation or project topic

8 What are the advantages and disadvantages of carrying out your project in your own sponsoring organisation?

9 How would you plan the content and sequence of your report?

10 How does a management report differ from an academic project report?

Answers in Appendix 4

FURTHER READING

ANDERSON, V. (2004) *Research Methods in Human Resource Management.* London: Chartered Institute of Personnel and Development.

JANKOWICZ, A. D. (1995) *Business Research Projects.* London: Chapman and Hall., 2nd edn.

MCKENNA, E. F. (1994) *Business Psychology and Organisational Behaviour.* Hove, East Sussex: Lawrence Erlbaum Associates Ltd.

ROBSON, C. (2002) *Real World Research,* 2nd edn, Oxford: Blackwell.

SAUNDERS, M., LEWIS, P. and THORNHILL, A. (2003) *Research Methods for Business Students.* Harlow: Pearson Education.

SCHOLARI SAGE. (2002) Methodologist's Toolchest (online) (cited February 2002). Available from URL:http://www.scholari.co.uk. In Saunders, M. Lewis, P. and Thornhill, A. 2003. *Research Methods for Business Students.* Harlow: Pearson Education.

VAN DE VEN, A. H. and DELBECQ, A. L. (1974) The effectiveness of nominal, Delphi and interacting group decision-making processes. *Academy of Management Review.* December, 606–615.

WALTON, R. (1991) 'From control to commitment in the workplace', in Steers and Porter (eds) (1991) *Motivation and Work Behavior.* New York: McGraw-Hill.

Writing it all up

CHAPTER OBJECTIVES

After studying this chapter you should be able to:

- write in a clear and concise style
- use plain and grammatically correct English
- use politically correct language
- clarify and refine your use of language
- plan your writing
- present your written work in an attractive format and style

INTRODUCTION

This chapter is about academic writing. Its purpose is to help you to write about your project in a clear, concise, correct and objective way. I will use the word 'project' here, but the contents of the chapter apply equally to essays, assignments, dissertations and any other items of academic prose. Where there are differences between these types of work, I will use the appropriate words. In this chapter, we discuss:

- The basic elements of clear and concise English
- Writing in grammatically correct terms
- Writing to meet the requirements of different types of reader, for example, a tutor who is to assess your project report and a manager in the organisation that sponsored your research who would be interested in the implications that the report has for the organisation.
- Political correctness.

THE IMPORTANCE OF GOOD WRITING

You will have noticed that when you are undertaking a degree or aiming for a professional qualification, a considerable amount of your time is spent on writing. Sometimes you are writing to yourself, such as when you are note-taking or drafting the results of research; at other times, you are writing to the tutors who assess your examination answers and project work. Cameron comments on this when she says that 'the credibility of any report you write at work will be reduced by poor expression. Grammatical or spelling mistakes may create doubt as to your competence in other areas. Lack of clarity in the way you write will imply a lack of clarity in the way you think' (Cameron 2001: 248).

Another important factor is that if you are on a business or HR course of any kind and you intend eventually to enter a business profession, those around you in the organisation who receive your e-mails, memos and other written communications will expect you to be literate.

WHAT MAKES GOOD WRITING?

Some say that writing is an art, and I suppose if you are a poet or a novelist it is, but academic writing is a craft that you can learn. You can learn to write well and, with experience, you can improve on what you have learned. Academic writing has to be *clear, concise, grammatically correct* and *objective.* These qualities are not in reference to the *nature* of the content, rather they concern how you use the language to articulate your arguments, express your findings and conclusions and the persuasiveness with which you 'sell' your recommendations to the reader. The ability to write well, therefore, is a very important skill to develop.

There are students who experience difficulty with expressing themselves in English. For some, English is their second language and while they may find it easier to express themselves when speaking, they may not be very fluent when writing. If this is you, then you should seriously consider taking a language course that you can start as soon as possible; it will pay enormous dividends. On the other hand, I have had native speaker students whose command of their own language is far from all that it should be; the advice to them is the same as the advice given to overseas students: take a course in English.

If you regard your command of English as reasonably good, you still might benefit from reading through the next section.

Loss of integrity

Some people have a particular difficulty when it comes to expressing themselves in writing. They find that when they are trying to transfer something, such as an idea or an explanation of a concept, from their head to a sheet of paper, they encounter a communication problem that is familiar to all communicators. The problem is the loss of integrity. For example, when the French sculptor August Rodin appraised a figure that he had just created, he was never completely satisfied with it. This is because when he had the image in his hands, it was not as beautiful as it was when it was in his mind. Every time a communication of any kind is transferred from one place to another, such as trying to turn an idea (which is in your head) into something tangible, it loses some of its integrity. Writing is like that. Writers are never entirely satisfied, but they can come close to it.

WRITING IN CLEAR TERMS

When you read something that has been published, there is a very strong possibility that it has been written at least twice and probably more times than that. Writers are continually asking themselves, 'what is the best way to say this?' They write something, they study what they have written and then they redraft it; and they keep on redrafting it until they get it 'right'. I do it all the time. One approach to achieving clarity is to read what you have written critically and objectively. If, for example, you have phrased something in a way that you think may not be clear and wish to improve it, put it aside for a while and go back to it later.

Syndicate journalists, who write well in advance of their deadlines, do that. I knew one who would put a piece of work aside for a few days, a week or sometimes even a month; when he went back to it, he could study it critically and objectively, treating it as if someone else had written it. If you decide to try this, the two main questions you would ask yourself while you are rereading and refining it are (i) to what extent is the reader likely to grasp the point I am trying to make and (ii) to what extent does it still retain its original meaning?

TRY THIS!

Read the following paragraph and keep reading it until you think you know what the writer is trying to say:

Less than 10% of manufacturing workers were employed in establishments with less productivity than the labour cost would allow. On the other hand, the most productive establishments had a productivity advantage five times greater, which demonstrates that manufacturing establishments with widely differing efficiencies co-exist in the market.

Now try to clarify the meaning of the paragraph by redrafting it.

You will find an answer (not *the* answer) at the end of the chapter.

I took the 'gobbledegook' paragraph in the example above from a real dissertation by a business student. It is possible to clarify and reduce it by 10 words!

Writing is a great leveller. This book contains some material of interest to foundation students and other material that would interest MBA students, but regardless of the level at which you are studying your writing standard has to be clear and concise. A quick and simple way to test your 'gobbledegook factor' is to read aloud to yourself what you have written – it really is surprising how quickly this method brings your 'fog factor' to the surface. Furthermore, if you record yourself reading it out and then play it back, any errors will leap out at you!

WRITING IN CONCISE TERMS

This means getting as much information as you can in the smallest possible number of words without losing any of the context, integrity or meaning of what you are trying to say. For example, instead of writing the previous sentence, I could have written: 'This is a reference to *word economy*'. The former is a sentence of 32 words; the latter is a sentence of seven words; it is concise and it saves 25 words.

ACTIVITY 13

Apply *word economy* to the following sentence:

The establishment of the organisation is represented by a complement of 42 managers, 280 professional functionaries, 323 administrative support staff, 28 ancillary workers and 14 drivers.

It can be reduced to five words!

Again, this is one that was taken from a student's management report.

You will find an answer on page 136.

As we said in the previous chapter, if the subject you have chosen is one in which you are interested and enjoyed researching, you will avoid some of the problems mentioned above. In your enthusiasm, you may have gathered so much information that you think the required 10,000 words is not nearly enough for you to say what you wish to say. If this happens, then you are in a healthy position, because you will be forced to exercise word economy in order to meet the word count requirement. Writing in concise terms gives a finishing touch to your project report because it:

- Makes what you are saying appeal to the reader's interest
- Is reader-friendly, looks professional and is easy to read
- Enables readers to retain what they have read
- Gives a crisp and precise air to the whole work.

WRITING IN PLAIN ENGLISH

Obviously, we cannot turn this chapter into a definitive work on the English language, but I hope the following guidelines will help you to write in a clear and acceptable style using plain English to draw your readers into your work and hold on to them throughout the whole piece.

- The introduction to the report is very important since this is where you draw your reader in. Always start with a short but meaningful sentence that makes the reader want to continue. For example, the first sentence of this chapter has only six words, but if you can keep it to less than 15 words, you should retain your reader's interest.
- To continue to retain the interest of your reader, avoid using long words; there are almost always shorter alternatives.
- Avoid long, convoluted sentences; they may confuse the reader and may even confuse you when you are writing them! If you use short sentences, the meaning you wish to convey will be clearer. If you have not done a thorough job on your project and if, as a result, the material for your report is a bit thin, you may be tempted to try to expand on your sentences in order to reach the required word count. This is a risky game to play. Firstly, if your sentences are too long, you risk writing unclearly and lapsing into gobbledegook; secondly, you risk boring your readers who will be wading through your 'fog factor' while waiting for you to get to the point; and thirdly, you risk losing the marks you were hoping to achieve.
- Do not exclude prepositions; these are words such as 'from', 'over', 'to', 'across', etc. At present, there is a fashion to exclude the word 'to', eg 'this will help you learn about writing', instead of '... to learn'. It seems to be acceptable for speech, but of course, speaking and writing are two different media that use the same language; you do not write in the way that you speak.
- Avoid using long paragraphs. It can be daunting (and somewhat boring) for your reader if he or she is continuously confronted with long paragraphs. The purpose of a paragraph is to communicate one particular aspect of your work. If there are subordinate issues involved in what you are saying, you can use sub-paragraphs, which we discuss later in this chapter.

WRITING OBJECTIVELY

Writing objectively means that what you have written is not influenced by your own personal feelings and opinions about what you are saying. Communicating facts without commenting upon them makes for objective writing. Some parts of your report will be totally objective; for example, near to the beginning of an investigative management report, you will give an objective account of the problem. What you think about the way things are is irrelevant at that point in the report. You will have opportunities to stamp your own personality on the report when you get further into it.

WRITING CORRECTLY

This refers to two main areas of concern. Firstly, it refers to legitimacy in terms of copyright and secondly, it refers to academic style, which relates to adopting the conventions of academic writing.

Legitimacy

The law on copyright provides legal protection to the creators of many different types of original work, including written work. Copyright may be infringed in several ways and for a variety of reasons; for example, in Chapter 7 we discussed the main variations on cheating. Probably the most despicable type of cheating occurs when plagiarists knowingly pass off someone else's work as their own. This can also happen accidentally, when, for example, the writer produces work from his or her notes having forgotten to include the source of the information, but this is not a legitimate excuse. The kindest word one can apply to this is carelessness, although the penalties are the same as those for doing it deliberately. Legitimacy also includes correct citing and referencing (see Appendix 1). Chris Hart, after listing the various types of cheating, says that all of these problems can be avoided by paying attention to detail. This means being scrupulous in your record keeping and ensuring all details of works used are fully and correctly cited (Hart 1998).

Academic style

I alluded to this earlier when I said that you would get an opportunity to stamp your personality on your work. In this context, your style is the way in which you express yourself in writing. For example, in your report you might decide to say something like, 'I carried out a survey' or 'in my opinion'. . ., or 'I think that this is owing to . . .' etc. We call this kind of expression your *active voice* because whatever it is that you 'did' or 'think' or have an 'opinion about' is attributed to the researcher who is writing, which of course is you. If, on the other hand, you are the kind of person who, like most academic researchers, does not wish to risk seeming immodest, you might decide to use your *passive voice,* in which case you would say 'a survey was carried out' or 'it may seem as if' . . ., or 'it is thought that'.

The passive voice can be used to good effect when you are constructing your argument. For example, when, in your literature review, you are comparing and contrasting what other writers have said about a particular subject, you might use such phrases as 'while the primary data are inconsistent with the views of Smith (1999), they do support the views of Jones (2000) and Robinson (2001), who maintain that . . .'. (Obviously, the above citations are hypothetical.)

USE OF PERSON AND TENSE

We have just referred to the first person as the active voice because the action of the verb (I carried out a survey) is attributed to the writer. However, you do have to be careful with your use of the first person. It can be annoying if throughout the whole report, you subject your reader to 'I did this' and 'I did that'. It tends to appear mostly in the methodology section of a proposal or report, which seems to be the most difficult section in which to avoid the first person. While the views of universities on this matter vary, it is safe to say that most advise against the use of the first person. I know of one that forbids it in any part of the report on pain of losing marks. They say that it is not in keeping with normal academic convention.

In grammar, there are three classes of personal pronouns and verb forms:

- You use the *first person* when you say *I, we or us*
- You use the *second person* when you say *you*
- You use the third person when you say *he/she, him/her, they* or *them.*

I have used the first and second person in this book in order to establish an element of informality with you. I believe it has the effect of putting people at their ease and that some readers may find the continuous use of the third person a little intimidating.

Tense refers to the *past, present* and *future.* While tense is easy to understand, some students seem to become confused when, for example, they are drafting a dissertation proposal. Most of the proposal should be written in the *future tense* because you are writing about something that you propose to do in the future. I have seen proposals that have been written in the *past tense,* usually because the writers have carried out an initial literature search and included the data they have collected.

This brings us to a further difficulty, which I mentioned earlier. How can *I* write about what *I* propose to do without using the first person? The answer is to use the passive voice, eg 'the aims and objectives of this proposal are to ...', rather than 'my aims and objectives are, etc.' One approach to avoiding these problems is to write up your '*possible (or projected) findings*' section first. Logically, the *future tense* is the only tense you can use when you are drafting what you expect to find. This will help to get you into using the future tense for the rest of the document.

ACTIVITY 14

Convert the following sentences into the third person and future tense:

'My intention with this investigation is to identify the possible advantages that my company might gain from making particular changes; especially in terms of market penetration.'

'In my search of the literature, I discovered case studies; elements of which match my organisation's current situation.'

COMMON ERRORS IN CHOICE OF WORDS

Some words seem to appear in the mind in pairs, such as *advice* and *advise.* Others are simply misunderstood, such as *imply* and *infer.* The term 'misused words' is meant to include (i) words that are used in the wrong context because their meaning is misunderstood by the writer, (ii) words that are commonly misspelled (or misspelt – either is acceptable) and (iii) American spellings, some of which can be used in your reports and others which are not transferable into your writing. There are many words that are commonly misused, some of which are included in the following section. For a list of these errors, see Appendix 2.

GRAMMAR

The very word grammar strikes fear in the heart of many students. It makes your thoughts go back to your schooldays when you had to write *compositions* and other items of prose. When my English teacher had marked and returned my work, I used to think that she must have taken advantage of a special offer on red ink at the local stationery shop! Still, I have since been grateful to her, because she taught me how beautiful and versatile the English language can be.

COMMON GRAMMATICAL ERRORS

Do not worry. In this section, I am not going to have a pernickety 'go' at the shockers I have seen in the work of some students. The idea here is simply to offer a few tips in a discussion about some of the common grammatical errors that people make. The main problem seems to be in sentence construction, which is what grammar really is about. Technically, the word grammar refers to the study of words and the rules that relate to their use and to their relationship to each other in a sentence.

Prose that is written in grammatically correct terms is more likely to convey accurately the meaning of what you are trying to tell your reader. It is a little like driving a car in that if you follow the rules, you are less likely to have an accident, since the other drivers (hopefully) are following the same set of rules. We share a language that has rules and those same rules are observed by those who assess your work. Try not to drive carelessly, because if you do, you risk joining the ranks of those who had the following accidents:

'Bill Gates is one of those who confounded Microsoft'

'Schein (1980) says that this is only true in the wildest sense'

'One such organisation is General Fools'

'As he was talking unclearly (at the interview), I asked him if I could tape it'

'. . . the Sexual Discrimination Act (1975)'!

'Personnel managers overlook recruitment and selection'

'Everyone agreed to the proposal, accept one'

NUMBERS IN YOUR TEXT

If you wish to use single numbers in your text: 1, 2, 3, etc, normal practice is to spell them out instead: one, two three, etc, up to nine. Beyond nine, it is fine to use the figures. However, if you wish to start a sentence with a figure you should always spell it out. If you are working with percentages, the same rules apply.

TRY TO AVOID

- The word 'proven'; 'proven' is correct, but 'proved' is preferred. In any case, applications of the research methods of the social sciences seldom *prove* anything, so you should not use the word very often.
- Using signs such as = instead of 'equal to'. Obviously, signs that are used in mathematics are fine for the analysis and presentation of data, but when they are used in the middle of text, they look and are incongruous. I have even seen 'we had a 1-2-1 interview'; and 'I conducted four interviews & 1 survey'!
- Using text message language, such as 'I'll wait 4U'.
- The word 'cool'. To the average examiner, *cool* is a matter of temperature.
- Jargon, eg, 'I used a D4 to get the message to the Customer Services Manager.' When questioned, the student who wrote this worked for a company in which a D4 is a customer complaints form! How could he think that I would know that? In a similar vein, avoid using phrases that are known only to the employees of your organisation.

WRITING IN POLITICALLY CORRECT TERMS

Political correctness (PC) is concerned with the avoidance of actions and spoken or written expressions that may be considered discriminatory or pejorative. In this context, the term *to discriminate* means to indicate a *favourable or unfavourable* attitude towards one type of person or another; or towards one thing or another. The word *pejorative* means to express disapproval, to write, speak or act against something or someone in a disparaging or derogatory way.

It may also be said that to be *discriminatory* or *pejorative* relates to the way we treat and refer to particular groups, especially minority groups on the grounds of their race, disability or age.[1] In addition,

---

[1] The legislation on age discrimination will not come into force until the year 2006. However, many organisations have been actively preparing themselves for this by drafting interim policies and codes of conduct in order to accustom their employees to what will be accepted practice.

these terms apply to the way we refer to people in terms of their sex, sexual orientation and their marital status. There is legislation that is designed to monitor and enforce these principles, although in terms of promoting general awareness and bringing about change, employing organisations and external pressure groups have had considerably more success than Acts of Parliament.

Here, we are concerned with the terms that you use when delivering an oral presentation or writing up a dissertation or management report. In any circumstances, you should not express yourself in discriminatory or pejorative terms when referring to individuals and groups as mentioned above.

Writing in non-sexist language

Political correctness sprang from the initiative to achieve equal treatment in respect of people regardless of their sex, marital status, sexual orientation, race, colour and ethnic origin. In all democratic, secularly administered nations, this principle applies not only in the workplace, but in all walks of life. The rules apply to all of our behaviour. Here, we are concerned with speaking and writing, which is where a few problems may arise.

In terms of writing, one of the problems is that it is often difficult to draft a sentence that is grammatically correct *and* non-sexist. 'Indeed, one of the arguments against the use of non-sexist language is that it leads to awkward sentence construction. On the other hand, there are many good reasons for avoiding sexist terms and constructions in your writing ... I can only suggest that you take it seriously, and that a clear style is compatible with non-sexist constructions given a little practice and forethought' (Jankowicz 1995).

An argument that has more subtle implications for academic writers is that if PC is allowed to influence the writing style of papers that carry the factual results of rigorous research, it may also influence the integrity of how those results are expressed. This problem is more likely to be encountered by social scientists than any other academic researcher.

Avoiding sexist language

Generally, you should try to avoid incorrect grammar while adhering to PC. This can be achieved in several ways. For example, where it is appropriate, you can construct your sentence using the plural, eg 'middle managers are responsible for allocating work to their staff', instead of 'a middle manager is responsible for allocating work to his or her staff'. The latter type of sentence, if extended, can become quite complicated and difficult to read, eg 'a manager might decide to enter his or her workplace via the shop floor where he or she can greet his or her staff before going into his or her office'. Obviously, that kind of prose is to be avoided at all costs.

On the other hand, I prefer to use 'he or she' because in cases where it would be inappropriate to use the plural, the only other alternative is to use 'their' or 'they', which would make the sentence grammatically incorrect. For example, I often see 'when a manager is delegating a task, *they* should ...' etc. Sadly, this approach, which should be avoided, has been widely adopted. One style that has come into use is 's/he', meaning he or she; and 'his/her', meaning his or hers. For the maintenance of reader-friendliness, it is important that the style you adopt is consistent throughout the document.

As a tutor, I never allowed politically incorrect behaviour in the classroom, and I believe that if this proscription were to be practised widely, the concept of political correctness would be carried through to students' written work. If you can attain the total concept of *equal treatment*, and internalise it to the extent that it influences the way you think, there is a very good chance that political correctness will find its place in your writing style naturally. Most universities and professional institutions have developed their own PC codes of practice, and it would be wise to get hold of a copy. Meanwhile, I thought it might be

Table 16   *Writing style – guide for equality*

Instead of	Try	Instead of	Try
Air stewardess /hostess	Airline staff, flight attendant	Manpower	Workers, employees, staff, human resource
Businessman	Business manager, boss, business/woman/chief	Manning	Staffing, jobs, job levels
Cameraman	Photographer, operator	Man-made	Synthetic, artificial
Newsman	Journalist or reporter	Ford men voted	Ford workers voted
Fireman/men	Firefighter, fire crews	Male nurse	Nurse
Dustman	Refuse collector	Woman doctor	Doctor
Foreman	Supervisor	Housewife	Depends on context. May mean women, shoppers or consumers
Ice cream man	Ice cream seller	Mothers	Often means parents
Policeman/men	Police officer or just police	Girls (if over 18)	Women
Salesman/girl	Assistant, shop staff	Spinster/divorcee	Such words are factual but should not be used in an insulting fashion
Chairman	Chairperson/woman	He/his	Change sentence construction to plural (they or theirs)
Best man for the job	Best person/woman	Mrs/Miss	Some women prefer Ms
Man or mankind	Humanity, human race, humans, people	John Smith and his wife Elsie	Elsie and John Smith
Manhood	Adulthood	Authoress	Author: avoid 'ess' wherever possible
Man-in-the-street	Average citizen/worker	Spokesman	Official, representative

Source: Adapted with the kind permission of the National Union of Journalists

helpful to tabulate a list of commonly used terms and phrases that may help you to avoid making statements that could be construed as 'non-PC'. Clearly, this is not an exhaustive list; the intention is to present the idea of political correctness in writing. The main aim is to avoid using words and phrases that imply gender (see Table 16).

Avoid use of the suffix 'ess': words such as actress, manageress and so forth are now as out of date as sempstress. Do not confuse the title of an official office with the sex of the person. For example, a woman may be a Lord Mayor or a Lord Lieutenant and (one day, who knows?) the Lord Chancellor. These are the titles of the office and are not changed to match the gender of the office-holder.

GETTING DOWN TO IT

The structure and sequence of the sections in a report need to be planned, and we discussed that in Chapter 9. Here, we are more interested in planning the contents of each section. If you followed the guidance given in previous chapters, you will have expanded your notes to give them their full meaning and collated them to match the sections or chapters in your report. In this way, you will have a file of notes labelled *methodology* and another labelled *recommendations* and so forth. That is what some students do. But many students do not plan their approach to this task. You can save yourself a lot of work by planning how you will write your dissertation or management report. If you try to do it randomly, by writing things down as they occur to you, there will be a considerable revision job to do afterwards. On the other hand, if you do it systematically, you will have only minor revisions to do.

Note that the structure that is given in Chapter 9 breaks the job down into sections that are comparatively small and, therefore, easy to manage when tackled one at a time. However, try to avoid treating each section as a discrete entity; you need to keep an holistic eye on the total task, so that while you are drafting any one particular section, you are aware that you are doing so within the context of the whole report.

READER FRIENDLINESS

Each of the sections should be 'bridged' so that as the reader finishes one s/he travels smoothly into the next. In other words, write the closing statements of each section in a way that opens the door to the next. In a management report, for example, the *methodology* section should conclude with an indication of the contents of the *findings and analysis* section.

EXAMPLE 11: BRIDGING YOUR SECTIONS

Methodology finishes with: An analysis of the data that was collected through these methods is presented in the next section/chapter.

Findings and analysis starts with: The purpose of this section is to present an analysis of the information that was collected and to explain the implications of these findings for the organisation.

MOTIVATION TO WRITE

Some of the world's greatest writers find it difficult to get started. Knowing that they have to do it, they still leave it and go for a walk or make themselves a cup of tea – anything rather than sit at the keyboard and start work. As the deadline approaches, fear may set in, yet still they cannot start. A well-known approach to breaking through this barrier is to train your brain to swing into action at particular times of the day or week; individual differences dictate that this does not work for everyone, but it is worth trying.

One world-renowned writer says that she can force her brain to switch itself on. She manages to achieve this by going to the keyboard and typing anything that comes into her head, from her name to Baa Baa Black Sheep and even the alphabet, until eventually her brain gets the message: 'it is time to write and, therefore, it is time to think'; writing and thinking are synonymous. Mind you, she first has to force herself, physically, to go to the keyboard!

She says that she also tries to motivate herself by considering the consequences of not writing. What would motivate you to get started? Your advisers are probably not allowed to use hypnosis or the Colt 45 method; all they can do is to advise you. The advice they offer would probably be similar to that given by Valerie Anderson who includes in her book a table entitled 'Making yourself write' (see Table 17 overleaf).

VISUAL PRESENTATION

While the actual content of your report will be the examiner's main concern, a report that looks attractive claims attention and is more likely to be taken seriously. Conversely, if a report that has a scruffy appearance

Table 17 *Making yourself write*

Planning to write	Divide the word count and set limits for each of the chapters or sections. Set yourself a writing timetable and deadlines. Draft out the structure for the section of the chapter you are about to write. Break down the main parts of the section or chapter into smaller parts – it is much less daunting to produce 200 words than 2000. Use outlines, structures and plans to keep you focused.
When to write	Begin early – the closer you get to the deadline, the more the pressure mounts up. If you write something *now*, there will be time to improve on it. Create time – ('prime time') for writing. – put off other jobs so that you are not exhausted when you begin writing. Write regularly and develop a pattern or rhythm of work on the report. Try never to miss a writing session. If the going gets tough, try writing at a different time of the day of the week. Write up a section as soon as possible.
Develop your own individual writing habits	Engage in your own personal writing rituals that might help you to get going (music in the background, sharpening your pencils, etc). Begin wherever it is easiest – start in the middle, if that's what it takes! Don't expect perfection – you are *drafting* something – you can improve on it later. Reduce interruptions – do what it takes to work for a defined period without distractions. Find a regular place for your writing (particularly if you are using a laptop). Familiarity with the surroundings means they won't distract you. Don't waste time getting everything out and putting it away again if you can avoid it. If you need to, start by speaking your ideas aloud, tape-recording them and then transcribing them. If you get stuck, take a short break and then come back to it after a walk, cup of tea, etc. Don't leave it for too long, however. Try not to stop mid-way if you can. If you can struggle through to the end of the troublesome section, you can revisit it another day, when you are fresh, and you will find that you can improve it then. Where possible, stop writing at a point from which it is easy to resume work again next time.
Monitoring your progress	Set yourself a target for writing a given number of words each week or month. Reward yourself when you achieve significant word count targets. Allow someone else to oversee your writing progress (partner, child, colleague?). Get someone else to read what you have written. This is hard but well worth it because he/she can comment on how understandable your material is and can point out some easy ways of making your work much better. Ask your supervisor/tutor to read your drafts so that you can identify any writing problems early on and deal with them. Plan to finish – look forward to the day when you submit the project report and can then forget about it if you want to.

Sources: Anderson (2004); Blaxter *et al* (2001); Robson (2002); Neuman (2003); Jankowicz (2000).

and looks like as if it has been cobbled together in a last-minute rush, the examiner might conclude that the author does not regard the report as important; and more seriously, may assume that the academic work was put together with a similar attitude.

Front cover

Binding the report in an attractive and robust cover is a good start. It shows that you have taken trouble over it and that you do regard it as important. It should also be borne in mind that by the time the report is returned to you, several people will have handled it and a sturdy cover will protect it. Put the title of the report in the centre of the page and then type under it any other information that your study centre requires. It is best if the title is in a typeface that is bold and slightly larger than you have used inside the report, but do not overdo it. Fourteen point is probably large enough. I have seen sizes in excess of 30 point, which looks not only ugly, but somewhat amateurish.

Internal style and format

For the purposes of uniformity, many organisations have their own distinctive reporting style and format. The advantage of this is that managers, who are normally busy, often need to read only part of a report, and if all company reports are similar in style and format, the manager will know where to find what he or she needs from it.

The most commonly used report format that is generally regarded as acceptable has a flexible and useful format (see Figure 18).

Each section of the report focuses upon just one area of the subject matter, such as the *conclusions* or the *recommendations*. The area concerned is broken down into numbered paragraphs within the section, and each of these relates to just one single aspect of the area dealt with in the section. Then, if there are subordinate issues around that one single aspect, the paragraph is further broken down into sub-paragraphs, which are used to deal with the subordinate issues one by one. This format lends itself easily to the addition of further material without disturbing the numbering sequence of the surrounding paragraphs and sub-paragraphs. All modern computers will follow this format and automatically revise the numbering system as and when necessary.

Finally, here is a list of hints and tips that might help you to produce a report that is attractive and reader-friendly (see Table 18 overleaf).

Section 4: Managerial style, climate and culture

4.1   The purpose of this section is to examine and comment upon:

   (i) those aspects of the internal culture of the company which are influenced by the style with which the managers communicate with the employees and the organisational climate that naturally follows from this

   (ii) the effect that the internal culture of the company has upon the attitudes of the employees towards the company as a whole.

4.2   *Culture* The information shows that the company has grown partly organically but mainly through acquisition, so that as other companies integrated with the organisation, their respective cultures converged.

   4.2.1   In the retail sector, when similar businesses integrate, changes in the social aspects of the culture are usually most evident at and near the top when directors, senior managers and other employees in and around the head office are forming new relationships, etc, etc.

   4.2.2   The information shows that the managerial style in the company is authoritarian, aggressive and critical and that from this, a hostile culture has evolved, etc, etc.

Figure 18   *Example of a page layout of a report*

Table 18 *Hints and tips on presentation*

- Use 12-point typeface and 1.5 line spacing in the text; never type in single space
- Use 14-point bold for the section titles, then reduce to 12 point for sub-headings and text
- Use **bold type** for sub-headings
- Keep your paragraphs short and concise
- Start each section/chapter on a fresh page
- Start your page numbering on the first page of the summary
- Do not interrupt the reader's 'flow' by cluttering the copy with material that should be an appendix
- Collate your appendices in the same order as you refer to them in the text
- Do not cover pages with plastic sleeves
- Write only on one side of the paper.

CHECK YOUR UNDERSTANDING
Questions

1 Explain four factors that make good academic writing

2 How might an idea or concept lose some of its integrity?

3 How would you test your 'fog' or 'gobbledegook' factor?

4 What is meant by writing in concise terms?

5 What should you avoid in order to maintain the interest of your reader?

6 Write down one sentence in the *passive voice* and one in the *active voice.*

7 What is the difference between *management* and *manager?*

8 How might poor grammar affect the assessment of your research?

9 Some researchers worry that political correctness can contaminate their findings. What is their particular concern?

10 What steps would you take to motivate yourself to write?

Answers in Appendix 4

Answer to 'Try this' on page 126

Manufacturers with negative wage-productivity ratios employ less than 10% of workers, while the ratios of the more productive organisations vary by up to a factor of five, demonstrating that organisations with differing efficiencies co-exist in the market.

Answer to Activity 13 (page 126)

The organisation employs 925 people.

FURTHER READING

ANDERSON, V. (2004) *Research Methods in Human Resource Management.* London: Chartered Institute of Personnel and Development.

BLAXTER, L., HUGHES, C. and TIGHT, M. (2001) *How to Research.* Buckingham: Open University Press.

CAMERON, S. (2001) *The MBA Handbook*, 4th edn. Harlow: Pearson Education.

HART, C. (1998) *Doing a Literature Review.* London: Sage Publications.

JANKOWICZ, A. D. (1995) *Business Research Projects*, 2nd edn. London: Chapman and Hall.

JANKOWICZ, A. D. (2000) *Business Research Projects*, 3rd edn. London: Chapman and Hall.

NEUMAN, W. (2003) *Social Research Methods: Qualitative and quantitative methods.* Boston: Wiley.

ROBSON, C. (2002) *Real World Research: A resource for social scientists and practitioner researchers.* Oxford: Blackwell.

Drafting citations and bibliographic details

It is almost impossible to write academic prose, such as an essay or a dissertation, without reference to previously published material. There are several reasons for this:

1   For the work to be worth anything at all in terms of credibility, the writer has to demonstrate scholarship in the ways in which he or she has carried out research in order to support the argument being made. The rigour and thoroughness with which this is done includes making oneself aware of what was previously known about the topic, which means searching and reviewing literature and other data sources.

2   It is vitally important for writers of academic work to draw clear distinctions between their own concepts, thoughts and ideas and those of others.

3   It is a normal courtesy to identify other writers whose work you have used to support or contradict your own thesis.

4   When you cite other writers and provide their bibliographic details, you give your reader/s the opportunity to locate the sources you have used, should they wish to do so.

5   It is essential that all ideas, arguments, evidence and quotations that you take from the work of others be fully acknowledged. By doing this, you will avoid an accusation of plagiarism.

USING THE HARVARD SYSTEM

While there are several referencing systems in common use, the one most favoured for its simplicity is the Harvard System. It is the system that is used in most universities, but it is wise to check with your course tutors if the method is acceptable and if it is appropriate for your subject.

One of the advantages offered by the Harvard System is that it eliminates the need for footnotes (for references) by including the author's name in the body of the text and giving a complete list of references at the end of the text.

For ease of understanding, I will refer to the references you place in the body of your text as *citations*. A *reference list*, which you include after the final main section of the report, is an alphabetical list of the full bibliographic details of all of the sources you have cited in your main text. A *bibliography* is an alphabetical list of all of the relevant sources consulted and used, but not necessarily cited in the text.

CITING YOUR SOURCES

This is about the style you use at the point in your text where you give appropriate credit to others, an example of which is shown in the following short paragraph:

> Smith (1999) maintains that an organisation's technology has the effect of creating different types of work group. On the other hand, Stedman and Clarke (2001) have shown that, (etc).

Where a book has more than two authors, you can cite them as Jones *et al* (2000). The term *et al* comes from Latin and means 'and others'.

If you wish to float a citation in the middle of a paragraph, or maybe you wish to refer to an article or book in the middle of a sentence, you can do it as follows:

> With regard to this particular area of analysis, Jones (1999) makes the point that the difference between British and Japanese methods of production is that ... etc, while Smith (2002) maintains that ... etc.

QUOTATIONS

A complete quotation from a source should appear *after* the quotation itself, eg 'brand names and trade-marks are sometimes chosen to strengthen the desired brand image' (Crawford 1960).

Likewise, if you are merely using the general tenet of the author's argument (loosely paraphrasing), it is sufficient to give just the year of publication. If, however, you are paraphrasing a specific paragraph you should treat this as if it were a direct quotation and include the page number, eg (Wilson 1987, p136); or alternatively (Wilson 1987: 136).

If you want to quote the exact words used by someone, this should be indicated by enclosing them in quotation marks, eg 'Sales along with a sense of fun are key characteristics of this culture' (Capon 2000: 5). If you are only quoting a few words, you can easily include them within your own sentence.

Longer quotations should be included as an appendix or, if only a short paragraph of, say, one or two sentences in length, may be started on a new line and indented. This can be given a suitable lead-in as follows: eg, Hussey, on the other hand is in sympathy with this viewpoint:

> Given the risk involved it was only proper that they should have sought to find an alternative route, even if this meant delaying the experiment further (Hussey 1985: 203).

Different authors – same surname

If you are citing different authors who have the same surname and both have published works in the same year, you should include their initials in the citation, eg Hussey, D. E. (1985); Hussey, R. (1985).

Likewise, if an author has published more than one book in the same year you can identify which it is by placing a suffix letter after the date, eg 'while Jackson (2002a) considered this to be true ...' etc, and '... while Jackson (2002b) seems to refute this suggestion ...' etc.

IMPORTANT!

The style with which you cite references in your main text should be uniform and consistent throughout.

CITING SECONDARY SOURCES

In some cases, you may wish to quote from a work that was cited in an article or a book that was published a long time ago. Depending on the general reliability of the source, you may decide to accept that the author of the secondary work is reliable and accurate in terms of the content of the original work. Wherever possible, however, you should try to locate and read the original work and refer directly to that. When you do this, you can also assess the context in which the original statement was made. Truly, it is not always possible to locate some sources, and if that happens to you, your text must make it clear that that you have not read the original text but are referring to it from a secondary source. You must therefore refer to both sources in your text. The following is an example of this:

Annett (1974) says that there is a basic difference between a theory of learning and a theory of training: 'The aim of the former is to elucidate the processes underlying learning (although this is denied by some) referring to the physiological process of information storage and retrieval in the brain' (Annett 1974: 17, quoted in Kenny and Reid 1986: 116).

CITING SEVERAL SOURCES

You refer to several authors in the same citation when, for example, two or more authors agree about something. Your critical review and discussion sections, for example, are where you build and strengthen your argument. Citing several authors can help you to do this. Inserting such a citation into your text is quite a simple process, but it is important to do it correctly. The authors should be set out chronologically and then alphabetically within each year of publication. Use a semicolon to separate each individual citation, eg

Robinson (1997) remarks that some students become worried and confused when they encounter such words as criticise and argument in relation to the kind of work they have to do. Robinson's work has not gone unchallenged (Brown 2000: 47; Green 2000: 131; Allsop 2002).

REFERENCES AND BIBLIOGRAPHIES

A *reference list* is a list of all of the sources you have cited in the body of your text and in the appendices that are your own work, although where there are citations in an appendix, some tutors like to see a brief reference list attached to the end of the appendix.

A *bibliography* is a list of all of the works and other sources you have consulted in the preparation of your work, whether you have referred to them in your text or not.

Strictly speaking, a reference list is not necessary if you are using the Harvard System since these details are easily determined from your bibliography. However, some tutors prefer a reference list and bibliography while others require only a reference list. The layout of a reference list is the same as that of a bibliography. If you are in doubt about the requirement at your university, ask your tutor. In this respect, most universities have a handbook that contains descriptions of the conventions that should be observed. If they use the Harvard System, the following will apply:

- The bibliography should be arranged in alphabetical order by the surname of the author
- Where a book has more than one author, use the first name in the published sequence to determine its location in your list
- If the author has more than one initial, use all of them; it helps to make identification easier
- Where you refer to more than one book by the same author, list them in the order of the date of publication.

The sequence of each entry should be as follows:

1 The surname of each author of the book, followed by a comma, followed by his or her initial/s with a full stop after each initial, eg Smith, H. and Brown, J. B.
2 The year of publication in brackets, eg (2001)
3 The title of the book in italics, eg *Work and the Nature of Man*
4 The place of publication followed by a colon, eg Oxford:
5 The name of the publisher.

FURTHER ACCEPTED RULES AND CONVENTIONS

- If you refer to two or more works by the same author published during the same year, they should be identified in the text *and* in the references/bibliography as, for example: (2001a), (2001b), etc.

- To distinguish between books articles, conference papers and other works, the accepted rule is that a published volume, which can be a book, journal or report etc, has its title in *italics,* whereas the title of a chapter, an article in a journal or any unpublished work is *not* italicised, but is placed in quotation marks. References to journals and periodicals also require you to give the month or volume number and the relevant pages.

- Note that some books are beginning to appear that include the ISBN of the book in the bibliographic listing. There is no specific requirement to include this, although it does identify the book clearly and simply.

SETTING OUT BIBLIOGRAPHICAL DETAILS

The sequence of the information is the same for reference lists and bibliographies. The following examples illustrate how to set out a broad range of types of publication. This list is by no means exhaustive.

BOOKS, ETC

One author: JANKOWICZ, A. D. (1995) *Business Research Projects*, 2nd edn. London: Chapman and Hall.

Two authors: HUCZYNSKI, A. and BUCHANAN, D. (2001) *Organisational Behaviour – an introductory text*, 4th edn. Harlow: Pearson Education.

Multiple authors: SAUNDERS, M., LEWIS, P. and THORNHILL, A. (2003) *Research Methods for Business Students.* Harlow: Pearson Education.

Institution/association as author: Confederation of British Industry (1989) *Towards a Skills Revolution.* London: CBI.

Papers presented at conferences, symposia, seminars, etc: ROLLINSON, G. B. 'Budgetary Management as a Control System'. *Annual Conference of Institute of Management, 1999.* Birmingham: IM.

Theses or dissertations: Page, E. (1991) 'Central Government Instruments of Influence on Local Government'. Unpublished PhD thesis. Strathclyde: University of Strathclyde.

ARTICLES IN JOURNALS, ETC

Journals: BRAVERMAN, H. (1974) 'Labor and Monopoly Capital: the Degradation of Work in the Twentieth Century'. *Monthly Review Press* (New York): p36.

Newspapers: 'The new Class War' (2004). *Daily Mail,* 18 September: pp16–17.

CITING ELECTRONIC SOURCES

As well as print sources, you also need to cite any electronic sources you use. As with printed sources, it is important to provide the reader with the information they would need in order to find the Web page easily. On a reference list or bibliography, the different types of source that you have used should be grouped separately from each other; each type has its own sub-heading. The accepted form is to put books first, then websites and so on.

CITING REFERENCES TO CD-ROMS

These are probably to easiest electronic sources to cite, since they parallel familiar print sources. The following is an example:

> 1: authors; 2: year of publication in brackets; 3: title and type of medium; 4: place of publication. Example: Victoria and Albert Museum and the Corning Museum of Glass (1995). *The Story of Glass* [CD-ROM]. London: Reed Interactive.

This information may be found on the introductory screens as the CD-ROM loads; also on screens within the CD-ROM, about the CD-ROM, or on your university library's catalogue record for the CD-ROM.

CITING REFERENCES TO WEB PAGES

Web pages can be more of a problem because their creators may not include all of the information you need. However, you must bear in mind that the whole point is to provide sufficient information to enable your reader to trace the document. To cite this source in your text, you have to follow the same pattern as that for printed sources, using the author's name and year of publication. Where an author is not identified on the Web, use the institution as the author; also, to help your reader, you could include the title. This information is used to locate the full bibliographical reference, but, to be safe, ensure that whatever details you give match up and will guide the reader to the source.

Web pages can be lengthy and they rarely include page numbers. If a page has internal divisions, use them to indicate the part of the text to which you are referring, eg (Jones 2002: Introduction).

URLs should never be used as citations in your main text. What you should include is as follows: 1: author/s; 2: year of publication or last update; 3: title in *italics*; 4: place of publication; 5: name of publisher. Available from URL [date accessed].

FURTHER NOTES

1   URLs in your bibliography should appear exactly as they do in the location or address box when viewing a page. An easy way to do this is to use the *Edit/Copy/Paste* function from the Windows toolbar to transfer the data into your bibliography.

2   Some detective work might be necessary to find the information you need from a Web page. Look carefully at the URL, the top and bottom of the Web page, or go to the homepage and trace the route from there. Some Web pages will include this information in the <head> section of their sources files, which you can look at through the *View/Source Code* option. Web pages will often have an organisation as author, as in the example given above, with no individual author being cited. Still, if all else fails, you can use the page's title.

3   In some cases, the Web page to which you wish to refer will be an online version of a standard publication. Most pages, however, exist solely on the Web. Do not worry if some information is not there. Include as much as you can and indicate where something is available. Also, do not leave it blank; this could be construed as laziness. Remember to include the date of access, in case the page has changed or no longer exists!

4   If you are going to rely heavily on electronic information to substantiate your argument, it would be wise to save the page to disk or to print it while it is on screen and include it as an appendix.

CITING ARTICLES FROM E-JOURNALS

This section provides the correct format for citing *Internet journals* and *databases.* The brackets and the italicised words and phrases indicate the information that should be in brackets or italicised.

To cite articles from Internet journals. The format is as follows:

> 1: author/s; 2: (year of publication); 3: *title of article*; 4: [type of medium]; 5: volume number (part number); 6: available from URL [date of access].

To cite articles from databases. The format is as follows:

> 1: author/s; 2: (year of publication of article); 3: title of article; 4: *title of journal*; 5: [type of medium]; 6: volume number (part number or publication date). Available from: database name and other information where available, eg the database may give a unique number for the article, or have a URL (date of access).

GETTING FURTHER HELP

There may be times when you need to cite or refer to something that does not fit into the main categories, such as those above. If this is the case, you should see your tutor or your information librarian for guidance. The main points to remember, however, are as follows:

1   Give credit where it is due by citing your information sources in your text

2   Include sufficient details in your final reference list to make it as easy as you can for your readers to locate your sources

3   With resources such as Web pages, which are likely to change, include the date on which you accessed them or, better still, make a hard or electronic copy of such documents while you have the original on screen and include this as an appendix. If you do this, there can be no argument as to the validity of the information.

4   The details of format and punctuation may vary, but be consistent in the format of your citations in the main text, your reference list and bibliography.

SOME USEFUL ABBREVIATIONS

anon	anonymous	nd	date unknown
ed(s)	editor/s	sl	place unknown
edn	edition	sn	publisher unknown
dir	director	p	page
wr	writer	pp	pages
prod	producer	ibid	in the same book or article
et al	and others (used when more than two authors)	op cit	in the work already quoted

Use ibid and op cit with care. For example, when you rewrite elements of your text and decide to insert or delete words or phrases, you can easily put your referencing out of sequence. Direct entry of each reference, although less elegant, is less likely to lose position with subsequent amendments.

Commonly misused words and their meanings

Accept – except *Accept* means to receive or to take something. To *accept* an invitation to do something, such as attend a function or make a speech. It also means to agree with something, such as to *accept* responsibility for something that has happened, or to *accept* what someone has said. *Except* means to leave out, to exclude, or to not include something, eg 'everyone went to the seminar except Jane'.

affect – effect To *affect* something means to change it, eg 'only the managers were *affected* by the new procedure'. To *effect* something means to do, or to cause something to happen, eg 'The board of directors *effected* the new procedure.'

Usage: 'The new procedure was effective; all of the managers were affected by it.'

both – either *Both* means two, eg 'the bridge has supports at *both* ends'. *Either* means one or another, this or that, eg 'you can put your tray at *either* end of the table' (meaning at one end or the other). Misuse of the word *either* occurs when people say, 'the bridge has supports (or a support) at *either* end' (which, if true, the bridge would fall down!).

councillor – counsellor A *councillor* is a person elected to represent the people in a geographic area, eg, a local district council. A *counsellor* is someone who provides guidance and support to another person. Barristers are often referred to as *counsel*.

Usage: 'I think I need to see a *counsellor* before I complain to my *councillor*.'

datum – data *Datum* is the singular and *data* is the plural, eg 'the data *have* been collected' and 'the data *are* in statistical form'.

formerly – formally *Formerly* means *were, was* or *before*, eg 'The CIPD, formerly the IPD, has its headquarters in London.' *Formally* means conforming to accepted rules or convention, eg 'Tonight's event is a formal affair, so I will have to dress accordingly.'

Usage: 'Formerly, the atmosphere of the meetings was relaxed, but now they are formal.'

imply – infer To *imply* is to suggest something without stating it directly, eg 'He *implied* that I am likely to get the job.' To *infer* is to draw a conclusion about something, eg 'judging by what was said, I *inferred* that he is going to leave'.

Usage: 'Roger *implied* that I would get the job, but from what the others said, I *inferred* that I may not.'

incredible – incredulous *Incredible* means unbelievable or hard to accept, eg 'I thought his behaviour was incredible.' *Incredulous* means showing disbelief, eg 'when I told her what I'd done, she looked at me incredulously'.

Usage: 'The word *incredible* implies that there may be some doubt about whether or not something should be believed, whereas the word *incredulous* means definitely not believed.'

inter – intra *Inter* means between two separate entities, eg 'Inter-group activities' means two or more groups interacting. *Intra* means confined within an entity, eg 'the exercise was strictly an intra-group event'.

Usage: 'The exercise began with intra-group activities and was then extended to involve the other groups so see if inter-group activities produced the same solutions.'

ideal – idealistic *Ideal* means exactly right or perfect, eg '*ideal* weather for cricket'. *Idealistic* means foolishly optimistic or unrealistic, eg 'the way you are planning it is *idealistic*'; this means if you go about it that way you will never achieve it.

Usage: 'I thought I'd produced an *ideal* project proposal, but my tutor said I was being *idealistic.*'

its – it's *Its* is a possessive word; it means belonging to, eg 'I like *its* colour' or '*its* speed belies its cubic capacity'. *It's* is short for 'it is', eg '*It's* the right colour for me.'

lead – led When the short pronunciation is used, *lead* is a metal and sounds like led. When you use the long pronunciation, *lead* sounds like *leed* and it means to occupy the front position, eg 'Nobody had been appointed to run things so Sam took the *lead.*'

Usage: 'Kelly Holmes did not take the *lead* until the race was in its final stage, whereas Paula Radcliffe *led* from the beginning.'

less – fewer *Less* means reduced, as in a reduced quantity, eg 'because of the new technology, it will take *less* time to …' etc. *Fewer* means smaller in number, eg 'because of the new technology, we will need *fewer* employees'. It would be incorrect, therefore, to say, '… we will need *less* employees'.

media – medium *Media* is the plural and *medium* is the singular, eg 'The *media were* all agog about this event'; 'Television *is* a versatile *medium.*'

Usage: 'Most of the *media* ran the story, but this particular *medium* was reluctant to do so.'

moral – morale The word *moral* is concerned with the goodness and badness of human character, eg 'we maintain high *moral* standards'. *Morale* refers to the state of human moods or spirits.

Usage: '*Morale* in the company was high after the directors made what the employees regarded as the right *moral* decision.'

principal – principle *Principal* can mean the most important or main thing or person, eg 'the *principal* reasons for doing this were …' or it can be used to describe the first person in rank, eg 'Lesley Jackson is the School *Principal*'. The word *principle* may also be used in two ways. Firstly, it can refer to a code of conduct, eg 'George is a man of *principle*'; secondly, it can be used to describe the validity of something, eg 'in *principle*, the main elements seem to be right, but there are doubts about the detail'.

Usage: 'They appointed Lesley as *principal*, knowing her to be a *principled* woman.'

stationary – stationery *Stationary* means not moving or it does not move, eg 'the train was *stationary* at the time'. *Stationery* means writing materials and other office accoutrements (example of usage not necessary).

whose – who's Both words relate to possession, eg 'Whose book is this?' *Who's* is short for *who is* or *who has*. Possession is also indicated in sentences such as 'George, *whose* movements are a mystery, is a man *who's* often late for an appointment.'

your – you're *Your* means belonging to you, eg 'this is *your* book', whereas *you're* is short for *you are*, eg 'I know where *you're* going.'

Usage: 'When *you're* going to town, do you take *your* car?'

COMMON MISSPELLINGS AND ALTERNATIVES

These are more often attributable to carelessness than any other reason.

adviser – advisor Both spellings are accepted, but most writers use *adviser.*

business – buisness The first spelling is correct.

forty – fourty The first spelling is correct.

management – manager *Management* is a process; it is something you do, not something you are; *manager* is something you are, eg 'the *managers* are responsible for the *management* of the organisation'.

organisation – organization Both spellings are accepted although universities do vary in their preference. There are many words in which the use of the letters 'z' and 's' are interchangeable.

program – programme The first spelling is American. In the UK it is fine to use it if you are writing about a computer program; otherwise it is the American spelling. In the UK, when writing about say, a training programme, then you should spell it out in full.

satellite – sattelite The first spelling is correct.

separate – seperate The first spelling is correct.

AMERICAN AND ALTERNATIVE SPELLINGS

You should usually use English (UK) spellings. I say 'usually' because there are a few exceptions. If, for example, you are citing an American author's work, which obviously will have American spellings in the text, you should use his or her spellings in your quotation. If you have cited an American author, whose book is entitled say, *Organizational Behavior*, then that is how you should be spelling it in your reference list.

The same principle applies to other authors who use alternative spellings. For example, if throughout your report you prefer to use *organisation*, while one of the authors you are citing has used *organization*, then you should use organization in the citation. The principal point here is that you should not alter an author's spelling.

Glossary of terms used in this book

Abstract: an introduction to a report from which the reader should be able to identify the topic you have chosen, your approach to the research, the results and the conclusions you have drawn. Typically, it is kept down to about 100 words.

Active voice: the voice in which the action of the verb is attributed to the person, eg: I carried out a survey (see *passive voice*).

Assessment criteria: written sets of standards against which your work is assessed. They vary between types and levels of work.

Assignment brief: a document detailing the nature of a particular assignment, including what you are expected to achieve.

Bibliographic details: the details from which a reader can locate book titles and other information sources used and/or cited in the text of a research report.

Bibliography: an alphabetic list (by authors' surnames) of the bibliographic details relating to all of the authors and others sources used in a study, but not necessarily cited in the written work.

Brainstorming: random thinking with a particular subject in mind. Its purpose is to generate a particular item, such as a topic for research. It may be carried out alone, but is usually more effective as a group exercise.

Browser: for example, Netscape Navigator or Microsoft Internet Explorer (see *client software*).

Cache: an area of memory on your hard drive that stores frequently used images when browsing.

Client software: software held on your hard disc, often called a *browser*, which reads and interprets html documents delivered from the Web.

Crawlers: software packages that search the Web for items to be included in large databases. You can then search these databases using a search engine.

Critical review: the evaluation of the information, ideas and theories of other writers on a particular research topic, in which the researcher compares and contrasts the writers' works and demonstrates how his or her own research fits into and builds upon the main body of knowledge on that topic (see *literature search*).

Database: an organised and structured bank of data held on a computer in a relatively meaningless form, although it is capable of storing, manipulating and presenting data in a meaningful form (see also *information*).

FAQs: frequently asked questions (and their answers): usually a good source of hints and tips on using a specific site.

Hits: the URLs (and other information) returned by a search engine that match with your search criteria.

HTML: hypertext mark-up language, strictly speaking not a language but a protocol for writing documents that can be read by client software running on any computer platform.

Hyperlink: in an HTML document, typically some words of text or an image, which can be clicked to download another document from the Web.

Hypothesis: a proposition in which the relationship between several concepts can be tested.

Individual assignment: as opposed to a *group assignment*: an item of coursework that you carry out alone. It is usually set in an organisation where a problem needs to be resolved.

Key words: subject-related words generated in order to drive the search for data.

Literature review: see *critical review*.

Literature search: an information-gathering process in which subject-related data are selected from authoritative sources (see *critical review*).

Parameter: has several meanings. For our purposes, it is '*a limit* or *boundary* applied to a subject of discussion'.

Passive voice: the 'voice' in which the subject of the sentence goes before the verb; for example: 'a survey was carried out' (see *active voice*).

Peer assessment: a structured method of assessment, in which students assess the performance of their classroom colleagues.

Population: the term we use to describe the main group of people from which a sample is drawn for research purposes. A population, therefore, may be an organisation's workforce, a management group or a group of customers.

Primary data: data that have been obtained directly by the researcher specifically for a particular research project. It is data that did not previously exist, such as in the analysis of completed questionnaires or interviews.

Primary information: primary data to which meaning has been added. In other words, the data have been analysed, inferences were drawn and, thereby, *meaning* has been added.

Primary research: research that produces data that are only obtainable directly from an original source. In certain types of primary research, the researcher has contact with the original source of the data.

Process words: verbs that direct the actions of a researcher towards a particular end, such as *analyse, criticise, compare and contrast, evaluate, explain, discuss, illustrate,* etc.

Purposeful reading: reading that is directed towards the discovery of particular information that is relevant to a research topic; it is reading with the target data continuously in mind.

Reference list: an alphabetical list of the sources cited in a research report.

Sample: a representative cross-section of people drawn from a population so that their responses may be studied.

Secondary data: data that have been collected for another purpose and which may be reprocessed and evaluated for relevance to a new topic. Typically, found in company documents, government reports and the results of other research.

Semi-structured interview: an interview in which the interviewer has a pre-set type and order of questions, but is prepared to add to the number of questions, vary the theme of the interview and the order in which the questions are asked if doing so is of benefit to the research objectives.

Server: a CPU that holds Web pages and runs the information transfer to and from them.

Spiders: see *crawlers*.

Structured interview: an interview in which the interviewer simply reads out a set of questions in a particular order and notes the interviewee's responses.

Study unit: a subject-centred segment of a course at a particular level. For example, a marketing course may have study units entitled *marketing communications, marking research, marketing strategy*, etc.

Survey: a data collection technique in which a *sample* of prospective respondents to a questionnaire is selected from a *population*. The results are then analysed and inferences drawn from them. In a sense, a series of interviews may be regarded as a 'talking survey'.

Technical dictionary: a dictionary in which the contents relate to a particular subject, such as the *Dictionary of Psychological Terms.*

Tertiary data is data accessed through a *tertiary literature source*.

Tertiary literature source: a source that is organised to assist in the location of primary and secondary literature.

Unstructured interview: an interview in which the interviewer starts with a single theme; some questions may be written down but the whole ambience is one of informality, so that the interviewer may explore the several aspects of a complex issue in depth.

URL: Uniform Resource Locator (the address that identifies a specific Web-accessible file).

How was your understanding? – Answers

Chapter 1

1 You could use a Gannt chart as suggested in this chapter. Certainly you are more likely to meet your deadlines by scheduling your time in some way. Remember, you may be juggling with this kind of work on four concurrent study units. It is important.

2 To the *tutor*, the purpose of an essay is to test your knowledge of a subject and to appraise your ability to manipulate, develop ideas and arguments into a logical and planned response to a question. *Your* purpose is to demonstrate your ability to research and write about a subject; and to learn from the experience of carrying out all of the above.

3 The first step for most students is to search and survey the literature and other data sources, looking for what other writers have said about the topic and for what has gone on record about it. You could also discuss it with your colleagues and the tutor, taking careful note of their ideas.

4 A methodology is the theory of how research should be carried out. You will have chosen particular methods and ordered them into a systematic approach to researching your topic. The *methodology* is your rationale for this.

5 Because it helps to clarify your thoughts, drafts the themes into a logical order and provides you with a plan for the whole work. The act of writing tends to clarify your thoughts, and you may even alter your original intentions.

6 (i): relevant literature; (ii): primary sources such as: surveying; interviewing key people; observational methods; (iii): secondary sources such as: company documents, statistics, public records and so forth; (iv): lectures, seminars and tutorials and the accompanying notes and handouts; (v) the experience of carrying out case study work in groups.

7 Primary information is gathered by you, specifically for your research, and usually results from carrying out interviews and conducting surveys. Secondary information is information that already exists and is found in company documents, such as policy statements and minutes of meetings, public records, statistics, and in research results, for example, from surveys conducted by others.

8 The purposes of a literature review are: (i) to learn what other writers have said about your topic; (ii) to compare, contrast and critically review what has been said and (iii) to demonstrate the relevance the chosen literature to your topic. Also see Chapter 9.

9 A dissertation is academically orientated, while in a major project, it is the practical values that predominate. A major project report, however, does have to include evidence of academic work, such as searching and reviewing relevant literature, especially when the author is on an award-bearing course, such as a master's degree of the final year of a professional course. In general terms, it is safe to say that a dissertation should contain evidence of the author's ability to carry out academic research at a significant level in terms of its breadth and depth, while in a major project report, the author has to demonstrate competence at a high level.

10 A report is divided into logically sequenced sections, which are preceded by a contents list, an executive summary and introduction. An essay is usually written straight through, although it is advisable to introduce the reader to the topic by drafting a meaningful title and question and, perhaps, including a little more detailed explanation in the first paragraph. Universities vary in the demands for particular formats, especially essay formats.

Chapter 2

1 The main purposes of a lecture are to (i) disseminate information about a specific topic; (ii) to provide the foundation upon which the study unit is based; and (iii) to analyse and explain complex issues and generally add to your knowledge of the central framework of the whole course.

2 Listen carefully to the *nature* of the information and classify each element of it as *facts* and *concepts*. The lecturer will pay particular attention to his or her explanations of these.

3 At a lecture, your principal role is that of a listener and note-taker. The lecturer may allow a little time at the end for questions, but opportunities to go into deeper discussion are usually fairly limited. At a seminar, however, the whole purpose is for you to participate in discussion and, for you, there is an even balance between listening and talking to your colleagues and the tutor.

4 There are several different kinds of seminar. Often, they are an opportunity to analyse and discuss the subject of a recent lecture. There are *structured seminars* in which you carry out problem-solving exercises, work through case studies or analyse and discuss an issue or question set by the tutor.

5 Firstly, you would research the topic that is going to be discussed. Do a little background reading and take notes on what you find. Participation comes more easily if you have learned something about the subject. Taking your notes into the seminar will lend authority to your contribution. Also, you should go in prepared to listen and consider what others have to say.

6 *Active listening* is a strategy that enables you to get the most from what someone else is saying. It keeps your input to the conversation brief and simple. Listening actively means observing the emotional as well as the factual content of what others are saying.

7 Active listening would be an advantage if you are (i) carrying out a semi-structured or unstructured interview; (ii) at a lecture; (iii) at a seminar; (iv) at a consultation or individual tutorial.

8 For linear note-taking, you can prepare formatted sheets in which you allocate defined spaces for particular types of information; this assumes that you know the kind of information you will be gathering. Diagrammatic or mind mapping are freestyle techniques in which you structure each page at the event, as the facts and concepts unfold.

9 Note-taking is what you do at a lecture, interview or during a literature search. Note-making means expanding on your initial notes as soon as possible after the event while the substance of it is still fresh in your mind. If you decide to add your own comments at this stage, ensure that they are clearly separated and identifiable as your own.

10 The main advantage is that you will have an organised and easy to access record of all of your notes, handouts, cuttings and any other relevant information you have collected.

Chapter 3

1 Three of the types of group in which you would work are (i) informal discussion group, (ii) structured learning group and (iii) assessment group.

2 To ensure that you will have a contribution to make, in advance of the session, you would research the subject of the case study or exercise and the situation or context in which it is set.

3 You would organise a meeting along the lines of an informal discussion group. At first, this may be a 'getting to know you' meeting, after which the purpose is to develop a strategic approach to the task. Together, you analyse the case and study the brief in order to reach agreement over exactly what you were required to do. Next, allocate individual tasks to each member and arrange a second meeting, where everyone reports on their research findings. The meetings would continue until the whole task, including the preparation of the presentation, had been completed.

4 If you take the group and teamwork on your course seriously, you will benefit from the experience

when you get into an employing organisation. Now, more than ever before, organisations form their employees into teams to carry out the work.

5 Firstly, the most important and effective stress buster is to know your material thoroughly. Having a familiar route in front of you boosts your confidence. Secondly, learn to relax before you make the presentation. There are techniques that can be learned, and there is plenty of literature on the subject. Thirdly, be genuinely interested in your subject. Your enthusiasm for it will be communicated to your audience, you will become involved in what you are doing and will forget that you were ever nervous. Fourthly, be aware of and control your speech. Talking too quickly, which for some students is an escape strategy, will make you feel even more nervous. Look at your audience and talk naturally, even a little more slowly than usual, without, of course, boring them. This can calm things down and give the audience the time to take in what you are saying. Then you can take charge of the session and run it to the best of your ability. The more you do it, the less nervous you will be.

6 Firstly, you benefit from carrying out the presentation; it is experience that you can carry with you into an employing organisation. Secondly, your student colleagues will learn from what you have to tell them. Interaction with your audience produces mutual learning benefits.

7 You need to know who they are and how much they are likely to know already about the subject. This will help you to 'pitch' your talk at the right level.

8 You divide the presentation into three in this approach. The sandwich is the analogy because the introduction (what you're gonna tell 'em) is the bottom layer of bread. The central part of it is the contents of the sandwich (tell 'em) and the summary is the top layer of bread (tell 'em what you've told 'em).

9 Firstly, you can invite 'on-the-hoof' questions, in which you are prepared to take questions at any random point in the presentation. Secondly, you can take questions at the end of the presentation; or thirdly, you can stop at appropriate points and invite questions.

10 The main difference is that when you are doing it alone, you are responsible for everything, including the timing and the visual aids, etc. With a group, you can work as a team, but remember to consider the other team members. Do not encroach upon their ground in terms of time allocation and handling questions.

Chapter 4

1 An essay is an answer to a question. Sometimes you are given a subject and have to develop the question yourself. It is a test of your general understanding of a subject, but you should also regard it as a test of your ability to manipulate and structure information and ideas, and develop your arguments into a planned and logical response to the question. It is, therefore, *an* answer; it is *your* answer. Given the same subject, someone else might draft a different question and, therefore, provide an answer that is different from yours.

2 Tell them to study and analyse the essay brief. This is the best for them to clarify their understanding of what they are expected to do. They can check any elements they do not understand by talking to the tutor. Analysing the brief is a crucial task since your understanding determines all of the research and other activities you have to carry out before sitting down to draft the final version of the essay.

3 Process words are verbs. They describe how the tutor expects you to handle the topic. The tutor might want you to *investigate* something; to *compare and contrast* what is said in literature; to *critically evaluate* something; to *explain* something or to *discuss* it. You should maintain a keen lookout for process words in an essay brief.

4 The range of the topic is an important concept since it more or less determines your angle on the topic. Before finally deciding on an approach, you should explore the variety of avenues that you

find to be relevant to your aims and objectives. Avenues lead to further invitations to explore, and you find that having started with a broad concept, you begin to rethink and refine your ideas. Do not, however, turn this exciting journey into a perilous one by failing to keep note of *what* you have found and *where* you found it. When, at a later stage, you are making the final decision about your approach, you will be lost without a record of what you have done. The range of the topic also refers to the breadth and depth of your study. As you progress through the years of your degree, you find that the demand for breadth and depth intensifies and becomes more complex. The breadth and depth you are expected to achieve may be reflected by the required word count in which those who set the essay in the first place think that sufficient breadth and depth could not be achieved in fewer than a certain number of words.

5 Your most important source of information when writing an essay is literature. You have to search for literature that is relevant to your question, and critically review it by comparing and contrasting what they have said. This will form the bulk of the information you gather. On the other hand, it is also important to search elsewhere for information, such as by scanning the Internet and using the university's library and information service to access CD-ROMs and other electronic and hard sources (see Chapter 4).

6 If you have a correct understanding of the assessment strategy, you will know the standard to aim for. You will know what the examiner expects to find, and you will also know how marks are allocated across the elements of the essay in terms of their importance.

7 The main features of a good essay title are: (i) attractiveness: does it provide a fair indication of what the essay is about? (ii) accuracy: is it a sensible and logical version of the question? (iii) the number of words in the title. If it is more than seven words it is less likely to hold the reader's attention.

8 There are several answers to this question. Firstly, you should aim for the top because if your results fall short of your expectations, the likelihood that you will still have achieved something creditable is increased. Also, if you aimed for the top and got there (or thereabouts) then the work you carried out in order to achieve that will have been worthwhile.

9 How many items did you get? If you got seven, give yourself a pat on the back. For five, give yourself a little revision. For less than five, give yourself a lot of revision! You should find: the topic in the form of a question, instruction or abstract; details about how you are expected to handle the topic; the assessment criteria and information about what the examiner will be looking for; the required length of the essay; the date it is to be handed in; some guidance about the format and style of the essay and an initial reading list.

10 You should regard the reading list as the starting point of all of your reading. It is an *initial* list, which is included to guide you towards further reading and other information sources.

Chapter 5

1 The obvious answer is that it is there so that you will know what the examiner is looking for, but it is also there to improve your understanding of the exact requirement. It gives you a standard to aim for, and the allocation of varying marks to each element of the assignment demonstrates the importance that the examiner attributes them.

2 Your first task is to analyse the assignment brief in order to clarify your understanding of what you are expected to do. If there is something in there that you do not understand you can consult your tutor. It is your understanding of the requirement that determines all of the assignment-related activities in which you engage from that point onwards. If you are unsure, you will have a hard time deciding upon a research strategy and finding the information sources that are likely to lead you to a solution to the problem.

3 It is a good idea because the very act of writing up a proposal clarifies your thoughts about how you are going to approach the problem. At the very least, it becomes a checklist of everything you need

to do to complete the assignment. If you make a thorough job of it, it becomes a set of guidelines to take you through the whole process.

4 Always check it out first with your immediate boss to make sure that (i) he or she agrees that it is a problem that needs to be addressed; (ii) that you will be permitted to do it; (iii) that you will be allowed access to information sources within the organisation in order to progress the work, especially in the area of research. Ordinary common sense tells you that it is a matter of courtesy to let him or her know your intentions. By doing this you will increase the likelihood of getting cooperation from your boss, and it will sharpen your focus on the possibilities before you go to see your tutor to discuss it further.

5 In most cases, the professional institution provides a reading list for the whole course. The items on that list are sectionalised so that each section relates to a particular element of the course. The sections are then augmented by the tutors and are issued at study unit level. What you get on your list, therefore, should be regarded as the starting point of your reading. Neither the university nor the professional institute regard it as a definitive list. You can increase the breadth and depth of your reading by extending it to the works cited by the authors on the reading list.

6 There are several answers to this. Firstly, it must be on time because of the availability of the people who assess your work. Secondly, you can lose marks by failing to deliver on time; most universities have a system in which the maximum marks available are reduced for late deliveries. Thirdly, delivering reports on time is a discipline that you have to get used to if you are working in industry. For example, if your manager asks you to look into a particular issue and wants your report on it for a Monday morning meeting, say, in six weeks, it is going to be totally useless if you deliver it on the Tuesday. Fourthly, late delivery implies that you have not organised your time efficiently and that other items of work may also suffer from the same problem.

7 If you study the sequence, you will see that there it is logic. Think of the reader. The sequence has to have a natural flow to aid the reader's understanding. The sections are progressively interdependent, which means that each section is dependent on the section that preceded it; it would be silly, for example, to present the findings before explaining the methodology, or to write up the conclusions before presenting the findings upon which they are based. It is a matter of 'reader friendliness'.

8 Methodology is the analysis of, and rationale for, the particular method or methods used in a given study, and in that type of study in general (Jankovicz 1995: 174). It is, therefore the rationale of, or argument for, the way in which you decided to approach the problem. It is a description of the methods you have decided to use to collect the kind of data that you think are most likely to lead you to a set of solutions to the problem.

9 Primary data are data collected specifically for the research project being undertaken (Saunders *et al* 2003: 486). Another way of putting this is to say that primary data are data that do not exist in any other form or are available through any other medium because they are data that you collect directly from an original source, such as through a survey questionnaire, a series of structured or semi-structured interviews, or from the use of observational techniques carried out specifically for a given study.

10 This is a vital part of your research strategy. You need to resolve a workplace problem or issue, and it is natural to turn first to the place where the problem exists and you think about interviewing people about the problem or carrying out a survey. Truly, these are the practical aspects of carrying out an assignment, but how do you know that your methods are correct; and, most importantly, where is your knowledge base? What you do already know about how to carry out practical research, and what do you already know about the subject of the problem? It is essential to find out *how* to carry out research, and it is also vital to discover what other writers have said about your subject. It is in this way that you learn.

Answers to questions on page 53

1 With her tutor, Jenny might wish to discuss the task that she has been given by Margaret to confirm its suitability as an assignment that would satisfy the requirements of the study unit. She might also wish to discuss the timing of the events, since the required delivery date for the action plan extends beyond the date by which the assignment report has to be handed in.

2 The tutor's main concern would be to discuss Jenny's task in detail to assess its suitability and to offer her advice about what she should include in the assignment proposal.

3 Jenny's immediate priority would be to complete her assignment proposal and have it approved. The task she has been given by her boss will be time-consuming, and if the proposal turned out to be a 'non-starter', her work and study times would be difficult to handle.

Chapter 6

1 There are several answers to this question. Firstly, you need to find out what other writers have said about your subject, which could be a topic or problem. Secondly, you need to learn as much as you can about the subject, so you study the authors who have contributed to the main body of relevant knowledge. Thirdly, armed with appropriate information you are in a good position to present a convincing argument in support of your academic thesis or problem-related recommendations. Fourthly, students attend universities in order to develop themselves and grow psychologically. By studying respected authors, you are adding to your own personal bank of knowledge.

2 A literature search is an information-gathering process in which you select subject-related data from authoritative sources. According to Collis and Hussey (2003: 84), a literature search is the process of exploring the existing literature to ascertain what has been written or otherwise published on your chosen research topic, how previous research has been conducted and how this impacts on your own research problem.

3 The Internet provides a vast amount of freely available and immediate information through a wide range of sources. This has speeded up the rate of research and has increased the amount of information being sought and used.

4 The basic difference is that data are meaningless but information has meaning. It has been said that data are only meaningful to those who understand the aims and objectives of the researcher who originally produced them, but by definition data have, at that stage, become information because meaning has been added. Otherwise data are just a mass of meaningless facts and figures.

5 The techniques for identifying key words are numerous. They include: (i) using dictionaries and encyclopaedia; (ii) 'cherry-picking' them from your lecture notes and classroom handouts; (iii) review articles in academic and professional journals; (iv) the works of relevant authors from your reading list. You can brainstorm ideas and/or use relevance trees.

6 A relevance tree is a hierarchically formed diagram, the content of which is constructed from a central concept. They can be used for developing a research subject or for identifying key words to drive a literature search.

7 Boolean logic is a system through which you can control the result of a search by linking key words with conjunctions or 'link' words. Like an experiment, your control of the inputs and the process determines the outcome.

8 Storing and backing up your information is vitally important. After all, it would be tragic to lose what you have got after all the time and trouble it took to get it. The same principle applies to storing the references to the sources you accessed, regardless of whether you gained any data. You need to store and back up:

i   the names of the writers

i   the titles of their publications

iii the dates of publication

iv the address of the sources where they were found.

You need all of these (i–iv) in case you need to revisit your sources. To lose data through a computer fault can be very stressful, especially when it happens just before the deadline date, which of course, is the reason for backing everything up. It is best to adopt a 'belt and braces' attitude towards it.

9 The vital and rather obvious key lies in the location of the sources, which is your university library. Note what we said earlier about library facilities and resources. Truly, there is much you can do from home on your PC, including access to the university library, but the specialist staff can offer you a multitude of services and considerable assistance.

10 There is no numerical answer to this question because the only answer is: 'as many as it takes'. Certainly you will have to carry out an initial brief trawl through the literature when you are sure about your research subject. It was mentioned earlier that you will carry out several literature searches. What you should find is that with each successive search you are narrowing your search down, doing more in-depth searches and refining the data you collect.

Also, writing up the results of your searches activates your thought processes, and the new ideas that you produce will lead to searching for further information; again, even at the report-writing stage, the very act of writing clarifies and refines your thinking; and you may decide to search again.

Answer to MedSun Tours Limited, page 72

Susan's first step will be to ensure that she has a thorough understanding of the problem that she has been set. When she is in that position, and knows the parent discipline, she can set about identifying key words.

1 This is a double-edged case in which first, she has to produce the *marketing* plans for the launch of the company and second, she has to produce plans for the development of the company. Parent disciplines, therefore, will be: *Marketing*, which should lead to strategy and planning; and *Business planning,* which should lead her to development and overall strategy.

2 Firstly, her methodology could include a set of structured interviews with the owners of MedSun to clarify their expectations. Secondly, she would carry out a literature search and review her findings about the technical aspects of handling a new marketing venture. Thirdly, she could also carry out *secondary research* to identify the state of the Mediterranean tour market and assess the success rate of other tour operators. It is unlikely that, for her purposes, Susan would gather much useful data from adopting a quantitative approach, although quantitative data could emerge from her secondary research.

3 Having been asked to include a methodology in her report, she is required to provide a rationale or argument to support her approach to the problem. A written statement outlining *how* she proposes to collect data would be insufficient, since she would also have to justify her chosen methods by showing how she expected them to yield data that are relevant to the problem. This should include the sources from which she expected to retrieve relevant and appropriate data.

4 Case studies, from public, professional and technical media that describe how new organisations have made mistakes in their handling of new launches might be helpful in a cautionary sense. In researching case studies for this purpose, Susan need not necessarily have to stick with tour operating companies; some errors are universal and repetitive!

Chapter 7

1 The purposes of the literature review are to firstly, demonstrate to the examiners that you have made yourself aware of what is already known about your subject by searching for, finding, studying and critically analysing the literature that is relevant to your research subject. That is a minimum requirement. Secondly, you use the data you have found to support the argument you are making in your final written work.

2 You can say that your literature search is complete when you have finished writing the literature review. If you are satisfied with your review, then you do not have to go back to your data sources to recheck or find something new.

3 It changes. When you start to put something into words that others are going to read and assess, it clarifies your thoughts and sharpens your focus on what you are saying.

4 Narrowing down refers to your literature search in which you start at a broad and general level and progress towards finding and reviewing material that is more specifically relevant to your research subject, aims and objectives.

5 When we say *critically* reviewing, we mean that you need to provide a considered and detailed analysis of the literature within the area of your research subject, including an evaluation of its merits and demerits.

6 Hopefully, quite a lot of the data you have collected will be useful, but some items of data are more useful than others. You assess their usefulness by critically analysing the data and prioritising them in terms of the degree to which they are useful. Obviously, you are considering why you need each item while you are doing this. For example, with your argument in mind, you can assess which items support the main points of the argument and which support the subsidiary points.

7 You should not highlight or underline your notes if you wish to go back to them later with a fresh and more objective eye. Highlighting and underlining are fine if you wish to pick up the threads from where you earlier left off.

8 Soak time is the amount of time it takes for learning to be fully understood and settled in your mind. You may notice that when a good lecturer makes an important point, he or she will pause to increase the possibility that what has just been said will be properly internalised by the audience.

9 Reflection is a process that makes good use of soak time. It is important because you need to be sure that you gain as much as possible from the experience you are reflecting upon, which could be a seminar or lecture.

10 Scholarship is a personal quality that is possessed at levels that vary from one individual to the next. It is the intellectual capacity to learn the subject; it is the careful way in which you analyse what others have said; the care and honesty with which you separate your own ideas from those of the writers whose ideas and concepts you are using; your knowledge of the subject and the intelligence with which you interpret the work of others, compare and contrast it and use it to support the argument you are presenting.

Answer to Mini-case, page 79

Sailesh should have been more focused when he carried out his literature search. He should have deliberately set out to find literature that favoured and literature that opposed the argument he wished to present. So, what can he do now? Firstly, Sailesh should consider visiting new sources to obtain fresh and more up-to-date information, possibly from case studies, articles in academic and professional journals and the Internet. Secondly, he may find that if the data he has collected are sufficiently persuasive, he may modify his argument so that it still states a reasonable case in terms of presenting alternatives to some of the aspects of current thinking. Thirdly, he could consult his tutor and the appropriate librarian to see if he can get any leads from them. Fourthly, if he collected any primary or secondary data he could review the results from those. Fifthly, he should carry out a final critical review of all of the data he has collected to ensure that the literature he had found does not contradict the case he is trying to make.

Chapter 8

1 Primary data are data that were previously unknown and have been obtained by the researcher for a particular research project.

2 The three main methods of collecting primary data are through carrying out surveys, interviews and observation.

3 Triangulation is the use of several sources of data in a single study. It enables the researcher to compare, contrast and cross-check the data and to assess the degree to which all of the data are saying the same things.

4 A method is a systematic approach to the collection of data, whereas techniques are the steps you actually take when you are employing a method. Methods, therefore, tell you *what* to do; techniques tell you *how* to do it.

5 Qualitative data may be obtained from semi-structured or unstructured interviews. Quantitative data is obtained from surveys, fully structured interviews and observational methods.

6 Interviews are generally categorised as *structured, semi-structured* and *unstructured.* In structured interviews the questions are closed and are not conducive to discussion, but with semi-structured and unstructured interviews, questions are *open* and designed to invite discussion to draw out further information.

7 Interviews may be conducted (i) in a one-to-one face-to-face situation; (ii) in a one-to-one session on the telephone and (iii) in a one-to-several situation.

8 The five main points of questionnaire design are: (i) the general layout of the questionnaire form; (ii) a statement of the purpose of the survey; (iii) the number of questions or statements; (iv) how the questions or statements are worded; (v) the response system, eg tick boxes or a measured scale, and the conditions of response, such as the return date, anonymity and whether or not all questions should be answered.

9 The main disadvantages of using a recording device may be listed as follows:

   i   May disrupt rapport, especially at the beginning of the interview

   ii After the interview it is sometimes difficult to identify who said what when there were several interviewees

   iii Technical problems, such as expiring battery interrupting flow

   iv Transcribing recording can be very time-consuming

   v May cause interviewee to divide their attention between you and the machine.

10 From a pilot study, you would gain fresh insight into the type of questions you have formulated and, importantly, the wording of the questions. This would give you the opportunity to review and refine your questions before distributing the questionnaire to the target population. Those involved in the pilot study may also offer useful comments about the general appearance of the questionnaire form and its total contents.

Chapter 9

1 Your tutor can advise and guide you on (i) your choice of topic and your approach to it; (ii) the feasibility of what you are proposing; (iii) any potential problems you may encounter; (iv) your preliminary literature search and other aspects of your research.

2 Four of the criteria are:

  i *Relevance.* If you are a third-year undergraduate or a professional course student, the topic should be relevant to a discipline that is within the main syllabus of your course.

  ii *Interest.* The topic should be one in which you are interested; indeed, some writers suggest that it should be something that fascinates you! The reason for this is that the more interested you are, the more you will wish to find out about it and the more motivated you will be to pursue your studies in a professional manner.

  iii *Researchable.* It should be *possible* to research the topic you have chosen. Firstly, you would carry out a preliminary literature search in order to assess the research possibilities in the literary context. Secondly, you would check that the doors were open to you to collect primary and secondary data from the organisation/s in which you are carrying out the study. If these steps proved to be fruitless, you would probably have to abandon the topic.

  iv *Standards.* Many students become so preoccupied with the problem of choosing a topic that they forget about the standards they have to achieve. You should study the standards that are expected of you and ensure that you understand them. If you were given a handbook at the beginning of the year the standards should be in it. If they contain something you do not understand, see your tutor.

3 If your manager gave you a company topic, the important aspects to examine are its relevance to your subject, its size, how long it is likely to take, and the degree to which it arouses your interest. If any of these aspects are unfavourable, you should look at the possibility of abstracting a part of it and turning that into your topic.

4 Three types of problem-solving groups are (i) Delphi, (ii) interactive and (iii) nominal. The main differences are:

  i If you use the original format for a Delphi group, the members do not meet face-to-face and, therefore, do not interact over the issue in question. The problem, and its attendant features are conveyed to the members via a structured questionnaire.

  ii Interactive groups are widely used and very often referred to as the *Delphi technique.* They involve members interacting at a meeting in the process of generating ideas about how a particular problem might be tackled, leading to a group decision, often reached by majority voting.

  iii In nominal groups discussion is forbidden during the decision-making process. Members are physically present together and remain silent while they write down their views about the problem. After that, the discussion takes place, but the members do not introduce the views they wrote down earlier. After the discussion, each member in turn presents one idea to the group, using a flipchart or a whiteboard. After every member has made his/her presentation, they are silent again while they rank independently the ideas already presented to the group. The idea with the highest aggregate constitutes the final decision.

5 Three purposes that your project proposal may serve are as (i) a discussion document with your tutor; (ii) a framework for the main dissertation or management report; (iii) a means of clarifying and refining your thoughts about the topic and your approach to it.

6 Three factors that will determine the degree to which you will meet the required standards are (i) the level of study skills you have developed; (ii) the degree to which you are motivated to do well, which will be reflected in the amount of work you are prepared to put in; and (iii) the topic you have chosen, which may or may not lend itself to high achievement.

7 In our context, this question is related to the behavioural things you do when in search of a topic. When you think *rationally*, you are using your *intelligence* to generate ideas, such as being honest with yourself about your own strengths and weaknesses; and in practical terms, taking action to resolve your problem, such as discussion with friends and searching the literature. In this way, you

are using and examining things which already exist. When you think creatively, the action you take involves you in developing things for yourself, such as mind maps, relevance trees, a notebook of ideas and structures as *aide-memoire*.

8 The advantages are (i) that it is comparatively easy to identify a problem or issue that needs to be addressed; (ii) your familiarity with the organisation and its people augurs well for accessing people and places when you wish to carry out primary and secondary research; (iii) your own work experience and what you have learned from it. The possible disadvantages are: (i) over-familiarity with the topic may close your mind to the ideas of others; (ii) it is possible that you may not learn as much from investigating something that you see every day, since you already possess the necessary knowledge and skills to handle it.

9 Firstly, you would study the structure that your university recommends and use that as your basic structure, although in most universities, such structures are not regarded as hard and fast rules. Consult your tutor about this. Secondly, you would plan the content, which is a more complex task than planning the structure. You can plan the content against a graphical image of the structure by inserting the main themes into sectioned areas.

10 The management report is usually shorter in length than the academic report. Busy managers are not normally interested in how well you reviewed the literature, and they certainly should not need a description of the organisation. You would, therefore, curtail those sections. The only section that might increase in size is the recommendations section. For the management report, you may decide to include greater detail regarding timing, costs and the use of resources.

Chapter 10

1 Academic writing has to be *clear, concise, grammatically correct* and *objective*. This means using plain English, exercising word economy, expressing yourself in correct terms, and writing about what you have found out through research without allowing your opinions to predominate.

2 When you express an idea or concept, it loses some of its integrity in the process. You find yourself redrafting and refining your writing in order to express things as clearly as you can.

3 One way is to read aloud to yourself what you have written, whereupon a different way of expressing it will occur to you; to achieve the same effect, record it and play it back. Yet another approach is to put it aside for a day or two; by doing this you can read it more objectively.

4 This is a reference to word economy. Try to get as much information as you can by using concise terms. In this way, you can meet the required word count while making the report more interesting to read.

5 To retain your reader's interest, avoid long and convoluted sentences and long paragraphs. In addition, an attractive page layout will help in this respect.

6 A sentence in the *active* voice might be 'I carried out a series of interviews', while a sentence in the *passive* voice might be 'A series of interviews was carried out'.

7 Management is something you do; it is a process, eg 'time *management*', whereas the term manager refers to a person occupying a particular position in an organisation.

8 Poor or careless grammar may influence the examiner's assumptions about other aspects of the work you have carried out. For example, it may cause him or her to assume that the research was carried out with similar lack of care.

9 Their concern is that political correctness can lead to awkward sentence construction. If this is allowed to influence the writing style of papers that carry the factual results of rigorous research, it may also influence the integrity of how those results are expressed.

10 Most writers have this problem. Firstly, you need to ensure that you allow yourself sufficient time to write. Individuals differ with regard to the steps they take to motivate themselves. It is said that you can train your mind to 'switch on' to writing at particular times of the day or week, but that does not work for everyone. I tell my students to think about the rewards when it is all over; also, the deadline is a great motivator!

FURTHER READING

COLLIS, J. and HUSSEY, R. (2003) *Business Research*. Basingstoke: Palgrave Macmillan.

JANKOWICZ, A. D. (1995) *Business Research Projects*, 2nd edn. London: Chapman and Hall.

SAUNDERS, M., LEWIS, P. and THORNHILL, A. (2003) *Research Methods for Business Students*. Harlow: Pearson Education.

Index

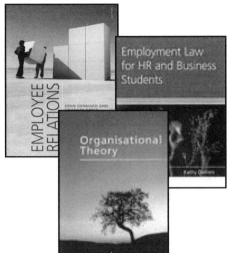

STUDENTS

Save 20% when buying direct from the CIPD using the Student Discount Scheme

Order online at www.cipd.co.uk/bookstore or call 0870 800 3366

The Chartered Institute of Personnel and Development (CIPD) is the leading publisher of books and reports for personnel and training professionals, students, and for all those concerned with the effective management and development of people at work.

The CIPD offers ALL students a 20% discount on textbooks and selected practitioner titles.

To claim your discount, and to see a full list of titles available, call 0870 800 3366 quoting '*Student Discount Scheme*', alternatively visit us online at **www.cipd.co.uk/bookstore.**

Membership has its rewards

Join us online today as an Affiliate member and get immediate access to our member services. As a member you'll also be entitled to special discounts on our range of courses, conferences, books and training resources.

To find out more, visit www.cipd.co.uk/affiliate or call us on 020 8612 6208.